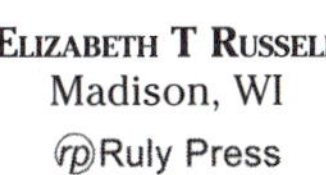

Elizabeth T Russell
Madison, WI
rp Ruly Press
www.rulypress.com

 Published by Ruly Press, an imprint of Harriet's Guides, LLC.

First printing 2014

Visit our website at www.rulypress.com

ISBN 978-0-9766480-1-7

Library of Congress Control Number: 2013913164

Edited and indexed by Caryn Sobel

Foreword by Jade Simmons (www.jademedia.org)

Illustrations, covers and interior design by Kay Lum (www.kaylumdesign.com)

Author photo by Kaitlyn Machina

TRADEMARKS. All trademarks appearing in this book are the exclusive property of their owners, and are used here solely for educational purposes.

PEOPLE. This book contains no intentional slights against any individuals or organizations. Any similarities between characters in the book, and real people, are purely coincidental.

THIS BOOK IS NOT LEGAL ADVICE. This book is intended to provide accurate information regarding the subject matter. It is distributed with the understanding that the publisher is not engaged in rendering legal, tax, accounting, or other professional services or advice. If legal advice or other assistance is required, the services of a competent professional must be obtained. Although the author and the publisher have conducted substantial research, neither the author nor the publisher assumes any responsibility for errors, inaccuracies, omissions, or inconsistencies in the book.

***ONCE AGAIN:* THIS BOOK IS NOT LEGAL ADVICE.** Neither purchasing nor reading this book creates a client-lawyer relationship with the author. Because the law is not static, and every situation is different, neither the author nor the publisher assumes any responsibility for actions taken, or not taken, based on information contained in this book. All principles expressed in this book are subject to exceptions and qualifications, and may vary significantly from state to state. Once again: if legal advice or other assistance is required, the services of a competent professional must be obtained.

ATTENTION SCHOOLS, COLLEGES, UNIVERSITIES, AND ARTS ORGANIZATIONS: Quantity discounts are available on bulk purchases of this book for educational, training, or fund-raising purposes. Special workbooks, booklets, or book excerpts can be created to accommodate your specific objectives. The author is also available for speaking and residency engagements. For information please contact the publisher via email: info@rulypress.com

Dedication

To my friends. You know who you are.

Contents

PART II: **Intellectual Property**

PART IV: **Business Issues You Might Have Overlooked**

ACKNOWLEDGMENTS

With great respect and gratitude to:

Caryn Sobel, an extraordinary editor and friend with whom it was a joy and a privilege to collaborate.

Kay Lum, whose artistic gifts invite readers to enjoy whimsy and color as they explore this book.

Those who read early drafts and provided guidance *(such as, "I know you get this stuff, but right here I have no idea what you're talking about....")*

Those who contributed generous statements of support: **Kathleen List, Terre Roche**, **Jade Simmons** and **Andrew Taylor**.

Karen Chelcun Schreiber; **Cindy Chelcun**; **Alicia Nall**; **Kathleen** and **Jackson Fonder**; **Bill** and **Kay Phillips**; **Margaret**, **Jim**, **Shirley** and the others who hang out on Fridays at Panera Bread; **Kaitlyn Machina**, **Laura V. Page**, **Adrianne Machina**, **Cecile** and **Matt Druzba**.

FOREWORD

Finally, an important shift is happening. Everyday artists are coming to realize that they are not just freelance makers of art and music. They are arts entrepreneurs. Truth is, we artists are about twenty years behind the rest of the commercial world when it comes to things like marketing, branding, and promotion. But even after we get current and learn how to make ourselves catchy and profitable, we're still mostly woefully uninformed in the legal actions we need to take and the processes we need to undergo to be the legitimate business we're aiming to be. Before now, our tendency was to jump in headfirst, figure things out in the midst of a mess, and hope for the best. But now, thanks to *Arts Law Conversations*, we can jump in equipped and confident that we know not only what we're doing, but also to what we're entitled.

Before I became a self-managed artist, and especially after I became one and took on my gargantuan workload, I used to think those were the lucky artists who got to pass all the nuts-and-bolts work of the business side of things to some higher power called "a manager." But there's nothing like the empowerment of knowing for yourself that you're creatively and legally on the right track. Every artist needs working knowledge of how the law works and of how the law can work for their art. And since we don't have time to muddle through legal jargon, thank goodness Elizabeth Russell took the time to put this powerful information in a wonderfully conversational format using easily understood language and often humorous storytelling along the way. This is crucial information, uncommonly communicated.

Jade Simmons
www.jademedia.org

PREFACE

In 2005, Ruly Press published the predecessor to this book: *Art Law Conversations: A Surprisingly Readable Guide for Visual Artists*. Several things became apparent. First, "ALC1" confirmed there was real need for a fun, understandable way to communicate complicated legal concepts to professionals in the creative industries. The book sold well and won awards.

Next, it became clear that practicing professionals weren't the only ones who needed this information. Fully half of all ALC1 sales were to college bookstores. Although not designed for that purpose, the book was being used in the classroom.

And creative entrepreneurs who didn't happen to be visual artists started saying, "what about us!?"

This book responds to those issues. It has been organized for use in the classroom; it follows a more logical sequence of topics; and it includes YOU TRY exercises to help readers learn more and test their skills. Still, this book welcomes all readers, retaining ALC1's conversational, easy-to-read style and good humor. And it's not just for visual artists. This is a fine point, but one worth noting: ALC1's title was "Art" Law Conversations; this book's title is "Arts" Law Conversations.

Here are a few notes, before you dive in.

Most of the terms you'll see in bold, are defined in the Glossary. If that's not the case, it's because the definition (I hope!) is clear from the context of the Conversation.

There is no answer key to the YOU TRY exercises. The law changes quickly, and over time it's very possible you will obtain different results from doing the same exercise. Ruly Press plans to implement a discussion forum so readers can compare notes and ask questions about the YOU TRY exercises.

Academics in the legal field make a big deal about employing "correct" format when citing cases. I have used the citation format generally prescribed by the courts in the State of New York. I have done this for two reasons. One is a nod to my New York roots. The other, quite candidly, is a personal act of rebellion against legal academics and their pointless obsession with the "Blue Book." Law Review was one of the most unpleasant experiences of my life, and it gives me great joy to say, "Guess what? You can still find the case without that #$%& apostrophe!"

This book has two things very much in common with ALC1. It's a starting point, not a treatise. For some, that will be enough. For others, it will provide a base for further study. Like ALC1, too, this book is for real people with busy lives. You don't have to wade through dense legal reading. You can read the book cover to cover, or you can just turn to the Conversation that addresses your issue of the moment. I hope this is a reference you'll actually enjoy using.

It is a reference I have truly enjoyed writing.

Elizabeth T Russell
Madison, Wisconsin

• PART I •

Navigating the Legal System

CONVERSATION #1

First Things First: The United States Constitution

It's not that complicated. Here is everything you need to know about the United States Constitution (for now!) in 25 simple bullet points.

THE US CONSTITUTION, IN 25 SIMPLE POINTS

- The **United States Constitution** is the foundation of our government and legal system, and it is the supreme law of the United States of America.
- After achieving independence from Great Britain, the United States operated under its first constitution, known as the **Articles of Confederation and Perpetual Union.**
- That didn't go well.
- In 1787 the Constitutional Convention convened in Philadelphia to revise the Articles of Confederation. George Washington presided.
- Fifty-five delegates from the original thirteen states (except Rhode Island) attended the Constitutional Convention.
- They ended up scrapping the Articles of Confederation.
- The Convention delegates are often referred to as the **Framers** because instead of amending the Articles of Confederation they "framed" a whole new government, set forth in what became the United States Constitution.
- There was plenty of discord among the Fram-

ers, but they were able to compromise and come up with the Constitution in fewer than 100 working days.

  - Nobody's quite sure whether this is or is not attributable to the absence of delegates from Rhode Island.

- The National Archives website (www.archives.gov) opines that the US Constitution stands as a model of cooperative statesmanship and the art of compromise.
- One of the reasons the Framers were able to get the job done is because they agreed right away on ten amendments to the Constitution. These ten amendments are called the **Bill of Rights**.
- The Bill of Rights appears for your convenience in Appendix 1.
- Amendments 11-27 to the Constitution are online at: http://www.archives.gov/exhibits/charters/constitution_amendments_11-27.html
- The Framers may have authored the Constitution, but **Jacob Shallus** was the scribe who physically etched the words on parchment.
- Jacob Shallus was paid thirty dollars for his services. He died in 1796 having no idea that he'd made history.
- We only needed nine, but eventually all thirteen states ratified the Constitution. So it became – and remains – the law of the land.
- The fundamental principle behind the Constitution is that our government's powers should be limited and that the government's authority derives from respecting and enforcing these limitations.
- The Constitution sets limits so that (theoretically) no person, group, or branch of government gets out of control and wields too much power.
- The Constitution establishes three branches of government, each of which checks the others:
  - Article I: The **legislative** branch makes the laws (example: Congress)

- Article II: The **executive** branch enforces the laws (example: US Attorney General)
- Article III: The **judicial** branch interprets the laws (example: US Supreme Court)

there are three reasons a law can be "unconstitutional"

- When you hear that a particular law is **unconstitutional**, that can mean the law is contrary to a provision in the Constitution. It can also mean the law is contrary to the manner in which a court has interpreted the Constitution. Another way the law can be unconstitutional is if the legislative body that passed the law acted without proper authority or in violation of Constitutional procedures.
- Congress can make laws about various issues only because Article I says it can.
- Article I, Section 8 says that Congress has the power *to promote the progress of science and useful arts, by securing for limited times to authors and inventors the exclusive right to their respective writings and discoveries.* That's why Congress can make copyright and patent laws.
- Article I, Section 8 also says that Congress has the power *to regulate commerce with foreign nations, and among the several states, and with the Indian tribes.* That's why Congress can make trademark laws.
- Article I, Section 10 forbids the states from doing certain things (such as entering into treaties, coining money, and granting titles of nobility).
- If the Constitution doesn't specifically give a power to the federal government (and Article I, Section 10 doesn't forbid it), the states can exercise that power. The Tenth Amendment says: *the powers not delegated to the United States by the Constitution, nor prohibited by it to the states, are reserved to the states respectively, or to the people.*
- That's why some laws (such as copyright and trademark) are federal and apply nationwide, and some (such as trade secret and visual art disclosure laws) are state-specific.

Got it?

CONVERSATION #2

Location, Location, Location: The State and Federal Courts

Now and then you'll read about some landmark decision from the Seventh Circuit Court of Appeals.

Or the Second Circuit Court of Appeals. Or the Ninth Circuit Court of Appeals.

Alternative dispute resolution

State and federal courts

Specialty courts

Jurisdiction

Venue

Do you know which Federal Circuit you live in?

Please welcome Sheila, an inquisitive artist, and Rick, a gifted attorney with a troubling sense of humor. In recent weeks Sheila and a gallery owner have been arguing about payments due to Sheila under a **consignment** agreement. The gallery owner had not wanted to use a written contract, but Sheila insisted and prevailed. Unfortunately, instead of retaining Rick to draft the agreement, Sheila and the gallery copied a contract they found on the internet (see Conversation #41).

And they got what they paid for. The internet contract had no provision for **alternative dispute resolution**; nor did it specify a **jurisdiction** or **venue** in the event of **litigation**.

Fade in to an increasingly frenzied Sheila and the always self-assured Rick:

Sheila: I can't let the gallery get away with this. What should I do?

Rick: You lookin' at me?

Sheila: Get over it, would you? I learned my lesson with the internet contract.

Rick: OK. Well, there's mediation and arbitration, two methods of alternative dispute resolution, or "ADR." Your contract doesn't provide for ADR, though, so unless the gallery agrees voluntarily, or we find a compulsory arbitration law that applies directly to this dispute, you probably can't force them into mediation or arbitration.

Sheila: They'll never agree.

Rick: Then you'll have to sue. How much do they owe you?

Sheila: $814,000.

Rick: So much for small claims court. Where's the gallery?

Sheila: New York City.

Rick: Do you live in New York?

Sheila: No, I live across the river in New Jersey. Why?

Rick: We have to decide where to bring the lawsuit.

Sheila: You mean, in New York or New Jersey?

Rick: I mean in state court or federal court.

Sheila abruptly leaves the room.

Sheila knew that Rick was about to launch into a tedious lecture on distinctions between the state and federal court systems. Sheila didn't have time for the speech. "Let Rick earn his money," thought Sheila, "I have art to make."

Sheila's choice (to exit the conversation) is understandable. State and federal court jurisdiction is extraordinarily complex and best left to the lawyers. On the other hand, all arts entrepreneurs should have a basic understanding of the courts and how they work.

As you may recall from Conversation #1, the United States

Constitution establishes three branches of federal government: the legislative, the executive, and the judicial. The legislative branch (Congress) makes the laws; the executive branch enforces the laws; and the federal courts (the judicial branch) interpret and apply the laws.

In addition to our federal courts, each US state has its own court system. Although the names and functions vary, state court systems typically have at least three tiers consisting of a trial-level court, an intermediate-level appeals court, and a top-level appeals court.

Federal courts are organized the same way. The United States is divided geographically into thirteen "circuits," each with a trial-level court called the District Court and an intermediate-level appeals court called the Circuit Court. The federal top-level appeals court is the United States Supreme Court.

in order to hear your matter, the court you choose must have jurisdiction (in this context, meaning control) over the person you are suing

Both state and federal courts also have trial courts for specialty issues, such as small claims, bankruptcy, etc.

In general (and this is a sweeping generalization to which there are many exceptions), state courts hear matters arising under state law and federal courts hear matters arising under federal law. Consignment agreements are contracts, and contracts are typically matters of state law. It was reasonable, therefore, for Sheila to have assumed Rick would bring the lawsuit in state court and that the only question was whether the appropriate state would be New York or New Jersey.

Let us pause. Why did Sheila assume that New York and New Jersey were the only available state courts? Could Rick bring the lawsuit in Colorado? Alabama? Tibet? Probably not, and here by way of explanation is a full semester of law school in two easy paragraphs. *(Note how the word "jurisdiction" has three different meanings!)*

1. In order to hear your matter, the court you choose must

have **jurisdiction** (in this context, meaning control) over the person you are suing. This is called **personal jurisdiction**. In order to establish personal jurisdiction, you (the **plaintiff**) need to show the court that the person you are suing (the **defendant**) has some sort of minimum contacts with the **jurisdiction** (in this context, meaning the state or federal district) in which the court sits. You can generally establish minimum contacts by showing that the defendant resides in the jurisdiction, owns property there, does business there, signed your contract there, etc.

2. The court you choose must also have **jurisdiction** (in this context, meaning authority) over the type of matter you are bringing. This is called **subject matter jurisdiction**. Think back to Rick's comment about small claims court. Small claims courts are typically limited in subject matter jurisdiction to matters where the dollar amount in controversy is relatively small (the actual threshold varies from state to state). In Sheila's matter the amount in controversy is quite large, so Rick will have to bring the lawsuit in a court with subject matter jurisdiction over matters involving larger amounts of money.

the court you choose must also have jurisdiction (in this context, meaning authority) over the type of matter you are bringing

OK. So Colorado, Alabama and Tibet are probably out unless Sheila can establish that the gallery has some sort of minimum contact with those jurisdictions. If Rick brings Sheila's lawsuit in state court, Rick will likely choose either New York (where the gallery is located) or New Jersey (if the gallery has minimum contacts with New Jersey, which it probably does.) The lawsuit could definitely move forward in an appropriate state court.

Why, then, was Rick talking about bringing it in federal court?

To bring the lawsuit in a federal district court (rather than a state trial-level court) Rick would need to establish that the federal court has **subject matter jurisdiction** over the matter. There are several types of federal subject matter jurisdiction. The two most common are known as **federal question** jurisdiction, which exists when the controversy arises under federal law or the United States Constitution; and **diversity of citizenship** jurisdiction. Federal law provides:

> *The district courts shall have original jurisdiction of all civil actions where the matter in controversy exceeds the sum or value of $75,000, exclusive of interest and costs, and is between –*
>
> *(1) citizens of different States....*
>
> 28 USC §1332 (a)(1)

Because the gallery is in New York and Sheila resides in New Jersey, and because the amount in controversy exceeds $75,000, Rick recognized that diversity jurisdiction might apply, making federal court a potential alternative for Sheila's lawsuit.

Quiz: There are federal district courts in New York and in New Jersey and, for that matter, all over the United States. Assuming Rick opts for federal court, could Rick bring the lawsuit in any district court, anywhere?

No. And this is the difference between jurisdiction and **venue**. We've already established that the federal district court has subject matter jurisdiction over Sheila's lawsuit. Subject matter jurisdiction is system-wide. That is to say: a federal district court sitting in Alabama would have **subject matter jurisdiction** over Sheila's matter. Alabama would not, however, be an appropriate **venue**. In addition to jurisdiction rules, there are also venue rules that specify, within the class of all courts at a certain level, the *particular* courts in which a **litigant** may bring an action. Usually, venue is determined by factors such as residence of the parties or where the disputed transaction took place. Venue for Sheila's action, for example,

usually, venue is determined by factors such as residence of the parties or where the disputed transaction took place

might be appropriate in a federal district court sitting in New York or New Jersey. But Alabama's got nothing to do with the dispute or anyone involved with it, so bringing the action in Alabama would not be appropriate.

Plain English summary:

1. Figure out which type of court (e.g., state court, federal district court, small claims court, bankruptcy court, etc.) has both **personal jurisdiction** over the defendant and **subject matter jurisdiction** over the controversy.
2. Then, once you've identified the proper type of court, figure out which specific court of that type (e.g., state court sitting in X county; state court sitting in Y county; federal district court sitting in Z state, etc.) is an appropriate **venue**.

Had Sheila not left the room so abruptly, she would now appreciate Rick's thoughtful contemplation regarding jurisdiction and venue. Sheila would also understand that the "Second Circuit" refers to the federal intermediate-level appeals court located...where? *(Hint:* see YOU TRY below)

YOU TRY

1. Find out where the Second Circuit is, and then find out what federal Circuit you live in: http://www.uscourts.gov/about.html
2. We just said there are thirteen Circuits. Why does it look like there are only eleven Circuits on the map? (Hint: First, look at the map more closely: http://www.uscourts.gov/courtlinks If you still can't see all thirteen Circuits, do a search by "Circuit." The pull-down menu will reveal the answer.)
3. Learn about the names, functions, and subject matter jurisdiction of your own state courts: http://www.ncsc.org/Information-and-Resources/Browse-by-State.aspx
4. Review from Conversation #1: Why do you think contract issues are governed by state law?

CONVERSATION #3

Don't Believe Everything You Hear: How to Check the Facts

In 2004 Dr. Steven Kurtz, an art professor, was indicted for federal offenses stemming from his alleged possession of biohazardous materials and the means by which he obtained them. The materials in question were relatively harmless bacteria known scientifically as *Serratia marcescens* and *Bacillus atrophaeus.* Professor Kurtz intended to use the bacteria in an educational art exhibit about biotechnology.

UNITED STATES OF AMERICA V STEVEN KURTZ

INDICTMENTS AND COMPLAINTS

USA PATRIOT ACT

THOMAS

ORPHAN WORKS LEGISLATION

GRAND JURIES

The Kurtz matter was highly charged, politically and artistically. Some felt that Professor Kurtz was unfairly targeted by overzealous prosecutors; others disagreed. Some felt that Professor Kurtz's overtly political work lacked artistic merit; others disagreed. The point of this Conversation is not to analyze those issues. Rather, the highly controversial Kurtz matter provides us with a great opportunity to think about the reliability of information we receive from the media, and the importance of developing one's own ability to do independent research.

Susan is a scientist by day and a potter in her spare time. She asked her friend Peter what the Kurtz case was all about. At the time, Peter was kind of distracted. He is a master craftsman and was busy building a boat. So Peter replied, "I can't talk right now. Just Google *Steve Kurtz*." Such a search does yield numerous accounts of the case, and all are presented as fact. Many, however, are inaccurate.

It's great to be passionate about a topic, and thanks to the US Constitution, we enjoy the right in this country to speak out. However: we further our own causes when we base our speech on verifiable facts. Here are some tips for checking yours.

In criminal matters the best place to learn about the background and alleged facts of a case is the **indictment**. In civil matters, such information appears in the **complaint**. These are the documents that charge a defendant with wrongdoing, and they contain allegations the charging party will eventually need to prove. (In criminal cases the charging party is the government; in civil cases the charging party is the **plaintiff** bringing the case.)

Indictments and complaints are one-sided. They contain only the charging party's view of the case.

Indictments and complaints are one-sided. They contain only the charging party's view of the case. Their allegations may or may not be true; that's what trials are for. So don't believe everything you read in an indictment or a complaint. Still, they are vital to our understanding of a matter because they frame the issues. So if you just want to know what a person's being charged with, read the indictment or the complaint.

Articles about legal matters often refer to **statutes** and other provisions of law that might affect the outcome of the matter. Almost all state and federal statutes are available for free, online. If you encounter such references, therefore, go read the statutes yourself. You might discover something the author of the article overlooked.

Here's an example. One article about the Kurtz matter referred to the USA Patriot Act and a bill known as "H.R. 3162." Susan wanted to know more, so she consulted THOMAS – the Library of Congress's online repository of federal legislative information (http://thomas.loc.gov). Here's what happened.

A new Congress convenes every two years, in the January following a November congressional election. Congresses have been numbered consecutively since the first Congress, in 1789. When Susan visited THOMAS we were in the 109th Congress, which began in January 2005. There was no bill numbered H.R. 3162 in the 109th Congress, so Susan's search came up empty. Then she remembered: she shouldn't have been searching in the 109th Congress, because the Patriot Act had passed several years earlier. (When a new Congress convenes, they start renumbering the bills – so it's really important to search in the correct Congress. It's possible, for example, that there could have been an H.R. 3162 in the 109th – but it wouldn't have been the bill Susan was seeking.) Susan didn't know exactly when the Patriot Act became law, so she clicked on "Search Multiple Congresses" and tried the 107th Congress, which had commenced in January 2001.

when a new Congress convenes, they start renumbering the bills – so it's really important to search in the correct Congress

On the first try Susan's search returned an impossibly huge number of documents because she forgot to use quotation marks (she entered H.R. 3162 instead of "H.R. 3162"). On the second try, Susan found what she was looking for: *Uniting and Strengthening America by Providing Appropriate Tools Required to Intercept and Obstruct Terrorism (USA PATRIOT ACT) Act of 2001, H.R. 3162.* She read the bill and was able to develop her own informed opinions about the Kurtz matter.

Several years later, Susan got caught up in the debate surrounding **orphan works** legislation. The visual art blogosphere was on fire with outrage about how such legislation would strip artists of their livelihoods in one fell swoop. There was such united and uniform hostility to the legislation that Susan jumped on the bandwagon, imploring her friend Peter to write his Congressperson in opposition.

Peter, however, remembered and was still impressed with Susan's research on the Patriot Act. He asked whether she'd similarly investigated and read the actual orphan works bills.

She had not, so together they took another trip to THOMAS. What they found surprised them both.

YOU TRY

1. Visit THOMAS: http://thomas.loc.gov Who is it named after? Repeat the steps Susan took when she was searching for H.R. 3162 in the 107th Congress. Then locate the Shawn Bentley Orphan Works Act of 2008 (it's in the 110th Congress). What do you think Susan and Peter found so surprising?
2. THOMAS has lots of additional information about the legislative process, the courts, and US history in general. Take some time to browse the site at your leisure.
3. Do a general web search for "indictment" and you will likely see some examples of actual criminal indictments.

Wanted: "The Law"

There is a lot of legal information online. And it's free.

Unfortunately, it's not all together in a neat little folder called "The Law."

Online legal research
Caselaw
Statutes
Regulations
Ordinances

The law takes many shapes and forms, and lives in many places. **Caselaw** is created by judges when they issue opinions. The higher the court, the more binding the opinion. Caselaw created by the United States Supreme Court, for example, is the law of the land. Caselaw created by a lower court (e.g., a federal district court) is typically binding on that court and on lesser courts in its jurisdiction, but it is not necessarily binding elsewhere. So if you're looking for caselaw to support your position, concentrate on the highest court you can find, in your jurisdiction. Caselaw is usually assembled in publications called **reporters**.

Another kind of law is that created by state legislatures, and by Congress. This type of law is called **statutory** law. Here's what usually happens:

- A legislator has an idea for a law, and introduces a **bill**.
- The legislature passes the bill, at which point it becomes an **act**.
- If the chief executive (i.e., the president or the governor) does not veto the act, he or she signs, and it becomes law.

- The jurisdiction organizes laws by number and topic, in volumes called **codes**.
- Once a law has been codified (i.e., given a number and put into a code) it is called a **statute**.

So, when you go looking for statutory law, you're going to be searching in the "Code" of your state, or, if you're looking at federal statutes, in the **United States Code** (USC).

In addition to laws, we also have **regulations**. These are rules adopted by **administrative agencies** to implement statutes. Regulations are typically found in a state's "Administrative Code" or, federally, in the **Code of Federal Regulations**. Don't overlook the importance of regulations, in your research. In Wisconsin, for example, you could search the statutes all day and never find anything on selling fine art multiples. Why? Because those rules, in Wisconsin, are regulations – not statutes. You'll find them in Wisconsin's Administrative Code.

once a law has been codified (i.e., given a number and put into a code) it is called a statute

One final thing. If the law you're looking for is local (as opposed to state or federal), it's probably called an **ordinance**.

Now that you know what you're looking for, here are some popular sources:

THOMAS (Federal legislation and US history):
http://thomas.loc.gov/

Cornell Legal Information Institute:
http://www.law.cornell.edu

FindLaw:
http://www.findlaw.com/casecode

General Code (Municipal Ordinances):
http://www.generalcode.com/webcode2.html

MUNICODE (Municipal Ordinances):
http://www.municode.com

Guide to Law Online:

http://www.loc.gov/law/guide/

United States Copyright Office:
http://www.copyright.gov (Click on "Law" and you've got the entire text of the US copyright law: Title 17 of the United States Code.)

US Courts:
http://www.uscourts.gov/courtlinks (Contains links to the websites for every federal court in the United States. Many post court documents online.)

National Center for State Courts:
http://www.ncsc.org/Information-and-Resources/Browse-by-State.aspx (Contains links to the websites for most state courts in the United States.)

You won't always find everything you're looking for at these free online sites. The lower the court, in fact, the less information you're likely to find. When that's the case, do some general searching and see if special interest organizations have made court documents available to the public. Or contact the parties themselves.

Now let's put some of this to the test.

Suppose you want to find out if your state has a specific statute governing artist-dealer transactions. First, go to one of the free research sites that links to the laws of every state. Click on your state. Then click on a link that says it's going to take you to your state's statutes. It might say "Revised Statutes" or "State Code" or "Code Annotated" or "Statutes Annotated" or just plain "Statutes." Any of those are OK; they're just different ways of describing the Code that contains your state's statutes. (Don't click on "Administrative Code," though. That will bring you to the regulations of your state's administrative agencies.)

you won't always find everything you're looking for at these free online sites

When you click on the link that takes you to your state's statutes, you're moving from the search site to a site maintained by your state. They're all different, so you have to use a little judgment and creativity to find what you're looking for. We'll use Iowa as a random example.

Having navigated to the Iowa Legislature's site, we figure the link marked "Current Version" is a good bet. We click. We then reach a screen with many intimidating pull-down menus, but also – hooray! – a search function. We enter, "art dealer." Bingo.

Now it's your turn. Retrace the steps we just described, to get a feel for how this all works. Then (assuming you don't live in Iowa), go back and do it for your own state. If you don't ultimately hit pay dirt, it's not necessarily because you did anything incorrectly. Remember: not every state has a statute governing the artist-dealer relationship; some states refer to art dealers by other terms (such as "merchants"); and some states' search functions are archaic and virtually unusable (not to name names, New York, but you know who you are.)

free information is never an acceptable substitute for professional legal advice

Legal websites offer a wealth of free information. Use them to become as informed as you can, or wish, to be. Remember, however, that free information is never an acceptable substitute for professional legal advice. It's always best to consult an attorney to make sure you didn't miss anything.

YOU TRY

1. Think back to Conversation #2, then do some research. Would it have been contrary to New York or New Jersey law for the gallery owner to take Sheila's work on consignment without a written agreement?
2. Library Resources

   Visual Art: For those of you with access to a research library and the patience to wade through some pretty heavy reading, there are two "must-consult" legal treatises. The first is *Art, Artifact & Architecture Law* by Jessica L. Darraby. The other is *Art Law: The Guide for*

Collectors, Investors, Dealers and Artists by Ralph E. Lerner and Judith Bresler.

Music: If you're serious about building your music law knowledge base, your first stop should be the very readable *All You Need to Know About the Music Business* by Donald S. Passman. Once you've mastered Passman, move on to *Kohn on Music Licensing* by Al and Bob Kohn.

CONVERSATION #5

Choosing Legal Advisors

As an entrepreneur you should have an attorney on your team. You need that attorney not only because you are in business but also because you are human. Everyone faces legal issues. Do you have a will? A financial power of attorney? A health care advance directive? Do you have children? A home? An attack dog?

CHOOSING A LAWYER
FEES
VOLUNTEER LAWYERS FOR THE ARTS
SELF-HELP RESOURCES

If you are like most people, these issues are a perpetual thorn in your psyche (no offense, children). You know you should be responsible, take care of business, get your affairs in order. But you put it off. You procrastinate. You spend precious energy on excuses and worrying. That's crazy! Let the attorney on your team take the lead, so you can nurture your business.

There are all kinds of lawyers. Yours should be a resource for navigating employment and labor law as you deal with unions, guilds, employees, and contractors. Copyright takes center stage in artistic endeavors and your attorney must — no exceptions — be an experienced intellectual property practitioner. He or she must also be familiar with the legal issues unique to your particular art.

In addition to competence in these core areas, your attorney must love contracts. Representing clients in the arts means spending hour after hour reading contracts, drafting contracts, tweaking contracts, perfecting contracts. It is what arts lawyers do, and it is an art unto itself. If the attorney does not take genuine pleasure in language, does not get a thrill from clear and succinct written expression—look elsewhere.

In an ideal world you would find a single attorney who is competent to handle your legal issues of daily living and your unique needs as an arts entrepreneur. Unfortunately, that is a tall order. There are not many attorneys out there who are competent in arts law *and* general practice. So remember this: nobody said you can have only one attorney.

You are building a team. Choose whomever you must to get all tasks accomplished and all needs met. Request an engagement letter from each attorney that specifically limits the scope of services that attorney will provide. You need not commit to long-term relationships. Test the waters by retaining an attorney to perform a single task, and make sure the engagement letter specifies that your client-lawyer relationship will conclude once that task has been completed. If you choose to use the attorney's services in the future, you may opt either to continue on a task-by-task basis or to establish a more formal retainer relationship. Either way, the choice is yours.

there are not many attorneys out there who are competent in arts law and general practice

Regarding money: you do not work for free. You expect reasonable compensation as determined by prevailing market factors. If you are a performer you expect travel and per diem reimbursements; you expect a certain level of accommodation. And rightly so. Why? Because you are a professional engaged in a business. As such, however, you must accept that those engaged in other professions are entitled to similar expectations.

So please don't ask a lawyer to work for free just because you are an artist and your work makes the world a better place. Said Rick, the attorney from Conversation #2, *I think my work with artists makes the world a better place, too, but I don't regard that as a compelling reason to ask my dentist for a free filling.* You need to budget for the necessary and reasonable expenses of professional services.

The definition of reasonable attorney fees will vary with factors such as geographic location, size of the law firm, and the present stage of your business or career. Entertainment firms on the coasts might charge more per hour than you pay in rent. Is that warranted? No. It's highway robbery. But that is the market rate.

If your attorney practices in a larger law firm the overhead is greater, and accordingly, so are the rates. A qualified solo practitioner or smaller-firm attorney is able to offer better rates due to lower overhead expenses. Do not sacrifice quality for cost savings, though. In the long run, bad advice can cost you far more than reasonable fees for quality representation.

Choosing a lawyer is an important business decision. Talk to others in your industry – those with legal issues similar to yours – and learn about their experiences with lawyers. Ask these colleagues not only for referrals, but for specific examples about matters the lawyers handled for them, and how the lawyers solved their problems. Then interview the lawyers themselves. Your objective in doing so is not to put the lawyer on trial! Certainly, you will ask about the lawyer's experience. But you don't need to grill him/her with difficult questions, for sport. Just talk. Is the lawyer truly listening and giving you his/her undivided attention? Is she looking you in the eye? Or does she seem bored, arrogant, and perfectly willing to take phone calls during your meeting? If the lawyer is a good match, he/she will ask questions that make you think, "This person gets me and knows what he/she is talking about. I feel comfortable."

That initial meeting might be free, and it might not. It's reasonable for a lawyer to speak with you for free, for the purpose of determining whether you are or are not a good match. If you expect the lawyer to offer specific legal advice, however, expect to pay a consultation fee.

To sum up: think and act proactively rather than reactively. Plan ahead. Do things right the first time. Avoid disputes. Make the investment up front.

think twice and three times before assuming you are an appropriate candidate for VLA or pro bono services

YOU TRY

1. Many states have "volunteer lawyers for the arts" (VLA) organizations. Some are simple projects of the local bar association; others are established stand-alone entities. If you can't afford a lawyer right now, check to see if there's a VLA group that serves your region. New York Volunteer Lawyers for the Arts has a great website that includes, among other resources, a listing of VLA groups nationwide: http://www.vlany.org/legalservices/vladirectory.php.
2. If you can't find an arts-specific legal services organization, consult your state and local bar associations and ask in general about their legal assistance programs. You can find contact information for practically any bar association, worldwide, at the Hieros Gamos website: http://www.hg.org/bar.html
3. Think twice and three times before assuming you are an appropriate candidate for VLA or pro bono services. Arts entrepreneurs need solid business plans to survive and thrive. (This applies to you, too, nonprofits!) It is up to you to show the world the arts will survive because they are economically vital, well-managed, and self-supporting. On this score your arts business is no different than a laundromat. Figure it out, and budget for your expenses.
4. If self-help is the only option, study hard. Nolo (http://www.nolo.com) and Allworth Press (http://www.allworth.com) specialize in self-help publications. New York VLA also has a list of useful books and publications on its website: http://www.vlany.org/resources/index.php.

CONVERSATION #6

Understanding Lawyers

Mary Ellen is a lawyer. When people who are not her clients ask Mary Ellen to comment on specific situations, she always says no. It's not because she doesn't want to help; it's because she's a lawyer.

CODE OF PROFESSIONAL RESPONSIBILITY

WHY LAWYERS SAY NO

This might sound ridiculous and it doesn't help the legal profession's challenges with image. But it is the responsible thing to do.

Here's why.

Lawyers are bound by a code of professional responsibility. The code exists to protect clients and to provide an ethical framework for the practice of law. A lawyer who violates the code is subject to disciplinary action, which could include disbarment.

It is important for you, the client, to understand how this works.

- You need to know why a lawyer might say "no" when you ask for help.
- You need to know why a lawyer might insist on spending more time on a matter than you think should be necessary.
- You need to know why somebody else's lawyer might refuse to speak with you.
- You need to understand why a lawyer might refuse to represent both you and your business associate.

And you need to know that in nearly all cases, none of this has anything to do with money. It has everything to do with the code of professional responsibility.

A note before we begin. Although each state's ethics code is slightly different, many are based on the American Bar Association's "Model Rules of Professional Conduct" (www.abanet.org/cpr/mrpc/mrpc_toc.html). For ease, our references will be to the ABA Model Rules.

Let's say you are a glass artist, and the local university wishes to commission a large-scale work for installation in a public building. This is a big deal, and you know there are many important issues to address in your written agreement with the university. You know you need legal advice. However, there are no arts attorneys in your region, and you do not have access to an arts-specific legal assistance group. So, when the contract arrives, you take it to your cousin Tim, a real estate lawyer, and ask him to "take a look." After all, a contract's a contract, right?

Tim can tell you if the contract is technically sound and legally enforceable, but as a real estate guy he's likely to miss the arts-specific issues that matter most

Wrong. Tim can tell you if the contract is technically sound and legally enforceable, but as a real estate guy he's likely to miss the arts-specific issues that matter most. These include, for example: copyright ownership; reproduction and licensing rights; title and re-siting restrictions; maintenance and attribution requirements; prohibitions against destruction and mutilation, etc. Almost certainly, you won't be getting the advice you need.

On top of that, what ethical dilemmas have you created for Tim by asking him to review your contract?

Once you establish a client-lawyer relationship, the lawyer owes you all of the many duties set forth in the Rules. These include, among others: duties of competence and diligence; duties regarding communications and confidentiality; and duties regarding conflicts of interest. These are very serious duties, and the lawyer who fails to fulfill them is subject to disciplinary action. Because this is such a big deal, lawyers have to be very careful not to establish client-lawyer relationships inadvertently.

Did you and Tim establish a client-lawyer relationship? If Tim agreed to review your contract, yes, you did — even if he offered his comments for free. The client-lawyer relationship commences when the client reasonably relies on the lawyer's advice. Tim now owes you all of the duties under the Rules, one of which is a duty of competence.

On the other hand, according to the Rules, if you communicated with Tim "unilaterally," without any reasonable expectation that he was willing to discuss the possibility of forming a client-lawyer relationship, none of the duties kicked in. This is why, when non-clients contact Mary Ellen with specific questions, her response is always (politely) that she cannot offer individualized legal advice to anyone who is not her client. If Mary Ellen were to respond substantively — without first running a conflict check, determining whether the issue is properly within her scope of practice and spending enough time to analyze the issue thoroughly — she could find herself owing duties she might not be able to fulfill.

Did you and Tim establish a client-lawyer relationship? If Tim agreed to review your contract, yes, you did — even if he offered his comments for free.

Next example. Suppose, when you showed up with the contract, Tim said he'd consider representing you, but that first he'd like to ask a few questions to see if you and he were a good match. Does that mean the two of you established a client-lawyer relationship? No, it does not. But even in this situation, Tim would owe you some (but not all) of the duties under the Rules.

Rule 1.18, entitled "Duties to Prospective Client," states that anyone who discusses with a lawyer the possibility of forming a client-lawyer relationship is a "prospective client." Even if a client-lawyer relationship does not subsequently ensue, the lawyer is still bound not to use or reveal information learned from the prospective client during the consultation.

There are other reasons why a lawyer might decline to speak with you. One stems from Rule 4.2, which says a lawyer may not communicate about a matter with a person the lawyer knows to be represented by another lawyer in the matter. For example, let's say you are an independent record label engaged in high-stakes negotiation with an artist. You have a lawyer, and the artist has a lawyer. You want to save time, so you call the artist's lawyer directly to discuss an issue related to the negotiation. The artist's lawyer won't take your call. You become angry, convinced those [*expletive*] lawyers are all in cahoots to squeeze out every last dollar.

a lawyer may not communicate about a matter with a person the lawyer knows to be represented by another lawyer in the matter

Not so. Rule 4.2 strictly prohibits the artist's lawyer from communicating directly with you. The ABA explains: [*Rule 4.2*] *contributes to the proper functioning of the legal system by protecting a person who has chosen to be represented by a lawyer in a matter against possible overreaching by other lawyers who are participating in the matter, interference by those lawyers with the client-lawyer relationship and the uncounselled disclosure of information relating to the representation.*

Lawyers also have to worry about potential conflicts of interest. Often, this concern arises when two or more business associates approach the same lawyer for joint representation. There are ethical ways for the lawyer to represent business associates; it happens all the time. Remember, though, the lawyer owes all of the duties under the Rules to every person with whom the lawyer forms a lawyer-client relationship. So when paradise sours and the business associates start fighting, the lawyer has a boatload of ethical dilemmas.

Best practice, when forming a business alliance, is for each person to consult his own lawyer. Once again, this is not a nefarious scheme to generate revenue. It's for your protection. You should expect the lawyer to insist that each individual sign a "multiple representation" agreement in which the lawyer discloses the possibility of conflict and seeks each client's written, informed consent. And if you find yourself in this situation, it's a good idea to ask another attorney to review the conflict waiver you are being asked to sign. Finally, if actual conflict does arise, do not be surprised if the lawyer withdraws altogether and refuses to represent you or any of your associates.

Always feel free to quiz your attorney about the Rules, as doing so is a good way to weed out practitioners you'd be better off avoiding. And when a lawyer says "no," don't take it personally.

The Rules exist for your protection.

· PART II ·

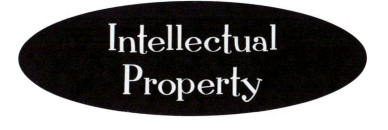

Intellectual Property

CONVERSATION #7

Novelty Teeth Can Make You Rich: Introduction to Intellectual Property

BILLY-BOB TEETH, INC. v NOVELTY, INC

TYPES OF INTELLECTUAL PROPERTY

PATENT AND TRADE SECRET LAW

MORE ABOUT STATUTES

Everybody's a comedian. The judges of the US Court of Appeals for the Seventh Circuit clearly enjoyed themselves in the matter of *Billy-Bob Teeth, Inc. v Novelty, Inc.* (329 F3d 586 [7th Cir 2003]). The court prefaced its opinion with the following:

> *When "International Man of Mystery" Austin Powers gazes at the comely British agent Kensington and purrs "groovy Baby" or "oh behave!" he always smiles, exposing a set of teeth that the best orthodontist in the world could not improve. They are ugly, and therein lies their beauty, at least from a financial point of view. This… case involves "novelty" teeth – oversized, crooked, and chipped teeth that fit over a person's real teeth. People wear them to get a laugh. Actor Mike Myers wore them when, as Austin Powers, he foiled the diabolical plans of Dr. Evil to achieve world domination.*

The **plaintiffs** in *Billy-Bob* were two friends. One of them (a dental student) designed a set of novelty teeth as a joke. The other friend saw the teeth, laughed like crazy, and realized that the teeth could generate serious cash. The two friends formed Billy-Bob, Inc., marketed the teeth, and soon cleared $5 million per year in sales.

At one point the **defendant**, Novelty, Inc., contacted

Billy-Bob, Inc. to obtain samples of the teeth, supposedly because Novelty wished to sell and distribute the Billy-Bob product. Billy-Bob sent the samples. Soon thereafter, Novelty told Billy-Bob they weren't interested after all. You can guess what happened next: Novelty started marketing its own line of ugly teeth.

The Novelty teeth were remarkably similar to Billy-Bob's, though allegedly of inferior quality. Billy-Bob sued for copyright infringement, and ultimately prevailed. Let's talk about why.

There are four types of intellectual property: **copyright**, **trademark**, **patent,** and **trade secrets**. Every entrepreneur should know how to tell one from the others.

Copyright protects *original works of authorship* that are fixed in any *tangible medium of expression* (17 USC §102; see Conversation #9). Copyright protects original expression. It does not protect ideas, methods, systems, or useful articles. It does not protect names, titles, slogans, or formulas. Copyright protects one's expression of an idea, but not the idea itself. It protects the expression of art affixed to an otherwise useful article (like a distinctive belt buckle), but it does not protect the utilitarian aspects of the article itself.

copyright protects one's expression of an idea, but not the idea itself

As a mechanical (utilitarian) means for covering one's natural teeth, Billy-Bob's teeth were not copyrightable. However, certain aspects of the teeth were protected by copyright as sculptural expression (see 17 USC §102[5]; Figure 1). Novelty ran afoul of copyright law not because it produced fake teeth, but because the teeth it produced infringed upon the original expression that was fixed in Billy-Bob's products. The nonfunctional design and appearance of Billy-Bob's teeth was sculptural expression. And that, copyright protects.

Trademark identifies the source of particular goods and services (see Conversation #36). Trademark law exists to protect consumers by prohibiting misleading uses of source indicators in the marketplace. Trademark law can protect words, slogans, designs – even sounds and smells – so long as the mark in question serves as an indicator of source. For example: "Billy Bob" was a trademark for the teeth produced by our heroes, because it provided the public with an indicator of source for their products. Similarly, "Novelty" was a trademark because it served as a source indicator for the competitor's product.

A secondary issue in *Billy-Bob* was **trade dress** (see Conversation #37), i.e., the extent to which the packaging of Novelty's teeth so closely resembled the packaging of Billy-Bob's teeth that a consumer would likely confuse the Novelty product for a Billy-Bob product. Trade dress is a branch of trademark law.

unlike copyright, patent's express purpose is to protect useful inventions like machines and processes

Patent grants an inventor the right to exclude others from making, using, selling, or importing her invention (see Conversation #8). Unlike copyright, patent's express purpose is to protect useful inventions like machines and processes. (And just so you know, patent law also protects asexually reproduced plants.)

Although patent wasn't at issue in *Billy-Bob*, let's pretend it was. We mentioned earlier that Novelty's trouble had nothing to do with the fact that it produced teeth, because copyright doesn't protect useful articles. (And notwithstanding one's personal views on novelty teeth, they are for purposes of legal analysis, "useful.")

Novelty was free to make ugly teeth so long as the appearance of its teeth didn't infringe upon the copyrightable expression fixed in Billy-Bob teeth. Had Billy-Bob obtained a patent, however, Novelty would have been precluded from manufacturing any teeth, regardless of their appearance, that infringed upon the numbered "claims" set forth in Billy-Bob's patent. For more about patents, consult the United States Patent and Trademark Office website (http://www.uspto.gov).

There's another branch of intellectual property, called **trade secret** law. Unlike copyright, trademark, and patent – all of which are governed by federal law – trade secret law is primarily state law. Most states have adopted some version of the Uniform Trade Secrets Act, which defines a trade secret as *information that derives independent economic value from not being known or readily available to others who could benefit from its use or disclosure, and is the subject of reasonable efforts to maintain its secrecy.* For as long as you maintain your trade secrets as… secrets… you may be entitled to the benefits of state trade secret protections. Potentially, this could be forever – unlike patent and copyright, which offer protection for limited terms only. Once your trade secret is "out," though, your protection ceases.

if a person keeps their trade secrets… secret… why do they need laws to protect them?

To sum up:

1. Copyright only protects original expression.
2. Trademark identifies the source of goods and services.
3. Patent protects useful machines, processes, and asexually reproduced plants.
4. Trade secret law protects valuable information for as long as you can keep it secret.
5. Novelty items can make you rich.

YOU TRY

1. Wait a minute. If a person keeps their trade secrets… secret…why do they need laws to protect them?
2. Use the research skills you learned in Conversations #3 and #4 and see whether your state has adopted a version of the Uniform Trade Secrets Act. (*Hint*: rather than going right to your state's site, look for a list of states that have adopted the Uniform Trade Secrets Act and see if your state is on the list.)
3. This symbol § is called a "section sign." You'll often see it

before the number of a statute. For example, §102 is the same as saying, "section 102."

4. Do you remember what a **code** is? (See Conversation #4). Codes are often divided up by topic, into **titles**. In the United States Code, for example, Title 17 contains the copyright statutes. So when you see 17 USC §102 that means: section 102 (the statute) of title 17 (the title) of the United States Code (the code).
5. In some cases the misappropriation of trade secrets can be a federal crime. Look into the Economic Espionage Act of 1996.

Conversation #8

The Macaroni Caper: Protecting Ideas

From Max: *I created a mixed media work of art. It was easy to create but the outcome is beautiful. My fear is, I sell one and someone recreates it and cashes in. How can I protect my idea?*

From Harriet: *I am a furniture maker and am completing a new chair design. How can I protect my ideas from being used by other furniture makers?*

Copyright fixation requirement

Original expression

Nondisclosure agreements

Utility, design, and plant patents

Write this down: ideas are not copyrightable. So at least initially, keep your mouth shut. If you share an idea with a friend, your friend can run out and use the idea and there's not much you can do about it. Are there legal theories you could advance against your ex-friend? Sure. But (a) they're just theories; and (b) they aren't much help unless you actually sue the person.

Let's apply this to Max, who invented the mixed media technique. For simplicity's sake, and with apologies to Max, let's say the technique consists of gluing macaroni to cardboard. The technique starts out as an idea in Max's brain. As long as it remains in Max's brain, it is safe and protected. Not so, once he shares it with others. Consider the following scenarios.

Scenario #1. Max has not yet created any actual work; he has not glued a single noodle to cardboard. When Bill comes over for tea, Max tells Bill about his idea. Bill excuses himself, goes home and empties his pasta pantry, creates a glorious work of art, and sells it for a million dollars. Too bad for Max; ideas are not copyrightable.

Scenario #2. Max made a prototype and showed it to Bill. Once again, Bill went home, made his own piece of macaroni art, and earned millions. Here's where things get sticky. (And not just because Max failed to rinse the macaroni.)

original expression isn't the idea itself; it's how you express the idea

Max's **work of authorship** acquired copyright protection the minute he **fixed** his **original expression** in a **tangible medium**. Those highlighted terms have specific legal meanings, and we will discuss them more thoroughly in Conversations #9 and #10. For now, it's enough to understand this: when Max glued the macaroni to the cardboard the resulting work was protected by copyright.

Well, let's clarify that. As it turns out, copyright only protects the **original expression** in a work. Max's original expression included, for example, the judgment he used to position individual pieces of pasta on the cardboard base; how he chose color, applied texture, etc. Copyright does not protect the idea of making art by gluing macaroni to cardboard, just as it does not protect the idea of affixing paint to canvas. Original expression isn't the idea itself; it's how you express the idea.

Whether Bill's work infringed upon Max's, therefore, depends on whether Bill's work copied protectible elements of Max's **original expression**. If Bill's expression (positioning, color, texture, etc.) was original and not "substantially similar" to Max's, Bill did nothing wrong (see Conversation #9).

Scenario #3. Max thought ahead and had Bill sign a **nondisclosure agreement** before he spilled the beans (and the macaroni). Nondisclosure agreements (NDAs) are contracts, governed by state law. Some states interpret NDAs very narrowly, so if you're going to use one it's best to consult an attorney who can draft an agreement likely to be upheld in your state.

NDAs are better than nothing and you should always try to have one in place before you disclose a valuable idea. If the other party misappropriates the idea, you have a potential remedy: suing them for breach of contract. It's important, however, to remember two things:

- First: you can't un-reveal a secret. So if keeping the idea a secret is what matters more than anything – regardless of any other remedy the NDA might provide – you still lose.
- Next: an NDA is only good if the other party actually agrees to it. You can ask movie producers, game manufacturers, publishers, etc., to sign your NDA – but don't be surprised when they refuse. When that happens, you have to weigh the risks against the potential benefits of revealing your idea (see YOU TRY, below).

Patent law

Sometimes you can use patent law to protect your work when copyright is not available. Sit down and open your checkbook, though, because pursuing patent protection is not simple and it's not cheap.

There are three types of patents. A **utility patent** may be granted to anyone who invents or discovers any new and useful process, machine, article of manufacture, or composition of matter, or any new and useful improvement thereof. A **design patent** may be granted to anyone who invents a new, original, and ornamental design for an article of manufacture; and a **plant patent** may be granted to anyone who invents or discovers and asexually reproduces any distinct and new variety of plant. (Basic Facts About Patents: http://www.uspto.gov/main/patents.htm)

NDAs are better than nothing and you should always try to have one in place before you disclose a valuable idea

Back to Max and Harriet. Max's work probably qualifies for copyright protection. But what about Harriet, the furniture designer? Copyright does not protect useful articles. More specifically: *In no case does copyright protection for an original work of authorship extend to any idea, procedure, process, system, method of operation, concept, principle, or discovery, regardless of the form in which it is described, explained, illustrated, or embodied in such work* (17 USC §102[b]). Bottom line: in the United States it is extremely difficult to obtain copyright protection for furniture and other types of **industrial design** (see YOU TRY, below).

copyright does not protect useful articles

Instead of copyright, Harriet might want to consider a design patent. (Please go to the glossary and look up **article of manufacture** before reading on.)

> *A design consists of the visual ornamental characteristics embodied in, or applied to, an **article of manufacture**. Since a design is manifested in appearance, the subject matter of a design patent application may relate to the configuration or shape of an article, to the surface ornamentation applied to an article, or to the combination of configuration and surface ornamentation. A design for surface ornamentation is inseparable from the article to which it is applied and cannot exist alone. It must be a definite pattern of surface ornamentation, applied to an **article of manufacture**.*
>
> *In discharging its patent-related duties, the United States Patent and Trademark Office (USPTO or Office) examines applications and grants patents on inventions when applicants are entitled to them. The patent law provides for the granting of design patents to any person who has invented any new, original and ornamental design for an **article of manufacture**. A design patent protects only the appearance of the article and not structural or utilitarian features.*

(Guide to Filing a Design Patent Application: http://www.uspto.gov/web/offices/pac/design/)

If you are considering patent law as a means of protecting your work, consult with a qualified patent attorney admitted to practice before the United States Patent and Trademark Office.

YOU TRY

1. Here are some useful resources:

   Circular 31: Ideas, Methods or Systems http://www.copyright.gov/circs/circ31.pdf

   Factsheet FL-103: Useful Articles

   http://www.copyright.gov/fls/fl103.pdf
2. Suppose Harriet had invented a new type of wheel for the chair. The novel wheel, itself, would probably qualify as an **article of manufacture**. What type of patent would she pursue to protect that invention?
3. It's not impossible to protect certain aspects of industrial design under copyright law–but it is difficult. In the United States, patent law is often the only available method of protection. Other countries, though, offer protection specifically for industrial design. To learn more: http://www.wipo.int/designs/en/
4. If you're in a situation where the other party refuses to sign your NDA, keep good records. If they do swipe your idea, you might be able to pursue remedies if you have strong evidence of: your efforts to maintain confidentiality (such as letters and emails prior to disclosure, expressing your expectations); their misappropriation of the idea following disclosure; and their unjust enrichment (and/or your damages) as a result of the misappropriation. If you're planning to do this, get legal advice before proceeding – and certainly before disclosing the idea!

Conversation #9

Hey, I Finally Get It! (Listening In On a Copyright Workshop)

Copyright protects *original works of authorship that are fixed in any tangible medium of expression*. In this Conversation we'll clarify what that really means, by listening in on a workshop led by someone whose initials are TS. The participants in this workshop happen to ask all the right questions, in perfect order.

Copyright basics
Works of authorship
Originality requirement
Feist Publications, Inc. v Rural Telephone Service Co., Inc.

To start, Karen asks: What is a **work of authorship**?

TS: The copyright law itself tells us what types of work qualify as works of authorship: literary works; musical works; dramatic works; pantomimes and choreographic works; pictorial, graphic, and sculptural works; motion pictures and other audiovisual works; sound recordings; and architectural works (see Figure 1).

Karen: So my work has to fall into one of those eight categories?

TS: For copyright purposes, yes.

Karen needs clarification.

Karen: I am a painter, and Jill is a choreographer. I don't consider either of us an "author." Are we?

TS: If you create copyrightable material you are its "author" even if the rest of the world considers you a painter, composer, sculptor, playwright, etc. Can you live with that?

Karen: I guess so. (Karen isn't so sure, but she's a good sport.)

Chris then raises his hand and asks: What makes a work of authorship **original**?

TS: Two things, really. The first is **independent creation**. The second is a requirement that the work display at least a **minimal level of creativity**.

Chris: The statute doesn't say that. It just says, "original."

TS: You're right. Over time, the courts have decided that originality means independent creation plus a minimum level of creativity.

Chris: Well, how on Earth were we supposed to know that?

TS: Respectfully, Chris, that's why you are attending this workshop.

Chris: Thank you. Please continue.

TS: Chris, what do you do for a living?

Chris: I am a graphic designer.

TS: Suppose you created a design, and by complete coincidence Aaron created the exact same design. Aaron never met you and had never seen your work. What would you think?

Chris: Seriously? It was a complete coincidence? I'd say I should be entitled to copyright the work, and not Aaron, because I created it first.

TS: It doesn't work that way. If you both honestly created the same work, independently, you are both entitled to copyright protection. That's what "independent" creation means.

Chris ponders this.

TS: Aaron, do you understand?

Aaron: Roger.

Chris: OK, what if by complete coincidence I created a copyrightable image that already existed but had passed into the **public domain**? Could I copyright it?

TS: Yes, you could. And others couldn't use *your* image without licenses from you. They could, however, use the one that was in the public domain. In an infringement situation it would be up to you to prove the infringer was using your work as opposed to the public domain version. That might sound ridiculous, but it is possible you could make that case.

over time the courts have decided, in specific cases, whether works do or do not reflect sufficient creativity

Harry is watching the clock because he has things to do. To move this along, he says: I think we get the independent creation part. What is the **minimal level of creativity**?

TS: Think of an imaginary line. If the work is above the line, it's sufficiently creative to qualify for copyright protection. If it's below the line, it's not.

Harry: That's not terribly helpful, TS. How do we know where to draw the line?

TS: Over time the courts have decided, in specific cases, whether works do or do not reflect sufficient creativity. We have to consider those court decisions, for guidance. The US Supreme Court said, *[t]he requisite level of creativity is extremely low; even a slight amount will suffice. The vast majority of works make the grade quite easily, as they possess some creative spark, 'no matter how crude, humble, or obvious' it might be* (*Feist Publications, Inc. v Rural Telephone Service Co., Inc.*, 499 US 340, 345, 111 S Ct 1282, 113 L Ed 2d 358 [1991]).

That "requisite level" is the imaginary line. And even though the bar is pretty low, it's important to remember that it does exist and not all work will be sufficiently creative. The white pages of the telephone book, for example, fell below the line. Said the Court: *[t]he selection, coordination, and arrangement of [the] white pages do not satisfy the minimum constitutional standards for copyright protection.... [The telephone company] simply takes the data provided by its subscribers and lists it alphabetically by surname. The end product is a garden-variety white pages directory, devoid of even the slightest trace of creativity* (*Feist*, at 361).

Harry: What else falls below the line?

TS: In the musical world, one court held that a "composition," consisting of two notes repeating back and forth to simulate the sound of a clock ticking, was insufficiently original.[1] Common shapes and designs fall below the line. Artists also run into originality problems in connection with realistic works based on nature.

Harry: Why is that?

TS: Because things that exist in nature are not the result of an author's independent creation.

Harry: So, for nature artists trying to be as realistic as possible, the artist with greater skill is less likely to obtain copyright protection for her work?

TS: Yes.

Harry has yet another question (that turns out to be an evil plan).

Harry: This is a lot to absorb. Can we take a break before somebody asks what **fixed in a tangible medium** means?

TS: Sure.

Harry went out for coffee.

---

[1] *Smith v George E. Muehlebach Brewing Co.*, 140 F Supp 729 (D Mo 1956), cited in *Levine v McDonald's Corp.*, 735 F Supp 92 (SDNY 1990)

YOU TRY

1. Remember Peter, the boat-builder from Conversation #3? He's particularly interested in chapter 13 of title 17 of the United States Code. Why do you think that is?
2. Did you get the football reference hidden in this Conversation?

FIGURE 1

Copyright Law of the United States

Title 17 of the United States Code

§ 102. SUBJECT MATTER OF COPYRIGHT: IN GENERAL

(a) Copyright protection subsists, in accordance with this title, in original works of authorship fixed in any tangible medium of expression, now known or later developed, from which they can be perceived, reproduced, or otherwise communicated, either directly or with the aid of a machine or device. Works of authorship include the following categories:

(1) literary works;

(2) musical works, including any accompanying words;

(3) dramatic works, including any accompanying music;

(4) pantomimes and choreographic works;

(5) pictorial, graphic, and sculptural works;

(6) motion pictures and other audiovisual works;

(7) sound recordings; and

(8) architectural works.

(b) In no case does copyright protection for an original work of authorship extend to any idea, procedure, process, system, method of operation, concept, principle, or discovery, regardless of the form in which it is described, explained, illustrated, or embodied in such work.

The Perils of Ice and Sand: Copyright's Fixation Requirement

Evanescent: Tending to vanish like vapor

Transitory: Of brief duration

Embodied: Made concrete and perceptible

Ephemeral: Short-lived

ix those dictionary entries in your short-term memory. We'll return to them in a moment.

Often, the art we experience live can be more powerful than art that's been fixed, or preserved in some other medium. When Jeff was growing up near West Point, New York, a highlight of summer was sitting under the stars at the Trophy Point Amphitheater as the concert band performed Tchaikovsky's *1812 Overture,* complete with fireworks and real cannons. He knew those blasts were coming, but every year he still jumped.

Copyright clause of the US Constitution
Fixation
Copies and phonorecords
Anti-bootlegging statutes
State law protections
Preemption

Not once has Jeff had the same reaction, listening to a recorded version of that work.

And yet: the recorded version gets copyright protection (as a sound recording) but the live performance does not, because it was not **fixed** in a tangible medium of expression. A live performance is the opposite of fixed. It is *evanescent* which (in addition to the dictionary definition) means: *No copyright for you!*

In copyright law, fixation is a big deal. Here's the

story.

United States copyright law derives from the US Constitution, Article I of which grants Congress its powers (see Conversation #1). Article I, Section 8, clause 8 states that Congress has the power *to promote the progress of science and useful arts, by securing for limited times to authors and inventors the exclusive right to their respective writings and discoveries.*

The Copyright Clause refers to *writings*. In the early days this was interpreted literally, to include only traditional writings such as books and papers. Over time, Congress and the courts interpreted the term to include other means of expression, such as musical notation, visual art and, most recently, sound recordings and architectural work. Congress and the courts continue to agree, however, that no matter how inclusive its interpretation, the term *writing* still means work in a fixed form.

Congress figured this was self-explanatory and never included an express fixation requirement in US copyright law until the Copyright Act of 1976. Today, the statute that establishes eligibility for copyright protection reads as follows:

> *Copyright protection subsists… in original works of authorship* ***fixed in any tangible medium of expression****, now known or later developed, from which they can be perceived, reproduced, or otherwise communicated, either directly or with the aid of a machine or device* (17 USC §102).

The law also defines what it means to be *fixed*:

> *A work is "fixed" in a tangible medium of expression when its* ***embodiment*** *in a* ***copy*** *or phonorecord, by or under the authority of the author, is sufficiently permanent or stable to permit it to be perceived, reproduced, or otherwise communicated for a period of more than* ***transitory*** *duration* (17 USC §101).

The law does not define *embodiment* or *transitory*, which is why we started this Conversation with those dictionary definitions. The law does define what a *copy* is, however, and interestingly, the definition of *copy* refers right back to the term *fixed*:

> *"Copies" are* ***material objects****, other than phonorecords, in which a work is* ***fixed*** *by any method now known or later developed, and from which the work can be perceived, reproduced, or otherwise communicated, either directly or with the aid of a machine or device* (17 USC §101).

So where does this leave us?

fixation means embodiment in a copy, and a copy is a material object

Well, in order to acquire copyright protection your work must be **original** (see Conversation #9) and it must be fixed in a tangible medium of expression from which it can be perceived, reproduced, or otherwise communicated. Fixation means embodiment in a **copy**, and a copy is a material object.

But that's not all. The fixation of your work (in that material object) also has to be permanent or stable enough to allow the work to be perceived, reproduced, or otherwise communicated for a period of *more than transitory duration.*

How long is *transitory*? There is no clear answer. But here are some thoughts.

Let's start with the obvious. Transitory refers to a period of brief duration. It does not mean permanent and it does not mean forever. Let's say that transitory (however long that may be) equals "T," and a period of *more than transitory duration* equals T+x. If your original work of authorship has been embodied in a material object for at least T+x, the work qualifies for copyright protection. That is so, even if shortly thereafter you destroy the material object in which the work was embodied. Reaching T+x is like a trigger. When that trigger goes off, copyright vests. And once vested, copyright lasts for the life of the author plus 70 years – regardless of whether the **copy** in which the work was originally **fixed** still exists.

T+x is a period of time longer than T; but the question remains: what is T? Most commentators agree that **evanescent** art (such as sand and ice sculptures) falls short of T. But what of an ice sculpture maintained in a freezer or in a part of Alaska that never thaws? Does such work reach T+x?

Here's another point. Don't confuse the word *transitory* with the word *ephemeral*. US copyright law suggests that ephemeral (which has nothing to do with qualifying for copyright protection) is quite a bit longer than transitory (which has everything to do with qualifying for copyright protection.) There is a provision of law, for example, that deals exclusively with **ephemeral recordings** (17 USC §112). These are copies or phonorecords of a work made for purposes of facilitating later transmission by a broadcasting organization. The law says they have to be destroyed within six months from the date of transmission to the public. So ephemeral, for this purpose, can mean six months or more.

US copyright law suggests that ephemeral is quite a bit longer than transitory

Let's take a brief time out. You may be wondering why the law keeps saying "copies or phonorecords." What's the difference? Not much, really. **Phonorecords** are just like copies, except they are the material objects in which sound recordings (as opposed to other types of work) are embodied.

Back to fixation and live performance. Josh, a jazz musician, gave the performance of a lifetime. It was completely improvised and not recorded. It was not, therefore, **fixed**. Well, it was not recorded by Josh – but Barry Bootlegger caught the whole thing on his cell phone. Does that count as fixation entitling Josh to a copyright after all?

No. The definition of fixation specifically refers to embodiment in a copy *by or under the authority of the author*. Josh did not authorize Barry's recording and had no idea it was even made. Part of the reasoning behind the fixation requirement is that an author has to care enough about obtaining a copyright, to take the steps to make it happen. If Josh didn't make the effort to record (fix) his performance, he shouldn't get the benefits of copyright protection.

does that mean Barry Bootlegger gets to copyright the performance?

Does that mean Barry Bootlegger gets to copyright the performance? Of course not. First of all, Barry Bootlegger is not the **author** of the performance. Second, although it's not technically a copyright statute, the copyright law contains an anti-bootlegging statute that states (in pertinent part):

Anyone who, without the consent of the performer or performers involved –

(1) fixes the sounds or sounds and images of a live musical performance in a copy or phonorecord, or reproduces copies or phonorecords of such a performance from an unauthorized fixation;

(2) transmits or otherwise communicates to the public the sounds or sounds and images of a live musical performance, or

(3) distributes or offers to distribute, sells or offers to sell, rents or offers to rent, or traffics in any copy or phonorecord fixed as described in paragraph (1), regardless of whether the fixations occurred in the United States,

shall be subject to the remedies provided in sections 502 through 505, to the same extent as an infringer of copyright (17 USC §1101)

So, performance artists: if you forfeited copyright protection by neglecting to fix your work in a tangible medium, this provision can at least offer some protection against bootleggers.

State law might be helpful, as well. In general, US copyright law **preempts** equivalent provisions of state law (17 USC §301). However, there's a very specific exception in the copyright law that states:

> *(b) Nothing in this title annuls or limits any rights or remedies under the common law or statutes of any State with respect to —*
>
> *(1) subject matter that does not come within the subject matter of copyright as specified by sections 102 and 103, including works of authorship* ***not fixed*** *in any tangible medium of expression (17 USC §301[b]).*

Translation: if your work is not copyrightable because it wasn't fixed, and there's state statutory or common law that would offer protection for such unfixed work, that state law is not preempted by US copyright law. You're free to proceed under the state law. California has a state law that protects unfixed works of authorship (Cal Civ Code §980[a][1]); New York common law protects certain sound recordings that are ineligible for copyright protection; and other states have similar provisions.

YOU TRY

The federal **preemption doctrine** kicks in when a state law conflicts with federal law. In such a case, the federal law wins. All of this arises under the Supremacy Clause of the US Constitution: Article VI, clause 2. Go find some cases and examples of state laws that have been preempted.

Conversation #11

Photographing Your Work: Who Owns the Rights?

Once your work is subject to copyright protection, the next question is: What does that mean? What rights do you get with your copyright?

The bundle of rights

Licensing

Derivative works

Fig. 2: *Bundle of Rights*

A misunderstanding between Sam and Meghan sheds some light.

Sam: Meghan claims she owns rights to my painting because she photographed it.

Meghan: That's right. I'm a skilled photographer.

Sam: But it's my painting!

Meghan: But they're my photographs!

You get the picture.

When one acquires a copyright, one really acquires a "bundle" of six exclusive, independent rights: the right of reproduction; the right to create derivative works; the right to distribute copies; the right of public performance; the right of public display; and, for sound recordings only, a limited right of public performance by means of digital audio transmission (17 USC §106; see Figure 1).

We will discuss each of the §106 rights in later Conversations. Right now, in order to make things right between Sam and Meghan, we must focus on the first two: the right *to reproduce the copyrighted work in copies or phonorecords* (17 USC §106[1]); and the right *to prepare derivative works based upon the copyrighted work* (17 USC § 106[2]).

Note: there has been much debate whether, when one photographs a copyrighted work, one is creating a **copy** (for which a reproduction license would be required under §106[1]) or a **derivative work** (for which an adaptation license would be required under §106[2]). If the photograph contains a sufficient amount of creativity (see Conversation #9), it's a derivative work (see http://www.copyright.gov/circs/circ14.pdf). If not, it's just a copy. Either way, the photographer needs a license from the owner of the underlying, copyrighted work. For purposes of this Conversation only, we will assume that Meghan's photographs are sufficiently original to be *derivatives* of Sam's copyrighted work.

if the photograph contains a sufficient amount of creativity, it's a derivative work

OK. Sam creates his painting. As its author, Sam owns the copyright to the painting. Sam's copyright includes all of the §106 rights that apply to paintings, including the right to prepare derivative works.

Sam needs photos of the painting for his portfolio, so Sam hires Meghan. Recall the bundle of rights. Without licenses (i.e., permission) from Sam, Meghan cannot shoot the painting. Why? Because the resulting photos would be both reproductions of and derivative works based upon the painting. Taking the photos without proper licenses would violate Sam's exclusive rights under §106 (1) and (2) and, thus, would constitute copyright infringement.[1]

So first, Meghan needs a license from Sam to photograph the painting. Sam and Meghan should have a written agreement, setting forth the terms and the scope of Meghan's license to shoot the painting. If they do not, i.e., if they have only a ver-

[1] The inquisitive Reader will start wondering why Sam doesn't own copyright in the photographs because he paid Meghan to create them. Hold that thought; we'll discuss it in detail in Conversation #28.

bal agreement that Meghan will do the shoot, it can be inferred that Sam has granted Meghan a limited, **nonexclusive license** to take the photos.

Query #1. At this point, who holds what rights with respect to the painting?

Well, Meghan has a license to reproduce and prepare derivative works of the painting. If Sam granted Meghan an **exclusive license** to do this, no one other than Meghan can photograph the painting, for the purposes specified, for as long as the license remains in effect. (Note: exclusive licenses must be in writing.) If Meghan's license is **nonexclusive**, Sam is free to license these rights to others in addition to Meghan, at any time.

think of the copyright bundle as a pile of firewood, and each of the six rights as separate logs on the pile

Think of the copyright bundle as a pile of firewood, and each of the six rights as separate logs on the pile. Sam (the copyright owner) can license away one or more of the "logs," and still retain the rest of the pile. That is, Sam does not lose his copyright just because he permits another party to exercise one or more of his rights under §106.

Sam still owns and controls his copyright bundle of rights, subject only to the licenses he granted to Meghan. For example, Sam still retains the right to license the painting for public display, to reproduce it in other media, etc. The only thing Sam can't do is violate the specific terms of Meghan's license.

Query #2. Who owns what rights with respect to the photographs?

Recall, we are assuming that the photographs contain sufficient originality (in their composition, lighting, etc.) to be derivative works based upon the painting. For that reason, Meghan owns a copyright interest in the photographs. That interest is limited, however, to the original, copyrightable elements that Meghan herself contributed to the photographs. Meghan does not own and has not acquired any copyright interest in the underlying work (the painting). Consequently, if Meghan wishes to use the photos for any purpose in the future, Meghan will still need licenses from Sam.

Query #3. Does Sam have any interest in the photographs?

It depends, but probably not. Unless Meghan specifically (and in writing) **assigned** copyright in the photographs to Sam, Sam cannot exercise any of the §106 rights, with respect to the photos, without Meghan's permission. Why? Because Meghan holds a copyright interest in the photos. Yes, it's limited in scope to composition and lighting, but that counts. Derivative works are separately copyrightable and, to the extent of the author's creative contributions, afford the author (here, Meghan) the full range of §106 rights. If Sam wished to reproduce, display, adapt or distribute the photos, therefore, he would need Meghan's permission to do so even though his own work constituted the subject of the photographs.

if Meghan wishes to use the photos for any purpose in the future, Meghan will still need licenses from Sam

Query #4. What happens if a third party comes to Meghan and asks for permission to exercise one or more of the §106 rights with respect to the photos?

In this case, the third party would need a license from Meghan (because Meghan has a copyright interest in the photos) and from Sam, because Sam's copyrighted material appears in the photos. Write this down: Anyone who seeks to use a derivative work must obtain an appropriate license from whoever holds a copyright interest in the derivative AND from the copyright holder(s) of any copyrightable work(s) upon which the derivative is based.

So Sam has not lost his copyright. Meghan has no rights at all in, or to, his painting. But Meghan does hold a limited copyrightable interest in the derivative works she created (i.e., the photographs).

With respect to any particular work, we must often pursue multiple paths to sort out who controls what, and then obtain appropriate licenses from everyone with copyrightable interests in the work.

If you are:	Sam	Meghan	A Third Party
...and you want to use the painting you need permission from	nobody	Sam	Sam
...and you want to use the photographs you need permission from:	Meghan	Sam	Meghan and Sam

FIGURE 2

§ 106. EXCLUSIVE RIGHTS IN COPYRIGHTED WORKS "BUNDLE OF RIGHTS"

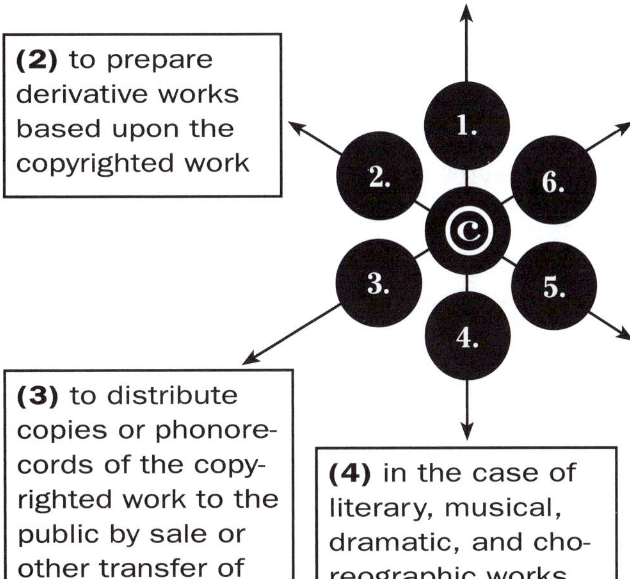

(1) to reproduce the copyrighted work in copies or phonorecords
(2) to prepare derivative works based upon the copyrighted work
(3) to distribute copies or phonorecords of the copyrighted work to the public by sale or other transfer of ownership, or by rental, lease, or lending
(4) in the case of literary, musical, dramatic, and choreographic works, pantomimes, and motion pictures and other audiovisual works, to perform the copyrighted work publicly
(5) in the case of literary, musical, dramatic, and choreographic works, pantomimes, and pictorial, graphic, or sculptural works, including the individual images of a motion picture or other audiovisual work, to display the copyrighted work publicly
(6) in the case of sound recordings, to perform the copyrighted work publicly by means of a digital audio transmission
1.
2.
3.
4.
5.
6.
©

PPSRDAT? What's That? (Licensing Music for Public Performance)

How do you use music? To enhance presentations; to create tension in films; to pacify (or enrage) customers while they wait on hold. As an arts entrepreneur you need to know how to license the music you use in your life and your business.

Musical works and sound recordings
More on the bundle of rights
ASCAP, BMI and SESAC
Dramatic performances
Statutory licenses
SoundExchange
Copyright notice and symbols

"Musical works" and "sound recordings" are separately copyrightable **works of authorship** and each gets its own **bundle of rights** under §106 (see Conversations #9 and #11, and Figure 2).

A **musical work** is a composition. It's the music the composer composed, and it can usually be represented on score paper. A **sound recording** is the fixation of sound. It is the particular recording – fixed by the performers and the recording engineers – of a musical work.[1] This is important: When you wish to use recorded music for a particular purpose, you almost always need two separate licenses. You need one for the sound recording, and another for the musical work (the composition) that is embodied in the sound recording.

In Conversation #11 we said that each copyrightable work of authorship (each original literary work, musical work, sound recording, etc.) gets its own bundle of rights (see Figure 2). Now it's time

[1] Sound recordings don't always embody musical works. They may also embody literary or dramatic works (e.g., audio books) and/or sounds not subject to copyright protection.

to reveal that the law has a few exceptions.

Sound recordings don't get #4 or #5 on the bundle.

Kevin (a recording engineer): Why not?

TS: The law just says so.

Kevin: Where?

TS: 17 USC §114.

Kevin: Where's that?

TS: Ask Susan, from Conversation #3. She's getting really good at legal research.

Kevin: What's her number?

TS: Never mind.

Sound recordings not being entitled to #4 and #5 is a big deal, so let's sort it out.

Q: Without a license from the copyright owner, can you **reproduce** a musical work or a sound recording?

A: No, because of #1 on the bundle of rights.

Q: Can you create a **derivative work** (e.g., an arrangement) of a musical work or a sound recording?

A: No, because of #2.

Q: Can you **distribute copies** of either?

A: No, because of #3.

Very good. Now it gets tricky.

Q: Can you **publicly perform** a musical work without a license?

A: No, because of #4 on the bundle.

Q: Can you publicly perform a sound recording without a license?

A: Yes, because sound recordings don't get #4.

Kevin: So if a bowling alley is playing one of my recordings, and the recording happens to be of Kaitlyn's composition, you're saying they need a license from Kaitlyn but not from me?

TS: That is correct.

Kevin: Seriously?

TS: Yes. It's controversial. But right now, with one exception, it's the law.

Kevin: What's the exception?

TS: #6 on the bundle of rights.

Even though sound recordings don't get #4, there is a limited public performance right for sound recordings in #6: the right to public performance by means of digital audio transmission. This is overly simplified, but in this context "digital audio transmission" means the public performance of sound recordings via satellite radio, cable TV, and webcasting services. The providers of such services need public performance licenses for the sound recordings they broadcast.

All of this leads inevitably to the following questions:

From Kaitlyn: How do people get licenses to publicly perform my musical works?

From Kevin: How do people get licenses to publicly perform my sound recordings by means of digital audio transmission?

We'll start with Kaitlyn.

Kaitlyn holds the copyright to a musical work. She lives in Montana. How is she supposed to know if a band or a restaurant or a museum in Alabama publicly performs that musical work? Copyright law (#4 on the bundle) says nobody can publicly perform her musical work without a license. But if she has no way of knowing, how can she enforce her rights?

Realistically, she can't. That's why she affiliates with a **performing rights society**.

We have three performing rights societies (PRSs) in the United States: ASCAP, BMI, and SESAC.[2] Musical work copyright owners (composers and music publishers) affiliate with one of the three PRSs. Accordingly, each PRS has a repertoire consisting of all the registered compositions of its affiliate members. (As an affiliate, you register each of your compositions with the PRS, one by one. If you don't register a particular composition, you won't collect any public performance royalties for that composition.)

Each PRS collects public performance license fees from venues that publicly perform the compositions in its repertoire.[3] Through a series of complicated formulas based primarily on airplay, the PRS then distributes those fees to its affiliates – and thus the affiliates (the copyright owners) get paid for public performances of their musical works.

performing rights societies only license one of the six rights on the bundle: #4, the right of public performance

The performing rights societies' scope is limited. They collect license fees for only one type of work: musical works. They do not, for example, license public performances of literary, dramatic, or any other work of authorship, including sound recordings. And as to musical works they only license one of the six rights on the bundle: #4, the right of public performance. Further limiting their scope, they only license <u>nondramatic</u> public performances. So if you're directing a theatrical production, don't rely on anybody's ASCAP, BMI, or SESAC license for the music you use in the production.

If you want to use something other than a musical work; or if with respect to a musical work you want to exercise a right other than #4 (or you need a license to perform the work in a dramatic context): the PRSs have no authority and you must deal directly with the copyright owner (or its agent) to obtain

[2] ASCAP is the American Society of Composers, Authors and Publishers (http://www.ascap.com). BMI is Broadcast Music, Inc. (http://www.bmi.com). SESAC (http://www.sesac.com) used to stand for Society of European Stage Authors & Composers, but now it's just plain SESAC.

[3] Each PRS has a different license for almost every type of venue you can imagine. By way of example, look at this: http://www.ascap.com/licensing/licensefinder.aspx

the license(s) you need.

Kevin: Interesting. Now can we talk about how people get licenses to publicly perform my sound recordings by means of digital audio transmission?

TS: Absolutely. Do you know what a **statutory license** is?

Kevin: No.

TS: OK, let's start there.

For certain types of licenses, the copyright owner doesn't have a choice. The license is compulsory.

As we'll see in the next Conversation, there are many different kinds of copyright licenses. Most of the time, if you need a license you negotiate directly with the copyright owner. The copyright owner might choose to grant you the license, or he/she might not. In most cases, it's their choice. For certain types of licenses, though, the copyright owner doesn't have a choice. The license is compulsory. In such cases, as long as you meet certain requirements you are absolutely entitled to the license, and its terms (rates, etc.) are set by law.

Kevin: Wait. Let me guess. The terms of the license are in a **statute** and that's why it's called a **statutory license**.

TS: Exactly!

Kevin. Cool. What does this have to do with my sound recordings?

TS: There are statutory license provisions for certain types of PPSRDAT.

Kevin: PPSRDAT? What's that?

TS: That's shorthand I made up so I don't have to keep saying, "public performance of a sound recording by means of digital audio transmission."

Kevin: OK. PPSRDAT.

TS: There are PPSRDAT statutory licenses available for digital cable and satellite television services; for non-interactive webcasters; and for satellite radio services.

Kevin: So if those types of providers come to me for a license, I can't say no?

TS: Right, but they won't come to you directly.

Kevin: Why not?

TS: There is an organization called **SoundExchange** that administers these statutory licenses on behalf of sound recording copyright owners.

Kevin: So those providers go to SoundExchange to get their licenses?

TS: Yes.

Kevin: Then how do I get paid?

TS: You register with SoundExchange.

Kevin: I'd better get on that!

TS: Right.

Kevin: I can think of other types of digital audio transmission that wouldn't fall into those three categories of statutory licenses. For example, what about on-demand services where you can choose what you listen to?

TS: For those uses licensing is not compulsory and the provider will have to negotiate with you directly.

Kevin: This sounds complicated.

TS: It is, but if you want to maximize your income it's worth taking the time to master.

Kevin: How do I learn more?

TS: Go to the SoundExchange website: http://soundexchange.com

YOU TRY

For comprehensive research about music copyright infringement cases from the mid-nineteenth century forward: http://mcir.usc.edu

Conversation #13

Song of the Century: More on Music Licensing

Music publishing
Mechanical licensing
Harry Fox Agency
Licensing music for films
Samples
Warranties, representations, and indemnification
Fig. 3: Types of Copyright Licenses

When Rebecca was in fifth grade she composed a song decrying environmental disaster. Creatively, she called the song, *Pollution*. It employed the only two chords she could play on the guitar and here is the entirety of its chorus:

It is pollution, pollution, pollution it is.

It is pollution, pollution, pollution it is.

Lucky for Rebecca (and as you will recall from Conversation #9) the originality threshold for copyright protection is rather low. So her musical work acquired a copyright and with it, the entire bundle of rights.

Pollution became an overnight smash thanks to the fifth-grade underground music scene. Music publishers throughout the land vied for the right to add *Pollution* to their catalogs. Big Giant Music Publishing (BGMP) won the deal. They had plans to earn buckets of money from the composition. To do that, though, they needed to own (or at least control) Rebecca's bundle of rights. So Rebecca transferred the entire bundle over to BGMP, in exchange for 50 percent of BGMP's **net income** from exploiting the composition.

Soon thereafter, recording artist KayP decided she wanted to sing *Pollution* on her next album. To record the song, KayP needed a license. Before reading on, take a moment to reflect on our prior Conversations. What kind of license(s) did KayP need, and why?

KayP needed a license for the first of the six rights: the right to reproduce *Pollution* in a **phonorecord**.[1] And because BGMP now controlled Rebecca's bundle of rights, KayP had to obtain that license from BGMP.

Or did she?

In Conversation #12 our friend Kevin introduced us to the concept of compulsory statutory licenses. Well, guess what? There's a compulsory statutory license provision that permits you to make and distribute phonorecords of musical works that have already been distributed to the public under the authority of the copyright owner (17 USC §115[a][1]). This type of reproduction license is called a **mechanical license**. If you are making your own recording (reproduction) of somebody else's musical work (composition), and your intent is to distribute copies of your recording to the public: you need a mechanical license. (Read that last sentence again, when you're working on YOU TRY #2, below.) And because mechanical licensing is compulsory, the copyright owner can't say no (provided all the requirements of the statute have been satisfied). For that reason, many copyright owners (mainly, music publishers) use a company called the **Harry Fox Agency** to administer mechanical licenses for them.

because mechanical licensing is compulsory, the copyright owner can't say no

OK, back to our story. As it turned out, BGMP used Harry Fox's services. So KayP obtained her mechanical license from Harry Fox and recorded her album. The physical objects she produced – the CDs themselves – were **phonorecords**. They didn't acquire any copyright rights, because CDs are just tangible "things," not **works of authorship**. KayP's performance, however, i.e., the actual sounds as fixed on each of those phonorecords, was copyrightable as a **sound recording**.

[1]Remember, a phonorecord is the material object in which a sound recording is embodied (17 USC §101). The term includes CDs, tapes, vinyl records, etc.

You knew that. But hang on. This is about to get more complicated.

Meg is a filmmaker.

Meg: Hi, TS. May I ask a question?

TS: Sure.

Meg: Jennifer and I love Rebecca's song, *Pollution*, and we would like to use it in our upcoming film. Are we good if we just go to Harry Fox and get a mechanical license?

TS: No.

Meg: Why not?

TS: Mechanical licenses do not cover reproduction of musical works for use in motion pictures or other audiovisual works.

Meg: So what do we do?

TS: You need a different kind of reproduction license, called a **synchronization** license. A "synch" license permits the mechanical reproduction of a musical composition for use in "timed synchronization" within a motion picture or other audiovisual work.

Meg: OK, so I go to Harry Fox and ask for a synchronization license?

TS: No. Harry Fox does not issue synchronization licenses.

Meg: TS, this is becoming a barrier to productivity. (Takes a breath.) Who do I ask?

TS: The copyright owner or music publishing company.

Meg: Is synchronization licensing compulsory?

TS: No.

Meg: So the copyright owner is free to refuse my request for a license.

TS: Correct.

Meg: Great.

TS (donning protective gear): There's something else you're not fully appreciating.

Meg: What?

TS: Well, the synchronization license only applies to the musical work, *Pollution*.

Meg: So?

TS: So there are many different recordings of *Pollution*. There's the famous John Denver version; there's Ozzy Osbourne's rendition; and of course KayP's new recording. Which one are you going to use in the film?

Meg: We want to use KayP's recording.

TS: OK, so think about it. In addition to reproducing Rebecca's musical work, you'll also be reproducing KayP's **sound recording**.

Meg: Uh oh. I think I see where this is going.

TS: That's right. You need a license from KayP to reproduce her sound recording.

Meg: And I suppose that license has some kind of special name?

TS: Yes. It's called a **master use** license.

Meg: Who do I ask, for the master use license?

TS: The copyright owner. That would be KayP, or, if she's signed to a label, her record company.

Meg: OK, TS. I know I'm going to regret this, but what else am I overlooking?

TS: Well, suppose KayP's master recording contains unlicensed samples or other material that infringes on somebody else's copyrights?

Meg: What if it does? That's not my fault.

TS looks at the floor.

Meg: No *!?#* way! Are you kidding me?

TS: If you use the recording in your film, and it contains infringing material, you are liable for copyright infringement right along with KayP.

Meg: So what are you saying? I can never safely use a recording in my work?

TS: No, I'm not saying that. But you do need to have well-drafted licenses in place that provide you with safeguards (**warranty** and **indemnification** provisions) assuring you that the material you are licensing does not infringe on somebody else's copyright (that's the warranty part) and that if it does – and you get sued – the licensor will pay your costs and make you whole (that's the indemnification part).

if you use the recording in your film, and it contains infringing material, you are liable for copyright infringement

Meg: Sounds like I should use a lawyer for that.

TS: Good ear, Meg.

YOU TRY

1. What's the difference between ℗ and the familiar ©? For the answer, check out Circular 3: www.copyright.gov/circs/circ03.pdf *(Then, for more on the copyright notice, stay tuned for Conversation #14.)*
2. What do music boxes and player pianos have to do with mechanical licenses? Do a little research. The answer is interesting!
3. A mechanical license permits you to exercise the copyright owner's right of reproduction. Look at the statute. Which other rights from the bundle does it also address?
4. Check out the Harry Fox Agency's website to learn more about their services: www.harryfox.com.

5. The danger is real. Without taking proper precautions, you can be liable for copyright infringement that somebody else committed if – even unwittingly – you use the infringing material. Enter the following phrases into a search engine and see for yourself how easily it can happen: "awkward tombstones" "santa claus" flickr
6. Come back to this after you've read Conversation #19. Do you think Qwest could have been held liable for the infrigement committed by Vilana? Assuming the answer is "yes" what could Qwest have done to protect itself?

There's No Such Thing As A Copyright License

By now it should be sinking in: when you want to use a copyrighted work you don't just ask for a "copyright license." You need to think about the bundle of rights; identify exactly what you intend to do with the work; and get appropriately specific licenses for each part of the bundle your proposed use will implicate.

The chart on the following page describes some of the licenses arts entrepreneurs are likely to need. For more information on copyright licensing sources, visit the Copyright Office website at: http://www.copyright.gov/resces.html

TYPES OF LICENSES

Work of Authorship	Bundle Number	For What	Examples	Type of License Required	Who To Ask
Musical work	4	Performing in public (non-dramatic)	Broadcast; live concert; background music; on-hold music	Public Performance	ASCAP/ BMI/SESAC (Conv. #12)
Sound Recording	6	Performing in public (via digital audio transmission only)	Webcasting; satellite radio; cable TV	Public Performance	Sound Exchange (Conv. #12)
Literary, dramatic choreography audiovisual	4	Performing in public	Staged readings; showing films; producing plays	Public Performance	Copyright owner or its licensing agent
Musical work	1	Reproducing in a recording	Recording a cover tune	Mechanical	Copyright owner or the Harry Fox Agency (Conv. #13)
Musical work	1	Reproducing in film/AV	Using a composition in your film	Synchronization	Copyright owner
Sound recording	1	Reproducing for any purpose	Sampling; using a sound recording in your film	Master Use	Copyright owner (Conv. #13)
All	2	Making a derivative work	Making a movie based on a book	Adaptation	Copyright owner
All except recordings	5	Displaying the work publicly	Images on websites; tattoos	Public Display	Copyright owner

CONVERSATION #14

Copyright Notice and Registration

STATUTORY DAMAGES
USING THE NOTICE
REGISTRATION
ELECTRONIC COPYRIGHT OFFICE

In years past, securing federal copyright protection wasn't quite as simple as it is today. Published work had to include a copyright notice. ("Notice" refers to use of the familiar © symbol.) Unpublished work had to be registered with the US Copyright Office (see Conversation #15 for a discussion about **publication**). Neither rule any longer applies. Today, copyright attaches as soon as copyrightable material is fixed in a tangible medium of expression (see Conversation #10).

This does not mean that notice and registration are unimportant. They are very important. So don't skip this Conversation.

Even though notice and registration are no longer required, they figure prominently in your ability to sue for copyright infringement and to collect damages when you win the case. You can't bring an infringement action until you've registered the work in question, so you might as well register now (17 USC §411). Plus, registration before infringement takes place (or within three months after **publication**) might qualify you for **statutory damages**. If not, you have to settle for **actual damages,** or the actual amount of your loss (and the infringer's gain) as a result of the infringing activity. Statutory damages can be significantly greater than actual damages (see Conversation #18).

Notice matters, too. Here's why. In a copyright infringement action the judge has discretion to award statutory damages to an eligible plaintiff *in a sum of not less than $750 nor more than $30,000* per infringement (17 USC §504[c][1]). If the infringement is found to be *willful*, the court has discretion to award up to $150,000 per infringement (17 USC §504[c][2]). If, on the other hand, the infringer *was not aware and had no reason to believe that his or her acts constituted an infringement of copyright*, the court may reduce statutory damages to not less than $200 per infringement (17 USC §504[c][2]). Whether you placed a notice on your work can be an important factor in determining whether infringing activity was *willful* or *innocent*. And that determination can mean the difference between $200 per infringement or, potentially, $150,000.

whether you placed a notice on your work can be an important factor in determining whether infringing activity was *willful* or *innocent*

Notice on published works should take the following form:

COPYRIGHT © [YEAR OF FIRST PUBLICATION] [YOUR NAME]

If your work is unpublished, an appropriate notice would be:

UNPUBLISHED WORK © [YEAR] [YOUR NAME]

For more information about copyright notice, see Copyright Office Circular 3 at: http://www.copyright.gov/circs/circ03.pdf

Is there an eCO in here?

Copyright registration takes place online at the US Copyright Office's Electronic Copyright Office (eCO). The Copyright Office has prepared some very useful tips and frequently asked questions, along with a step-by-step tutorial. All are available at http://www.copyright.gov/eco.

Can you learn to register your own work? Sure. But first get advice. Although the online forms appear to be simple and straightforward, it's easy to make errors unknowingly. If that happens you might very well receive a registration, yet not realize there's a problem until you need to rely on it. By then it will be too late.

YOU TRY

Copyright law changes frequently. If you want to know how the requirements for copyright protection have changed over time, turn to the YOU TRY section of Conversation #16. For now, know that there was, indeed, a time when notice and/or registration was required, and when registrations had to be renewed. So if you are seeking to use a "copyrighted" work don't just assume it is still protected. If the author failed to comply with whatever requirements were in place at the time, the work may have fallen into the **public domain**. You should ask a copyright lawyer to make this determination.

CONVERSATION #15

Copyright: Guess What "Publication" Means?

As we discussed in Conversation #14, registration with the Copyright Office is not required in order to obtain a copyright. Still, there are important reasons for choosing to register your work:

MORE ON THE IMPORTANCE OF REGISTRATION

MORE ON COPIES AND PHONORECORDS

UNDERSTANDING PUBLICATION

- A registration creates a public record of your copyright claim in the work.
- You cannot file an infringement suit in court unless you have registered the work.
- If you register within five years of the work's first **publication**, the registration constitutes *prima facie* evidence, in court, of the validity of your copyright and the facts stated in your certificate. (*Prima facie* means you don't have to submit evidence to prove the point. It's up to the other side to show you're wrong.)
- If you register within three months after the work's first **publication**, you can be eligible for statutory damages and attorney fees in an infringement suit.
- Registration allows you to record your copyright with United States Customs and Border Protection, to protect against the importation of infringing copies of your work. (For more information about this issue, visit http://www.cbp.gov/ipr)

So registration is important, and you may at some

point find yourself registering your own work with the Copyright Office. During that process, the online application will ask whether the work you are registering has yet been **published**. If you don't understand the legal meaning of **publication**, you might respond incorrectly and that could compromise the validity of your copyright registration.

What do you think **publication** means? Most people think literally, believing it refers to traditional print publication – as in a book or a magazine, or online. They figure, if the work didn't appear in one of those media, it was never "published."

if you don't understand the legal meaning of *publication*, it could compromise the validity of your copyright registration

Not so.

Here's how section 101 of the copyright law (17 USC §101) defines the term **publication** (emphasis supplied):

> *"Publication" is the **distribution of copies or phonorecords** of a work **to the public** by sale or other transfer of ownership, or by rental, lease, or lending. The offering to distribute copies or phonorecords to a group of persons for purposes of further distribution, public performance, or public display, constitutes publication. **A public performance or display of a work does not of itself constitute publication.***
>
> *To perform or display a work "publicly" means —*
>
> *(1) to perform or display it at a place open to the public or at any place where a substantial number of persons outside of a normal circle of a family and its social acquaintances is gathered; or*
>
> *(2) to transmit or otherwise communicate a performance or display of the work to a place specified by clause (1) or to the public, by means of any device or process, whether the members of the public capable of receiving the performance or display receive it in the same place or in separate places and at the same time or at different times.*

Section 101 also defines **copies** and **phonorecords**:

- *"Copies" are material objects, other than phonorecords, in which a work is fixed by any method now known or later developed, and from which the work can be perceived, reproduced, or otherwise communicated, either directly or with the aid of a machine or device.* ***The term "copies" includes the material object, other than a phonorecord, in which the work is first fixed****.*
- *"Phonorecords" are material objects in which sounds, other than those accompanying a motion picture or other audiovisual work, are fixed by any method now known or later developed, and from which the sounds can be perceived, reproduced, or otherwise communicated, either directly or with the aid of a machine or device.* ***The term "phonorecords" includes the material object in which the sounds are first fixed****.*

Further explanation appears in the Copyright Office's *Circular 1* (http://www.copyright.gov/circs/circ01.pdf):

> *"...it is clear* ***that any form of dissemination in which the material object does not change hands****, for example, performances or displays on television,* ***is not a publication*** *no matter how many people are exposed to the work. However, when copies or phonorecords are offered for sale or lease to a group of wholesalers, broadcasters, or motion picture theaters, publication does take place if the purpose is further distribution, public performance, or public display."*

So it comes down to this. Your copyrightable work is embodied in a material object (e.g., canvas; digital media; paper). If that material object (and/or additional **copies** of work) changes hands: your work has been **published**. If you simply display or perform your work but material copies of it do not change hands, your work has not been published.

Here are some additional reasons why it is important to understand about publication.

- A work's status as published or unpublished can affect the court's analysis in determining whether another person's use of your work was or was not **fair use**.
- "Published" or "unpublished" is the determining factor in certain cases involving library exemptions and protection for authors of other nationalities; it also affects whether you need to deposit copies of your work with the Library of Congress.
- Certain procedures for registering multiple works with a single application are available for published works; other types (with different rules) are available for unpublished works (see Conversation #17). If you don't know the difference, you might end up with an invalid registration.

Conversation #16

How Long Does It Last? (Copyright Duration)

For years, copyright lasted for the life of the **author** plus fifty years. In the Copyright Term Extension Act of 1998 (CTEA), Congress extended this period from life of the author plus fifty years, to life plus seventy.[1]

Eldred v Ashcroft
Calculating when work falls into the public domain

In January 2003 the United States Supreme Court decided *Eldred v Ashcroft* (537 US 186, 123 S Ct 769, 154 L Ed 2d 683 [2003]), a case challenging the constitutionality of the CTEA. With Justices Breyer and Stevens dissenting, a majority of the Court upheld the CTEA, finding that Congress acted within its constitutional authority by extending the duration of copyright protection, both for existing and future works.

In this Conversation we will examine the nuts and bolts of copyright duration. In short, we're going to do math.

But first, a few words about *Eldred*. The CTEA tacked on an additional twenty years to the term of copyright, both for existing work already subject to copyright protection, and for work yet to be created ("future work"). In *Eldred*, challengers conceded that extending the term for future work was within Congress's authority, because the US Constitution permits Congress to enact legislation

[1]Congress did so at the behest of the late Rep. Sonny Bono who, many believe, took his inspiration from an entertainment conglomerate facing the imminent expiration of valuable copyrights. You do the math.

securing to authors for limited times ...the exclusive right to their...writings (see Conversation #10). There can be no argument that the span of time defined as "life of the author plus seventy years" is a finite, *limited time.*

The challengers contended, however, that applying the extension to existing work, for which the duration clock had already begun ticking, violated the Constitution's *limited times* provision. The *limited time* in effect when a copyright is secured, they argued, *becomes the constitutional boundary, a clear line beyond the power of Congress to extend* (*Eldred v Ashcroft*, supra, 537 US 186, 193). The Supreme Court disagreed, finding that if life plus seventy is a *limited time* for future work, it's also a *limited time* for existing work. As the Court noted, Congress has extended the term of copyright numerous times since enactment of the Constitution's copyright clause in 1790 (most notably in 1831 and 1909), and in all cases the extensions applied to existing, as well as future, works. So our current reality is that Congress can change the rules, mid-game. And at the moment, the rule is "life of the author plus seventy years."

our current reality is that Congress can change the rules, mid-game

January 1, 1978, to present. "Life plus seventy" applies to works created and fixed in a tangible medium of expression on or after January 1, 1978. If the work happens to be a **joint work** in which two or more authors share the copyright (see Conversation #27), the term lasts for 70 years after the death of the last surviving author. Copyright protection for **work made for hire** (see Conversation #28), as well as anonymous and pseudonymous works, is 95 years from first **publication** or 120 years from creation, whichever is shorter.

Congress amended the Copyright Act in 1976. The 1976 amendments (which became effective on January 1, 1978) did away with the previous requirement that in order to secure copyright protection, a work had either to be published or registered with the Copyright Office. Now all an author has to do to get copyright protection is to fix her work in a tangible medium of expression (see Conversation #10).

Pre-January 1, 1978. Prior to the 1976 amendments copyright only lasted for 28 years. In order to obtain a second 28-year term (extending the total term of protection to 56 years), an author had to renew his copyright with the Copyright Office – and could do so only in the 28th year of the first term. If the author failed to renew within that narrow window of time, the work passed into the public domain.

The 1976 amendments tacked on an additional 39 years to the renewal term, bringing the total term of copyright protection from 56 years (28 plus 28, as above) to 95 years (28 years in the first term plus 67 years [28 plus 39] in the renewal term.) Until a subsequent amendment in 1992, you still had to renew your copyright in order to get those 67 extra years. After the 1992 amendments, renewal became automatic.

all of this ancient history actually matters today

All of this ancient history actually matters today. Suppose, for example, you wish to use a photograph in your work. If the photograph is a post-1977 work, you know that its copyright lasts for the life of the photographer plus seventy years, and it will not fall into the public domain until then. If the photograph was taken before January 1, 1978, though, you need to know about all of those prior rules and amendments, and which one(s) apply to the work in question.

Our Conversation so far has addressed pre-1978 work that was properly published or registered with the Copyright Office. What about pre-1978 work that had not been properly published or registered?

Work that had been created, but neither published nor registered before January 1, 1978, automatically got copyright protection under the 1976 amendments. In general, such work is now subject to the "life plus seventy" rule. As an additional perk, all such pre-1978 nonpublished, nonregistered work got a guaranteed period of protection for 25 years and a free pass until December 31, 2002. So the copyright for work in this category lasted for "life plus seventy" or until December 31, 2002, whichever was greater. And to make matters even more complicated, if the work happened to get published between January 1, 1978, and December 31, 2002, it got another 45 years, extending the copyright to "life plus seventy" or December 31, 2047, whichever is greater.

by now you're probably getting the picture: calculating copyright duration is not a simple task

By now you're probably getting the picture: calculating copyright duration is not a simple task. We haven't even discussed the old notice requirement or the special rules for work originally copyrighted between January 1, 1950, and December 31, 1963!

When copyright duration is at issue, your first question should be whether the work was published before 1923. If so, it is in the public domain. Chances are you'll be dealing with more recent works, however, in which case the cardinal question is whether the work was created before or after January 1, 1978. If the work was created on or after that date, and there is a single author, you're dealing with the familiar "life plus seventy." If the work was created before January 1, 1978, if it's a **work made for hire,** or if there is more than one author involved, be aware that calculating the applicable term requires more careful analysis.

YOU TRY

1. To learn more about copyright duration, consult the Copyright Office's Circular 15a, available online at: http://www.copyright.gov/circs/circ15a.pdf

2. These two charts are also great resources:

   http://copyright.cornell.edu/resources/publicdomain.cfm (By Peter B. Hirtle)

   http://www.unc.edu/~unclng/public-d.htm (By Lolly Gassaway)

CONVERSATION #17

Copyright: Registering Multiple Works Together

Groups

Collections

Single units of publication

Special considerations for photographs

Sara, a photographer, told TS she had registered several images with the Copyright Office. She asked, *Does a copyright registration cover all current and future pieces of my art – or do I have to register each one?*

Typically, a single application and fee covers a single work of authorship: that is, a single painting, a single book, a single recording, etc. The Copyright Office's Circular 40 explains (www.copyright.gov/circs/circ40.pdf):

> *Registration covers only the particular work deposited for the registration. It does not give any sort of "blanket" protection to other works in the same series [nor] any earlier or later [work].*

Not only that, every time you revise a work, you need to re-register. *Circular 40* states:

> *Each copyrightable version or issue must be registered to gain the advantages of registration for the new material it contains.*

That is not what Sara wanted to hear.

She brightened momentarily when TS told her it is possible to register more than one work, with a single application and a single fee.

Then TS qualified her answer. It's possible, but they don't make it easy. There are many rules and they're difficult to find. As TS explained: You can realistically learn to do simple, single-work copyright registrations on your own. Registering multiple works together is more appropriately a project for your copyright lawyer. If you do it yourself and make a mistake, your registration is vulnerable to being invalidated in a dispute.

Sara still wanted to learn more, so she and TS sat down for a chat. TS began by advising Sara to set her regular vocabulary aside, keeping in mind that words like **group** and **collection** have very specialized legal meanings.

Group Registrations

Copyright law *requires* that **group** registration be permitted for works by the same author that were all first published as contributions to periodicals.

registering multiple works together is a project for your copyright lawyer

Copyright law *permits* the **Register of Copyrights** to specify by **regulation** other types of work that are eligible for **group** registration. The Register of Copyrights has chosen by regulation to permit group registration for the following five types of work:

- Automated databases
- Related serials
- Daily newspapers
- Daily newsletters
- Published photographs

So. If the works you want to register together fall into one of the above categories, you might be eligible to pursue a **group** registration. Each of those categories, though, has its own set of regulations prescribing different requirements and procedures. That's why this is so tricky: the group registration rules are not the same for each permitted category of work.

Sara: Can you tell us more about the rules for group registration of published photographs?

TS: Sure, but let's do that at the end of this Conversation so our non-photographer friends can skip out if they want to.

Sara: OK.

Single Work Registrations

The second method for registering multiple works together (and hang on, because this is confusing) is called **single work** registration. (Thanks a lot, Copyright Office. Would it have been too much trouble to name this *multiple work* registration?) Anyway. If the works you are trying to register together are not in the categories that qualify for **group** registration, there are two types of **single work** registrations that might be available:

the second method for registering multiple works together is called *single work* registration

1. If the works you are registering have been published, you may register together those that were first published in a **single unit of publication**.
2. If the works you are registering are unpublished, you might be able to register them together as a **collection**.

But again, there are very specific requirements you're not going to find on the Copyright Office website (at least not easily), so if you want to submit a **single unit of publication** or a **collection** registration, you're best advised to seek advice from a copyright attorney.

Sara wondered, *If I register multiple works together in one of the ways TS just described, can my registration certificate list each individual work that's included?*

The answer reflects a positive development in registration procedure: Yes.

Prior to the introduction of **eCO** (the Copyright Office's system for registering works online), a multiple-work registration would only contain the single title you gave to the group or collection. Now it is possible to list and have included in the registration the title of each individual work that's included.

Sara (turning to leave): Great, thanks a lot.

TS: Wait, didn't you want to know more about the group registration rules for published photographs?

Sara: Oh. Yes, please.

The first place to look for information is Copyright Office Fact Sheet, FL-124 (http://www.copyright.gov/fls/fl124.pdf):

> *A group of **published** photographs may be registered on a single form with a single fee if <u>all</u> the following conditions are met:*
>
> *1. All the photographs are by the same photographer. If an employer for hire is named as author, only one photographer's work may be included; AND*
>
> *2. All the photographs **are published within the same calendar year**; AND*
>
> *3. All the photographs have **the same copyright claimant**(s).*

And here's an important note of caution:

> *If infringement of a published work begins before the work has been registered, the copyright owner can obtain the ordinary remedies for copyright infringement (including injunctions, actual damages and profits, and impounding and disposition of infringing articles). However, the owner cannot obtain special remedies (statutory damages and attorney's fees) unless registration was made before the infringement commenced <u>or within 3 months after first publication of the work</u>.*
>
> *To be certain that your application, deposit, and fee are received in the Copyright Office within 3 months of publication <u>of the earliest published photograph</u> within the group, you may wish to register fewer than 3 months of published photographs on a single application.*

As we learned in Conversation #14, registration within three months after publication is required if you want to collect **stat-**

utory damages. Otherwise you have to settle for **actual damages,** or the actual amount of your loss (and the infringer's gain) as a result of the infringing activity. *FL-124* is telling us that your three-month grace period starts ticking from the date of publication for the earliest published photograph in the group.

Example. Your group contains twelve photographs, each published in a separate month of calendar year 2050 (one was published in January, one in February, etc.). You figure you'll wait until January 2051 to submit your group registration, in order to get the most for your $35 fee. If someone infringes any of these photographs after March 2050, though, you're precluded from claiming statutory damages or attorney fees because your three-month grace period started ticking in January 2050.

Sara nodded and thanked TS. Then she called her copyright lawyer, to set up a regular schedule for registering her work.

Conversation #18

Copyright Damages: A Case for Registration

Bouchat v Baltimore Ravens, Inc.

Importance of registration

Actual and statutory damages

Summary judgment

This is the story of Frederick Bouchat, a Maryland security guard and amateur artist. When the Cleveland Browns® football team announced its move to a new city (Baltimore) and adoption of a new identity (the Ravens), Mr. Bouchat took it upon himself to sketch some new logo designs for the team. He faxed one of his designs (the "Winged Shield" design) to the Chairman of the Maryland Stadium Authority, along with a note asking the Chairman to forward the design to the Ravens' president. Mr. Bouchat asked the Ravens to send him a letter of recognition and an autographed helmet if they used the Winged Shield design.

Guess what happened?

Of course, they used the design. (This wouldn't be a very exciting story, otherwise). But they didn't send a letter, and they didn't send a helmet. So Mr. Bouchat sued for copyright infringement, and won (*Bouchat v Baltimore Ravens, Inc.*, 215 F Supp 2d 611, affd 346 F3d 514, cert denied 541 US 1042, 124 S Ct 2171, 158 L Ed 2d 732 [2004]). He had a jury verdict against the National Football League and it was upheld on appeal. Gotta be worth millions, right?

Wrong.

Had Mr. Bouchat registered the Winged Shield

design with the Copyright Office prior to the infringement, he would have been eligible for potentially enormous **statutory damages**. But he hadn't registered in time, so he had to settle for the consolation prize: his own **actual damages** (of which there were none) and profits of the infringer that were "attributable to the infringement" (17 USC §504[b]).

in order to measure an infringer's profits, the copyright owner needs to present evidence of the infringer's gross revenue

Here's how the damages statute works. In order to measure an infringer's profits, the copyright owner needs only to present evidence of the infringer's gross revenue. Then it's up to the infringer to prove that its profits were attributable to factors other than the copyrighted work. (This is called "shifting the burden of proof.") Mr. Bouchat's lawyers contended that at least some portion of all Ravens revenue was attributable to the infringement, so the lawyers merely submitted evidence of the gross receipts from all Ravens activities (e.g., ticket sales, merchandise, royalties, etc.)

The Ravens made a motion for **summary judgment** arguing that Mr. Bouchat had cast too wide a net by claiming profits from all revenue sources. (Stop. Go to the Glossary and look up **summary judgment**. It's important, in order to understand the rest of this story!) The court agreed, and granted the Ravens' motion, restricting the available pool from which the jury could award damages. The court allowed revenue from T-shirts, caps, souvenir cups, and a few other types of merchandise. Everything else (sponsorships, broadcasts, ticket sales, royalties and parking/concession revenue) was excluded from the pool. With apologies for mixing sports metaphors, this was strike one against Mr. Bouchat.

A damages trial proceeded, and the jury determined that the Ravens had submitted legally sufficient evidence that all profits – even from merchandise still in the pool – were attributable entirely to factors other than the Winged Shield design. Even though the Ravens had indisputably infringed, the jury awarded Mr. Bouchat absolutely nothing.

Strike two.

His only remaining hope was reversal on appeal. Mr. Bouchat argued that the lower court had erred by excluding so many categories of merchandise from the pool. His lawyers also contended that summary judgment in favor of an infringer – excluding portions of revenue from the damages pool – was not permissible. The Fourth Circuit Court of Appeals rejected these arguments.

Strike three.

Once you get through the legal gobbledy-gook, the point of the Fourth Circuit's decision is that **summary judgment** in favor of an infringer, excluding certain sources of revenue, is permissible, but only if: (a) there is "no conceivable connection" between the infringement and those revenues, or (b) despite the existence of a conceivable connection, the copyright holder failed to offer evidence of a "causal link" between the infringement and the revenue.

Wait a minute. The copyright holder failed to offer evidence...? We just said that the burden of proof had shifted to the infringer to show that their gross revenues were not attributable to the infringement. What gives?

That's what Mr. Bouchat wanted to know. In his view, he was entitled to the benefit of the presumption, under section 504 of the copyright law, that the infringer's revenues were entirely attributable to the infringement unless the infringer proved otherwise. Now all of a sudden it was he – the victim – who had to prove that the excluded categories were attributable to the infringement. Worse still, because summary judgment is a final determination made by a judge, he lost the opportunity to present his proof (regarding the excluded categories) to a jury. That just didn't seem right.

all of a sudden it was he – the victim – who had to prove that the excluded categories were attributable to the infringement

The appeals court, however, had no problem with this

approach so they set to analyzing the case under the "no conceivable connection" and "evidence of a causal link" tests. With respect to two categories of revenue (minimum guarantee shortfalls and free merchandise) the court found there was "no conceivable connection" between the Winged Shield and the revenue. Summary judgment excluding those two categories was upheld.

register your copyrights as soon as possible

With respect to the remaining excluded categories, the Fourth Circuit acknowledged that there could, conceivably, be a connection between the Winged Shield and the revenue. So the next question was: did Mr. Bouchat submit enough evidence to create a "question of fact" that profits from the excluded categories were attributable to the infringement? Please note, he didn't have to submit conclusive evidence at this point; to survive the summary judgment motion his lawyers only had to submit enough evidence to establish a "question of fact" for the jury.

Mr. Bouchat's lawyers had submitted nothing at all. In response to the summary judgment motion they simply relied, once again, on their evidence establishing the total gross receipts generated by all Ravens activities. They didn't submit a single thing drawing a causal link between those revenues and the Winged Shield design. Mr. Bouchat thereupon flunked the "causal link" test, and summary judgment on the remaining excluded categories was upheld.

Frederick Bouchat's pool had officially run dry.

This Conversation is somewhat heavy on the legalese. It's important to present this story fully, however, in order to convey two important concepts.

Important Concept #1: Register your copyrights as soon as possible. Had Mr. Bouchat registered in time to qualify for statutory damages, he might have collected upwards of $150,000 per infringement (see Conversation #14). That's a lot of money. Instead, he walked away empty-handed, with a hollow victory.

Important Concept #2: Lawyers make mistakes. No one is passing judgment on the performance of Mr. Bouchat's attorneys. This case might have turned out differently, however, had the legal team chosen to submit more evidence. In court, the "it should be obvious" argument rarely prevails. You want your lawyer to be meticulous about everything, and never to take anything for granted. Pay attention, and if something doesn't seem quite right, speak up. Make sure your case is being presented as clearly and as thoroughly as possible.

in court, the "it should be obvious" argument rarely prevails

CONVERSATION #19

Copyright Damages: Another True Story

GREGERSON V VILANA FINANCIAL, INC.

PUNITIVE DAMAGES

ATTORNEY FEES

DAMAGES FOR REMOVING WATERMARKS

PRO SE REPRESENTATION

Here's another true story with insights on digital watermarking, web-related copyright infringement, copyright damages, attorney fees, invasion of privacy, and representing oneself (***pro se***) in court.[1] This case also sports an interesting cast of characters and confirms that truth is indeed stranger than fiction.

Here's the story.

Chris Gregerson is a photographer. He licenses stock images, both on a single-use basis and for purchase as prints. In August 2002 Mr. Gregerson photographed a home in the Minneapolis area (the "Kenwood" photograph). In January 2004 he photographed the Minneapolis skyline (the "Skyline" photograph). Mr. Gregerson posted both photographs on his website. He placed a copyright notice underneath each image, along with visible and digital watermarks. He also posted the terms and conditions for licensing the photographs.

The defendants in this case are two Minnesota corporations offering mortgage, financial, and real estate services (the "Vilana" companies). Andrew Vilenchik is (or was) the principal shareholder of both corporations.

In May 2005 Mr. Gregerson discovered his Skyline photograph in a Vilana advertisement printed on

[1]*Gregerson v Vilana Financial, Inc.*, 446 F Supp 2d 1053 (D Minn 2006)

the inside cover of the 2005-2006 Qwest telephone book. The photograph had been cropped to remove the visible watermark. Reasoning that Qwest had printed approximately 500,000 copies of the telephone book, Mr. Gregerson estimated the fair market value for this use at $1,816. He sent defendants a letter demanding payment in the amount of $5,448, explaining that it was his policy to triple the charge for unauthorized use. He further stated that if payment were not received within two weeks, the fee would increase to ten times the normal charge, or $18,160.

Mr. Gregerson successfully defended the defamation claim and won the copyright case

The defendants chose to pay nothing.

Mr. Gregerson then discovered additional unauthorized uses of both the Skyline and the Kenwood photographs, in print and online. The Skyline photo showed up in advertisements in Zerkalo, a Russian-language newspaper, and on the *Zerkalo* website. Both photographs appeared in a Vilana trifold brochure.

Next (and for this part of the chronology we rely on statements Mr. Gregerson made on his website): Mr. Gregerson brought the equivalent of a small claims action against the defendants, seeking payment for the unauthorized uses. On his website, Mr. Gregerson also posted his thoughts about the dispute and about Mr. Vilenchik. His comments about Mr. Vilenchik were not complimentary.

Mr. Vilenchik (and company) sued Mr. Gregerson for **defamation** and **invasion of privacy by appropriation** (see Conversation #38). Mr. Gregerson then sued them, in federal court, for copyright infringement. Fast forward: after what one court deemed "a bout of litigation fever," Mr. Gregerson successfully defended the defamation claim and won the copyright case. Here are some of the highlights.

The "sauna defense" falls short. The defendants argued they were perfectly entitled to use the Skyline and the Kenwood photographs because they had commissioned them from the "real" photographer: a man named Michael Zubitskiy. Mr. Vilenchik testified that he met Mr. Zubitskiy in the sauna at a gym and, while in the sauna, commissioned Mr. Zubitskiy to take the two photographs. Let's jump ahead to the part where the court found: "*...there is no credible evidence to support a belief that 'Zubitskiy' exists or was the source of the controverted photos. It is highly implausible that after a brief meeting in the sauna... at which Zubitskiy did not provide contact information, references or examples of his work, Defendants commissioned Zubitskiy to perform the photography service."* The court found, bottom line, that "Zubitskiy" was a fabrication and that the defendants had unlawfully procured the photographs from Mr. Gregerson's website.

Copyright damages. As we just discussed in Conversation #18, you have two options for damages when you sue someone for copyright infringement. You can request "actual damages and profits" or (if you qualify) you can request "statutory damages." You have to choose one or the other; you can't ask for both.

the court found that "Zubitskiy" was a fabrication and that the defendants had unlawfully procured the photographs from Mr. Gregerson's website

Actual damages and profits are the actual damages you suffered as a result of the infringement, plus any profits of the infringer that are attributable to the infringement. **Statutory damages** allow the court to impose a sum of its choosing, within a range that the statute prescribes. Ordinarily, that range is between $750 and $30,000 per work. If the infringement was "willful," the court may impose statutory damages of up to $150,000 per work. Statutory damages are not available, however, unless you registered the work with the Copyright Office within one of several permissible windows of time.[2]

With respect to the Skyline photo, Mr. Gregerson sought actual damages. He claimed the fair market value for all uses of the photo was $4,462. Given his policy of increasing the fee

[2] 17 USC §§ 411, 412, 504

tenfold for unauthorized use, he sought $44,620 as actual damages. The court awarded $4,462. Here's why.

The law permits you to recover "actual damages and profits." It does not permit you to arbitrarily impose additional, **punitive damages** on those who infringe your work. As the court explained: *The Supreme Court has made very clear that the purpose behind the measure of damages set forth [in the actual damages statute] is to provide just compensation for the wrong, not to impose a penalty by giving to the copyright proprietor profits which are not attributable to the infringement.*

the burden is on the plaintiff to supply evidence establishing a direct connection between the infringing use, and the defendant's profits from such use

So: if you have a similar policy you might be able to enforce your penalty as a matter of contract law – but do not expect to do so under copyright law.

In addition to "actual damages," the law permits the owner of the infringed work to seek *any profits of the infringer that are attributable to the infringement and are not taken into account in computing the actual damages* (17 USC §504[b]). Accordingly, "profits of the infringer" might have been another source of damages for Mr. Gregerson, had he made that request – which he did not.

When asked for comment on this Conversation, Mr. Gregerson explained why he chose not to seek "profits of the infringer." As he had discovered, the burden is on the plaintiff (the owner of the infringed work) to supply evidence establishing a direct connection between the infringing use, and the defendant's profits from such use. Speculation is not good enough (see *Mackie v Reiser*, 296 F3d 909 [9th Cir 2002], cert denied 537 US 1189, 123 S Ct 1259, 154 L Ed 2d 1022 [2003]). In Mr. Gregerson's view, it would have been extremely difficult to secure admissible evidence establishing that his photo directly caused consumers to purchase Vilana products. (For a case where the plaintiff succeeded in establishing the required direct connection, see *Lucky Break Wishbone Corp. v*

Sears Roebuck & Co., 373 F Appx 752, 757-58 [9th Cir 2010, unpublished]).

With respect to the Kenwood photo, Mr. Gregerson sought statutory damages and a finding of willful infringement. He prevailed. The court found the infringement to be willful, and awarded statutory damages of $10,000.

removing the digital watermark was a slam dunk

Mr. Gregerson also sought attorney's fees. This claim was denied, principally because he did not have an attorney.

But he did receive one additional award, stemming from the defendants' removal of his digital watermark. There is a provision in the copyright law that states: *[n]o person shall, without the authority of the copyright owner or the law intentionally remove or alter any copyright management information* (17 USC §1202[b][1]). Removing the digital watermark, in this case, constituted a violation of §1202. (The court observed that removing the visible watermark might not have counted, due to a technical definition in the law. But removing the digital watermark was a slam dunk.) The range of statutory damages for violation of §1202 is not less than $2,500 and not more than $25,000. The court awarded Mr. Gregerson $5,000.

So, to sum up:

- Digital watermarks might be more valuable (financially) than visible watermarks.
- Adopting punitive penalty policies won't earn you any more in actual damages in copyright litigation.
- Have good contracts. (Would an enforceable website terms-of-use agreement have helped Mr. Gregerson?)
- Register your work in time to qualify for statutory damages.
- Don't rely on the sauna defense.

CONVERSATION #20

Using Copyrighted Work:

Asking for Forgiveness Is Not a Good Business Model

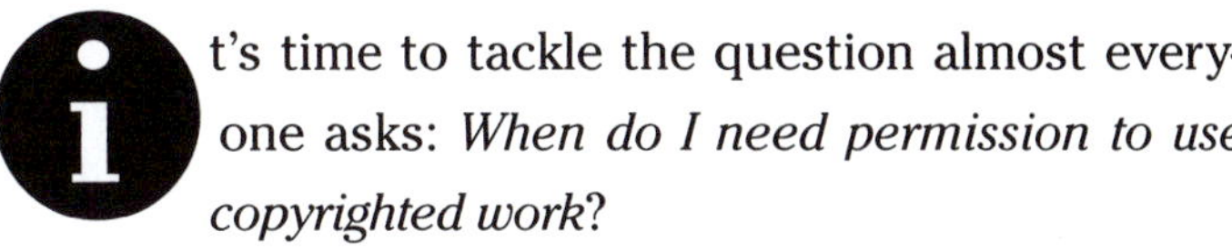

It's time to tackle the question almost everyone asks: *When do I need permission to use copyrighted work*?

Here are two extreme approaches.

Copyrightability
Public domain
Statutory exceptions
Fair use
Defenses to infringement
Fig. 4: Using Copyrighted Work

Emily is a high school English teacher. She loves teaching grammar because she always follows the rules. Always. When asked, *When do I need permission to use copyrighted work,* Emily's response is, "Always."

Mary is a dingbat. She's a wonderfully creative fiber artist and a joyous human being. But Mary is a dingbat, as she herself will happily concede. When asked, *When do I need permission to use copyrighted work*, Mary's response is, "What?"

The fundamental flaw with both of these approaches is that they seek the easy way out. They're trying to make the law black and white, and it isn't. The reality is that sometimes you need permission, and sometimes you don't.

Erring on Mary's side will obviously get us in trouble. But erring on Emily's side is just as dangerous (albeit for philosophical reasons). If we take Emily's easy way out and don't avail ourselves of the exceptions and legal principles that legitimately permit us to use copyrighted work without permission, we move closer to destroying the Constitutional balance upon which the copyright system is based (see Conversation #21).

There are a lot of myths out there. The greatest myth of all is that you may use another's copyrighted work so long as you change the work by some magical degree or percentage. Not true!

the greatest myth of all is that you may use another's copyrighted work so long as you change the work by some magical degree or percentage

There is no bright-line, across-the-board rule that permits you to use copyrighted work so long as you change it "enough." Rather, the only way to know whether you may use a copyrighted work is to conduct a thorough legal analysis. That's right. There's no way to sugar-coat this. You have to analyze every image, clip, poem, sample, passage, composition, recording.... This is a tedious procedure and it can cost money. On the other hand, this is your business. Clearing the rights to your work should be worth the investment.

There are six fundamental questions you need to ask (and answer) when you want to use someone else's copyrighted work. There are countless sub-issues related to each of the six questions, and that's why you should work with a lawyer. Still, you should study the six questions and their underlying concepts. With an informed appreciation for the issues, you'll be in good shape either to clear the rights on your own or to streamline your work with an attorney.

Question number one: **Is the work you want to use copyrightable material?** Not everything is subject to copyright protection. If the work isn't copyrightable at all, your analysis ends, and at least from a copyright perspective, you can use the work. Simple! What's not so simple is the fact that volumes of caselaw discuss what is and is not copyrightable. To be copyrightable the work must qualify as a "work of authorship;" it must be "original;" and it must be "fixed in a tangible medium of expression" (see Conversations #9 and #10).

Question number two: Assuming the work is copyrightable, **has it fallen into the public domain?** If the work is in the public domain, you can use it. Simple! What's not so simple is calculating when work falls into the public domain (see Conversation #16). At the Copyright Office website, *Circular 15a* addresses the issue of copyright duration (http://www.copyright.gov/circs/circ15a.pdf). Public domain calculations can be very tricky, so if more is at stake than you can afford to lose, be sure to consult a copyright lawyer.

OK. The work is copyrightable and not in the public domain.

Question number three: **Are there any statutory exceptions that would permit you to use the work without permission**? (See Conversation #21.)

Question number four: **Would your use of the work be an infringement of the owner's copyright?** We know that not all material is copyrightable. In the same vein, not all uses of copyrighted material are infringements. Nonlawyers can learn to answer many of their own legal questions. Determining whether a particular use is copyright infringement, however, falls into the category of "don't try this at home." Just know to ask this question before moving ahead.

if the work is in the public domain, you can use it

Question number five: Assuming your use would otherwise be an infringement, **can you assert fair use?** This one requires its own Conversation. So if you want to dive right in, turn to Conversation #21. For now, understand that fair use is a major consideration when the question is whether you can or cannot use copyrighted work without permission.

Question number six: **Do you have any other defenses to infringement?** Assuming you've struck out on questions one through five, your last hope for using a copyrighted work (and staying out of trouble) is to establish a defense to infringement. The defense of **independent creation**, for example, is available if you can establish that you did not copy the copyrighted work and that, in fact, any similarity between your work and the protected work is purely coincidental (see Conversation #9). Another possible defense: you copied, but you did not copy any protected elements of the copyrighted work (see Conversation #26).

If none of these considerations leads to the conclusion that you can use the work, there's only one thing left to do.

Emily knows what it is.

FIGURE 4

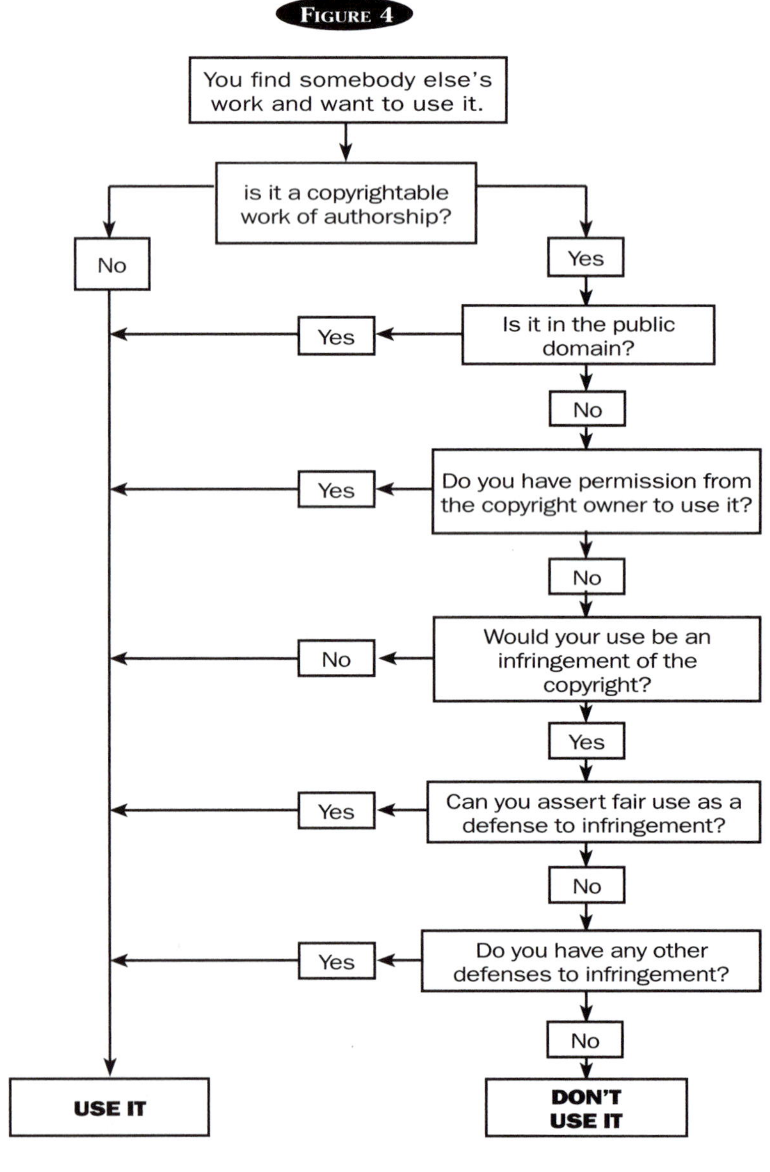

Conversation #21

Copyright: The Fair Use Doctrine

The statutory exceptions

Balancing rights of the author v rights of the public

Fair use analysis

The copyright **bundle of rights** is not absolute. That is to say, the rights are subject to certain limitations spelled out in the copyright law. These limitations (sometimes called **statutory exceptions**) appear in chapter 1 of title 17 of the United States Code (17 USC §§107-122). Refresh your statute-finding skills (see Conversation #4) and go take a look!

In plain English, the statutory exceptions mean: "Even though the work is copyrighted, you can {*use the work as the exception allows*}, without a license, as long as you satisfy all the terms of the particular statute." Example: section 110 says it's OK to perform or display works, without a license, in the course of face-to-face teaching activities at a nonprofit educational institution. There are several requirements you have to meet, in order to qualify for this exception. As long as you satisfy the requirements, you're in. You can take advantage of the exception.

Why do we have these exceptions? Because copyright is a balance between the rights of the author and the rights of the public. Remember, the US Constitution states that Congress has the power [*t*]*o promote the progress of science and useful arts, by securing for limited times to authors and inventors the exclusive right to their respective writings and discoveries* (see Conversation #10). That means we're going to give authors certain rights, for *limited times*, so they can make a living and keep creating. But after those *limited times* expire, we're going to allow works to pass into the public domain (so everyone can use them) in order to *promote the progress of science and useful arts* (see Conversation #16). It's not all about authors, and it's not all about the public. It's about balance. The statutory exceptions help to preserve that balance.

It's not all about authors, and it's not all about the public. It's about balance.

A cornerstone of this constitutional balance is the doctrine of **fair use**. Fair use is one of the more difficult exceptions to apply, and it is by far the most perplexing to understand. Its framework appears in section 107:

> *Notwithstanding the provisions of sections 106 and 106A, the fair use of a copyrighted work, including such use by reproduction in copies or phonorecords or by any other means specified by that section,* ***for purposes such as*** *criticism, comment, news reporting, teaching (including multiple copies for classroom use), scholarship, or research, is not an infringement of copyright. In determining whether the use made of a work in any particular case is a fair use* ***the factors to be considered shall include —***
>
> > *(1) the purpose and character of the use, including whether such use is of a commercial nature or is for nonprofit educational purposes;*
> >
> > *(2) the nature of the copyrighted work;*
> >
> > *(3) the amount and substantiality of the portion used in relation to the copyrighted work as a whole; and*
> >
> > *(4) the effect of the use upon the potential market for or value of the copyrighted work.*
>
> *The fact that a work is unpublished shall not itself bar a finding of fair use if such finding is made upon consideration of all the above factors.* 17 USC §107

There are two high-level steps to a fair use analysis. (Look at the sections of the statute in bold, above.) First, the proposed use must be for an acceptable purpose. The problem, however, is that the statute says "for purposes *such as*" criticism, comment, etc. In the words of various courts, those examples are "illustrative rather than limiting." So there's plenty of room for interpretation about whether a proposed purpose is or is not acceptable.

<u>Just because you have an acceptable purpose doesn't mean you're done</u>! You still have to balance the four enumerated factors to determine if the proposed use will be considered "fair." That's step two of the fair use analysis. The courts eloquently observe that balancing the four factors is an *open-ended and context-sensitive inquiry*. In other words: it's just shy of a crap shoot.

Well, not really. But courts have a tremendous amount of discretion in weighing and balancing the four factors. So predicting any outcome with certainty is very difficult.

Here is an acronym to remember the four factors: **PNAM**.

"P" **Purpose and Character of the Use**. In this first factor we look at your use of the copyrighted material. Why do you need it, and what are you doing with it? Are you using the material for a commercial purpose, or for an educational or expressive purpose? In general, educational/expressive purposes cut in favor of fair use while commercial purposes cut against. Another primary inquiry for this factor is whether your use of the material is "transformative." That is, have you used the material to create something new or to add new value or meaning to the original? Or (on the other hand) have you merely taken the material and used it as a replacement for its same original purpose?

"N" **Nature of the Copyrighted Work**. Next, you need to examine the nature of the work you are seeking to use. Was it the product of someone's creative energies? Or was it more a work of diligence? In general, the more creative the work, the more protection it will receive and the less likely you are to make a case for fair use. Was the image published (less protection) or not published (more protection); is it by nature entertaining (more protection) or educational (less protection)?

"A" **Amount Used**. This one can be misleading. In general, yes: the less you take, the better your case for fair use. Take only what you need to make your point or create your new transformative work... and no more. But it's not all about quantity. In fact, sometimes it's not about quantity at all; it's about *quality*. Even if you take just a tiny amount of the copyrighted work, you'll flunk this factor if what you take is the "heart" of that work. For example, if there is a three-note progression that absolutely identifies a famous song in the minds of others...and you take those three notes...you have taken the heart of the work. That's not OK. On the other hand, sometimes it's perfectly fine to take 100% of the work, as, for example, if you are reproducing a promotional concert poster for an acceptably transformative purpose. Of course you need to take the whole thing. It would look pretty silly (as would you) if you reproduced only the top left corner of the poster! Despite what you may have heard, there is no magic rule about "how much" is OK to take. This is a complicated issue, and you should seek advice from a copyright lawyer.

take only what you need to make your point or create your new transformative work... and no more

"M" **Market Effect of Your Use**. The fourth factor looks at whether, by using the copyrighted work without a license, you are undermining the market for the work or otherwise causing the copyright owner to lose income.

Final word from the courts:

> *The ultimate test of fair use...is whether the copyright law's goal of 'promoting the Progress of Science and useful Arts,' U.S. Const., art. I, § 8, cl. 8, would be better served by allowing the use than by preventing it.*

YOU TRY

1. Read the history and follow future developments in the

matter of *Cariou v Prince*. The Second Circuit Court of Appeals delivered an opinion on April 25, 2013. You'll see just how critical the question of work being "transformative" is, to fair use analysis.

2. Understanding fair use will always be a challenge. Here are some useful references:
    - Stanford University has assembled a collection of cases that helps us track how courts have applied the doctrine over time. Try reading the cases, or at least Stanford's summaries: http://fairuse.stanford.edu/Copyright_and_Fair_Use_Overview/chapter9/index.html
    - Columbia University's Copyright Advisory Office is a great resource. One of its offerings is a fair use checklist: http://copyright.columbia.edu/copyright/fair-use/fair-use-checklist
    - A coalition of stakeholders in the documentary film industry has prepared a publication called *Documentary Filmmakers' Statement of Best Practices In Fair Use*. Online locations frequently change, but at this writing the *Statement* is available on the website of American University's Center for Social Media: http://www.centerforsocialmedia.org/fair-use/best-practices/documentarydocumentary-filmmakers-statement-best-practices-fair-use
    - Prefer to get your information in comic book form? You're in luck, thanks to Duke University's Center for the Study of the Public Domain. Enjoy: *Tales From The Public Domain: Bound By Law?* http://web.law.duke.edu/cspd/comics/

CONVERSATION #22

That's Not Funny! (Parody, Satire, and Fair Use)

Copyright infringement

Rogers v Koons

Leibovitz v Paramount Pictures Corp.

Campbell v Acuff-Rose Music, Inc.

Dr. Seuss Enters., L.P. v Penguin Books USA, Inc.

Let's say you're a photographer. You were commissioned to photograph a married couple and their pets. Once the commission work was complete, you included the portrait in your portfolio. Later, you licensed it for reproduction on note cards. A famous sculptor purchased a set of the note cards and thought your image would make a great sculpture. So he physically ripped the copyright notice off your card, sent the card to fabricators in a foreign country, and instructed the fabricators to craft an exact replica of the image in your photograph. The sculptor's work garnered kudos and buckets of cash. When the sculpture was featured in a major metropolitan newspaper, you were not pleased. You were, in fact, livid. You sued the sculptor for copyright infringement. Do you know what happened next?

Chances are, you do know what happened next – because these are the facts of a highly publicized case: *Rogers v Koons* (751 F Supp 474, affd 960 F2d 301, cert denied 506 US 934, 113 S Ct 365, 121 L Ed 2d 278 [1992]). The photograph in question was entitled, *Puppies*. In black-and-white it depicted a man and a woman with eight newborn puppies. The sculpture, though colorized, was nearly identical. Evidence at trial confirmed, in fact, that the sculptor went to great lengths to ensure that details such as facial features and expressions were exactly the same as the photograph. The sculpture was entitled, *String of Puppies*.

Rogers v Koons is neither new nor particularly groundbreaking. Still, it's a good case for illustrating the concept of infringement. To establish infringement, the copyright owner must prove (a) that he/she owns a valid copyright to the work in question, and (b) that the alleged infringer copied elements of the work that are original to the copyright owner, without authorization.[1] In *Koons* the sculptor was found to have committed infringement.

had the sculptor expressed his own depiction of similar subjects, there would not have been a finding of infringement

Ideas are not copyrightable. You know that. The idea of depicting a man and a woman with a bunch of puppies, for example, is not protectible. Had the sculptor expressed his own depiction of similar subjects, there would not have been a finding of infringement. In this particular case, though, he blatantly reproduced elements of the photograph that were original to the photographer: shading (lighting), poses, and expressions. That was infringement.

> *Maybe so, argued the sculptor, but my work was a* ***parody*** *so I should be able to assert fair use as a defense.*
>
> *You can assert anything you want, said the court (in so many words), but that doesn't mean we're going to buy it. And in this case: we don't.*

The sculptor's parody-as-fair-use argument did not prevail. Here's why.

The *Koons* sculptor practiced "appropriation" art; i.e., the wholesale taking of an existing object or another work of art and suggesting an alternative meaning for the familiar image (think Andy Warhol, Marcel Duchamp). Notwithstanding the artistic value of this practice, in legal circles "appropriation" means stealing. In order to beat allegations of infringement,

[1]Refer back to the bundle of rights (Figure 2, Conversation #11). Exercising any of the rights in the bundle without permission can constitute copyright infringement; it's not just about "copying."

therefore, the appropriation artist needs to establish fair use.

The *Koons* sculptor explained that he'd appropriated *Puppies* for an exhibit at New York's Sonnabend Gallery called the *Banality Show*. He belonged to a school of artists believing that mass production of commodities and media images contributed to deterioration in the quality of society at large. His work in the *Banality Show* used commonplace images (such as a man, a woman, and their dogs) to advance this view.

The law encourages parody, because such criticism fosters creativity. As the sculptor would learn, however, it's not enough merely to proclaim that you have appropriated someone else's work to comment on society at large. If you're going to claim parody, the material you appropriate must itself be the object of your commentary.

the law encourages parody, because such criticism fosters creativity

The *Koons* court instructed, *the copied work must be, at least in part, an object of the parody, otherwise there would be no need to conjure up the original work.* With *String of Puppies* the sculptor was not making fun of the photograph, *Puppies*. He appropriated *Puppies* to make a comment about society in general.

Had *Puppies* been the object of a true parody, appropriating the *Puppies* image would have been necessary in order to conjure that original work in the viewer's mind. *Puppies*, however, was not the object of the sculptor's commentary, so there was no need to use that particular photo. The sculptor could have made the very same point with original or properly licensed material. **And that is the difference between parody and satire.** With a true parody, the original work is the object of commentary. In satire, the original work is simply appropriated to make an unrelated point. Unauthorized copying for purposes of parody supports the defense of fair use. Unauthorized copying for purposes of satire does not.

Now let's say you photographed a famous actress for the cover of a national magazine. In the photo, the actress is nude and eight months pregnant. She is depicted in profile with her right hand and arm covering her breasts and her left hand supporting her pregnant belly. A large ring adorns the middle finger of her right hand and her facial expression is serious, without the trace of a smile. Your cover causes this to become one of the magazine's best-selling issues of all time. Your name is Annie Leibovitz, the actress is Demi Moore, and the magazine *Vanity Fair* (August 1991).

Parody may or may not be fair use. Like any other use, parody has to be analyzed in light of all four of the fair use factors.

Two years later, Paramount Pictures starts to promote its movie, *Naked Gun 33 1/3: The Final Insult*, starring Leslie Nielsen. (And just to be clear: the late Leslie Nielsen was a man.) Paramount approves an advertising campaign in which Mr. Nielsen's mischievous, smirking face is superimposed on the photo of a similarly posed nude, pregnant woman (with a large ring on her middle finger) along with the words, "Due this March." You sue Paramount for copyright infringement, and lose.

Before we go on, a bit of history is in order. At one time (circa 1984), any unauthorized commercial use of copyrighted material was "presumptively unfair" (*Sony Corp. of America v Universal City Studios, Inc.*, 464 US 417, 104 S Ct 774, 78 L Ed 2d 574 [1984]). If you appropriated another author's material without a license, and you did so for a commercial purpose: the rest of the fair use factors were all but irrelevant and your fair use defense would probably fail. In 1994, however, the Supreme Court decided a case that changed things pretty dramatically. The case involved the musical group known as 2 Live Crew and its parody of Roy Orbison's hit, "Oh, Pretty Woman" (*Campbell v Acuff-Rose Music, Inc.,* 510 US 569, 114 S Ct 1164, 127 L Ed 2d 500 [1994]). The *Campbell* case stands for several important concepts, but for purposes of our Conversation this one is key: Parody may or may not be fair use. Like any other use, parody has to be analyzed in light of all four of the fair use factors.

OK, back to our story. In *Leibovitz v Paramount Pictures Corp.* (137 F3d 109 [2d Cir 1998]) the court dutifully applied the four factors to Paramount's claim of fair use. (Remember PNAM? If not, breeze through Conversation #21 as a refresher.) Whether the ad was or was not a true parody arose in the context of examining the first factor: the purpose and character of Paramount's use.

First Factor: Purpose and Character of the Use. Because Paramount claimed its use was a parody, the court had to determine whether the movie poster "commented" on the original photograph. As the court cautioned, *being different from an original does not inevitably 'comment' on the original.*

Because Mr. Nielson's smirking face contrasted so strikingly with Ms. Moore's serious expression, the court found that *the ad may reasonably be perceived as commenting on the seriousness, even the pretentiousness, of the original.* The court also observed that the poster might reasonably be perceived *as interpreting the Leibovitz photograph to extol the beauty of the pregnant female body and, rather unchivalrously, to express disagreement with this message.* The court contrasted Ms. Leibovitz's *serious portrayal of a beautiful woman taking great pride in the majesty of her pregnant body* with Paramount's *ridiculous image of a smirking, foolish-looking pregnant man.*

Paramount wasn't making fun of pregnant women in general: they were making fun of the Leibovitz photograph. To do so, they had to take at least enough of the original to conjure it up in the mind of the viewer. Importantly, too, the *Naked Gun* movie had a plot-line concerning pregnancy and parenthood. This "linkage of substance and content" was critical in establishing Paramount's parodic (as opposed to satirical) intent. The Paramount ad was therefore a parody, and as such, transformative.

The court also took up Ms. Leibovitz's argument that fair use should fail because Paramount used this poster for a commercial purpose. The court agreed: Paramount's use was commercial. And according to *Campbell*, a commercial use "lessens the indulgence" to which a parody is entitled. However, the court felt that the strength of the Paramount parody was so great as to tip the first factor significantly toward fair use, *even after making some discount for the fact that it promotes a commercial product.* "Less indulgence," said the court, "does not mean no indulgence at all."

The first factor thus tipped in favor of Paramount.

<u>Second Factor: Nature of the Copyrighted Work</u>. No one disputed that Ms. Leibovitz's work contained significant creative expression. That will almost always be the case, when an artistic work is the subject of parody. The second factor tipped in favor of Ms. Leibovitz.

commercial use lessens the indulgence to which a parody is entitled

<u>Third Factor: Amount and Substantiality of the Portion Used</u>. Remember, copyright does not protect ideas. It only protects original expression. In determining "how much" Paramount took from the original photograph, therefore, the inquiry focused not on each and every element of the photograph, but only on how much of Ms. Leibovitz's original expression (lighting, skin tone, camera angles, shading, etc.) Paramount copied. As it turned out, they copied a lot of her original expression--maybe even more than they needed to. But the court still tipped the third factor in favor of Paramount. The court did so because of language in *Campbell* suggesting that if the first and fourth factors favor the parodist, the third factor doesn't merit much weight. (Remember that comment in Conversation #21 about fair use being a crap shoot?) There may be flaws in this approach. At the moment we're just telling a story, though, and the story is this: the court tipped the third factor in favor of Paramount.

<u>Fourth Factor: Effect on the Market for the Copyrighted Work</u>. This one tipped easily for Paramount because Ms. Leibovitz essentially conceded the poster had no adverse effect on the market for her original photograph.

Weighing all four factors, the court upheld Paramount's claim to fair use.

The *Leibovitz* case involved a true parody. But what of **satire**? For that, we look at a case involving Dr. Seuss.

Theodore S. Geisel wrote and illustrated a series of famous children's books under the pseudonym "Dr. Seuss." One of his most famous works is *The Cat in the Hat,* first published in 1957. In 1995, following the celebrated O.J. Simpson murder trial, Alan Katz and Chris Wrinn, respectively, wrote and illustrated *The Cat NOT in the Hat!* satirizing the trial. They did not seek any kind of license, and litigation ensued.

The defendants claimed their work was a parody and that it constituted fair use. The court, however, found their work to be satire (*Dr. Seuss Enters., L.P. v Penguin Books USA, Inc.,* 109 F3d 1394 [9th Cir 1997]. As the court observed, *The stanzas and the illustrations simply retell the Simpson tale. Although* The Cat NOT in the Hat! *does broadly mimic Dr. Seuss' characteristic style, it does not hold <u>his style</u> up to ridicule*. The court went on to apply the four fair use factors, and resolved all four against the defendants.

If you're wondering why parody gets special treatment and satire does not, the reasoning is pretty simple. If you appropriate copyrighted work because you're making fun of it (as in parody), you pretty much have to copy it; otherwise your audience won't get the joke. Plus, the owner of the work isn't likely to grant you a license, knowing your intent is to mock the material. And that would stifle creativity.

If you appropriate copyrighted work because you're making fun of something *else* (as in satire), you don't necessarily need the particular work you're copying, to make your point. You could make the same point using other, properly licensed material, or you could create your own, fresh material to make that point.

Copyright is a balance between the rights of the author and the rights of the public. Permitting unauthorized copying for purposes of parody acknowledges the rights of the public. Prohibiting unauthorized copying for purposes of satire acknowledges the competing, equally precious, rights of the author.

Conversation #23

Quotations and Compilations

Quotations
Compilations
Databases
Taxonomies
Jokes

Linda asks:

I'm designing postcards with quotes by famous people. I see that many websites with collections of quotations have copyright notices. It is the same with books of quotations. This doesn't seem right. How can you copyright a quote by Picasso, Renoir, or Goethe?

Are quotations protected by copyright?

Let's review the copyright basics. First, we know that copyright does not protect names, titles, or short phrases (see *Circular 34*: http://www.copyright.gov/circs/circ34.pdf). If the quotation is a short phrase, it's probably not copyrightable at all.

Assuming the quotation is copyrightable, however, recall the other requirements for copyright protection: the work must be original and fixed in a tangible medium of expression (see Conversations #8 through #10). If the person to whom the quotation is attributed never fixed the quotation in a tangible medium of expression, the quotation is not protected by copyright. And if someone else fixed the quotation in a tangible medium it's still not protected. Why? Because in such case the quotation would not be original to that person.

What if the quotation is copyrightable and it was fixed in a tangible medium of expression by its original author? Then we determine whether the quotation has passed into the public domain (see Conversation #16). If the work was **published** before 1923 it is in the public domain. That pretty much clears quotations attributable to Pierre-August Renoir, who died in 1919, and Johann Wolfgang von Goethe, who died in 1823. Pablo Picasso, however, died in 1973. Theoretically, then, a work by Picasso – whether a painting or a copyrightable quotation – could still be subject to copyright protection.

compilers receive protection for their original contributions in assembling the compilation

If you suspect the quotation you wish to use might be protected by copyright and has not passed into the public domain (and there are no **statutory exceptions** for your proposed use) you must obtain permission to use it, either from the author him/herself or from that person's estate.

Those sites and books that Linda refers to are **compilations** of quotations. Under copyright law a compilation is *a work formed by the collective assembling of preexisting materials or of data that are selected, coordinated or arranged in such a way that the resulting work as a whole constitutes an original work of authorship* (17 USC §101, emphasis supplied). Copyright law protects original compilations (17 USC §103).

The copyright notices on those sites and books refer not to the underlying quotations themselves, but rather to the compilers' *selection, coordination and arrangement* of the quotations. As long as the compilers' editorial decisions reflect a threshold amount of creativity and judgment (see Conversation #9), the book or the website *as a compilation* qualifies for copyright protection.

Compilers receive protection for their original contributions in assembling the compilation – not (unless it's their original work) for the underlying material compiled. If a quotation resides in the public domain, therefore, it remains freely available notwithstanding issuance of copyright protection for any compilation in which it happens to appear. You can run into trouble if the quotation is not in the public domain, or if you copy protected elements of the compilation, i.e., its selection, coordination, and arrangement. However, as long as you use only the quotation itself (and it is, in fact, in the public domain), you are not committing copyright infringement.

if a quotation resides in the public domain, it remains freely available notwithstanding issuance of copyright protection for any compilation in which it happens to appear

Here's another example. Databases are compilations of data. If you assemble a database you are entitled to copyright protection for the compilation, i.e., your original selection, coordination, and arrangement of the data. But your compilation copyright does not extend to the underlying data itself.

YOU TRY

1. Do you know what a taxonomy is? Look it up. Then think about how, if at all, a taxonomy might be protected under copyright law. When you're ready, take a look at this case: *American Dental Assn. v Delta Dental Plans Assn.,* 126 F3d 977 (7th Cir 1997).
2. Our discussion about quotations also applies to jokes. As to both, if the material in question is copyrightable, it gets the full bundle of rights. But quotations and jokes are so "out there" it's often impossible to identify the author. How might **orphan works** legislation provide assistance? (See Conversation #3)

CONVERSATION #24

Owning the Piece (as Opposed to) Owning the Copyright

MORE ON LICENSING
ASSIGNMENTS
MORE ON STATUTORY EXCEPTIONS
TATTOOS

Paula:

A corporation wants to buy one of my art pieces and also use the image on brochures, catalogs, and flyers. I'm not sure how to handle this and I don't know if these are two separate transactions. Can they reproduce the image just because they own the piece, or do they need my permission? Am I entitled to a separate fee? Should I have a contract?

First of all: Of course you should have a contract. Please. Don't ever ask that again (see Conversation #41).

And yes, these are separate transactions. Remember, copyright is a bundle of rights (see Conversation #11 and Figure 2). Distinct components of the bundle include, for example, the right to reproduce the work, to distribute the work, to perform the work, to display the work publicly, and to create derivative works based upon the work.

When a buyer purchases your artwork, the buyer acquires the piece. The "tangible medium" in which you fixed your original expression. A material object. The buyer does not acquire your copyright in the work, nor any of the individual components of your copyright bundle. Those, you keep (17 USC §202). Within limits the buyer can do whatever she wishes with the material object (17

USC §109[a]), but unless you formally transfer the bundle of rights she acquires no copyright interest in the work. In order to acquire any copyright interest in the work, the buyer must obtain from you (in addition to the piece itself) either a **license** or a written **assignment** of copyright.

An assignment, which must be in writing, transfers your entire copyright interest, i.e., the entire bundle of rights, to another party. After you execute an assignment, you no longer own any copyright interest in the work (see Conversation #29).

an assignment, which must be in writing, transfers your entire bundle of rights to another party

A license transfers just one or more – but usually not all – rights from the copyright bundle. A license can be exclusive, meaning that once you have granted it to one party, you cannot grant the same thing to anyone else. **Exclusive licenses** must be in writing. A license can also be nonexclusive. In that case, you can authorize the same thing over and over, to as many parties as you wish. **Nonexclusive licenses** do not have to be in writing.

Let's return to Paula's questions.

The corporation purchases one piece of Paula's work. The corporation acquires the piece, and nothing else. The copyright law provides:

> *Ownership of a copyright, or of any of the exclusive rights under a copyright, is distinct from ownership of any material object in which the work is embodied. Transfer of ownership of any material object, including the copy or phonorecord in which the work is first fixed, does not of itself convey any rights in the copyrighted work embodied in the object; nor, in the absence of an agreement, does transfer of ownership of a copyright or of any exclusive rights under a copyright convey property rights in any material object.*

17 USC §202

Now the corporation wishes to reproduce copies of the work on its convention brochure. That's an entirely separate transaction, and one for which Paula should be separately compensated. The right to reproduce the work is a component of the artist's exclusive bundle of copyright rights. Even though the corporation owns the piece, it will be committing copyright infringement if it reproduces the work without a license. If the corporation wishes to reproduce copies of the work, it must first acquire a license from Paula to do so.

Paula's friend Randy seeks clarification.

> Randy: So, are you saying that a purchaser of my work cannot, under any circumstances, exercise any of my copyright rights?
>
> TS (knowing that Randy smells a rat): Not exactly. There are some exceptions.
>
> Randy: I KNEW IT!
>
> TS: Randy, where did you get that tattoo?
>
> Randy: What?
>
> TS: You heard me. Where did you get that tattoo?
>
> Randy: From Ryan's House of Ink.
>
> TS: Did Ryan herself design the tattoo?
>
> Randy: Yes. What does this have to do with ANYTHING?

In Conversation #21 we talked about **statutory exceptions** to the general rules of copyright law. If you need a refresher go take a look, because we're going to talk about them again, right now.

Above, we referred to section 109(a) of the copyright law which states (in so many words) that if you lawfully own a copy of a copyrighted work (e.g., a print; a book; a sculpture) you can sell or dispose of that copy without a license from the copyright owner. Section 109(a) is a statutory exception.

Section 109(c) is another statutory exception:

Notwithstanding the provisions of section 106(5), the owner of a particular copy lawfully made under this title, or any person authorized by such owner, is entitled, without the authority of the copyright owner, ***to display that copy publicly****, either directly or by the projection of no more than one image at a time, to viewers present at the place where the copy is located.*

17 USC §109(c)

Randy: Interesting. Let me see if I understand. If you buy one of my paintings, you don't get my bundle of rights.

TS: Correct.

Randy: Section 109(a) says you can sell your copy of my painting without my permission.

TS: Yes.

Randy: And if you do, ownership of the physical piece might transfer to somebody else, but I still own and control the bundle of rights.

TS: That's right, subject only to the various statutory exceptions.

Randy: Yeah, one of which appears to be section 109(c). That one says even though I have the exclusive right to public display (section 106[5]), you can display my painting publicly without my permission.

TS: Right, but look more closely. There's an important restriction.

Randy: I'm tired. Just tell me what it is.

TS: You can only display your copy *to viewers present at the place where the copy is located.*

Randy: So, if you hang my painting in your office that's OK because anyone viewing it will <u>also</u> be in your office and so *present at the place where the copy is located*?

TS: Yes! That's exactly right.

Randy: What's an example of something that would not be OK?

TS: Suppose I decided to make a movie about my exciting life. The crew filmed in my office, with your painting on the wall. When Tom goes to the theater to see my film, Tom (the viewer of the painting) is not in the same place as the painting.

the courts are still slogging through tattoo issues

Randy: The painting is on your wall, but Tom is in the movie theater.

TS: Right. So in that case, section 109(c) would not apply and I'd need a license for the public display of your work.

Randy gets a second wind.

Randy: I'm starting to understand why you were asking about my tattoo.

TS: Go ahead...

Randy: Well, it's a work of visual art and Ryan, its author, owns the bundle of rights. I didn't get the bundle of rights from Ryan; I just got a copy of the work inked into my skin.

TS: Right.

Randy: So this is really no different than my painting?

TS: Well, the courts are still slogging through tattoo issues. But right now, yes. It's the same.

Randy: So when I walk down the street, I am displaying the tattoo but that's OK because anyone who sees me on the street is also on the street, so they are in the same "place where the copy is located."

TS: Right.

Randy: But if I'm on TV....

TS: You'd better have a license from Ryan.

YOU TRY

1. Why is section 109(a) a statutory exception? If it didn't exist, what provision of section 106 would prohibit the owner of a copy from selling or giving that copy away to someone else?

2. What's the difference between a **sound recording** and a **phonorecord**? (Hint: see Conversation #13.)

3. When you acquire a phonorecord you're just getting a material object. Does that convey any rights to the underlying sound recording? Generally speaking, no. But there are some exceptions. Take a look at section 109(b). It's going to be dense reading, but you can do it.

4. For more on this topic use your legal research skills and check out (*Viacom Int'l v Fanzine Int'l,* 2000 WL 1854903, 2000 US Dist. LEXIS 19960 – 2000)

5. Technically, there's a difference between a "right" and a "license." Our discussion in this conversation was somewhat imprecise, in order to be understandable. But if you want to dig deeper, do some research on the legal meanings of each term.

Leaf Me Alone: First Sale and Derivative Works

National Public Radio (NPR) once carried a story about an innovative artist who works in chlorophyll. He prints images on leaves gathered from his mother's garden.

Copyright first sale doctrine

Derivative works

Munoz v Albuquerque A.R.T. Co.

Annie Lee v Deck the Walls, Inc. and A.R.T. Co.

The NPR report suggests that he takes the images from magazines and online archives. We'll give this artist the benefit of the doubt and assume he has appropriate licenses from the copyright owners of these images. For purposes of discussion, though – what if he doesn't? Is it OK to lift an image from a magazine, or from the internet, and print it on a leaf?

No, it is not OK. There is no difference between printing the image onto a leaf and printing the image onto a piece of paper. It's still copying; it's still reproducing the image, which is something only a copyright owner or licensee may do (see Conversation #11 and Figure 2).

What happens, though, if the artist (or anyone else) were to purchase a lawful copy of an image, affix that copy to a leaf, and then offer it for sale?

In this Conversation we explore copyright law's **first sale doctrine** and the concept of **derivative works**.

The first sale doctrine is a provision of copyright law stating that once a buyer has purchased a particular copy of a work, the buyer can dispose of that copy by sale or any other means (17 USC §109). The buyer does not acquire any copyright interest in the work (see Conversation #24). With certain limitations, however, the buyer may dispose of the particular copy she purchased in any way she wishes. This applies whether the copy in her possession is a one-of-a-kind original or one in a series of multiples. If there's only one copy, the doctrine applies. If there are thousands of copies, the doctrine applies to each individual copy.

If there's only one copy, the doctrine applies. If there are thousands of copies, the doctrine applies to each individual copy.

Last century (in the 1980s and 1990s), a company known as ART lawfully purchased multiple copies of an image, affixed each copy to a ceramic tile, and offered the individual tiles for sale. ART did this quite a lot and, consequently, was sued for copyright infringement by several artists. The artists claimed that ART's tiles were **derivative works** of their images and, since only a copyright owner can make a derivative work, creating the tiles was infringement.

ART replied, *Hey. We lawfully purchased each and every copy we put on a tile. The first sale doctrine says we can dispose of our copies however we wish. We chose to put them on tiles and dispose of them by sale. That's not infringement.*

Guess who prevailed?

Answer: The artists...and then ART Co.

Section 101 of the copyright law defines **derivative work** as follows:

> *A "derivative work" is a work based upon one or more preexisting works, such as a translation, musical arrangement, dramatization, fictionalization, motion picture version, sound recording, art reproduction, abridgment, condensation, or any other form in which a work may be recast, transformed, or adapted. A work consisting of editorial revisions, annotations, elaborations, or other modifi-*

> *cations, which, as a whole, represent an original work of authorship, is a "derivative work" (emphasis supplied).*

In 1993 a Federal court found that ART's tiles were, in fact, derivative works (*Munoz v Albuquerque A.R.T. Co.,* 829 F Supp 309, affd 38 F3d 1218 [9th Cir 1994]). ART had argued that placing the images on tiles was merely a form of display, akin to framing, and that this practice neither "reproduced," "recast," "transformed," nor "adapted" the images. The court disagreed, noting:

> *It is commonly understood that [framing] amounts to only a method of display.... [I]t is a relatively simple matter to remove the print or painting and display it differently if the owner chooses to do so. [But] neither of these things is true of the art work affixed to a ceramic tile.... [T]iles lend themselves to other uses such as trivets (individually) or wall coverings (collectively).*

The court essentially found that using epoxy resin to bind a legitimately-acquired image to ceramic tile constituted creation of a derivative work and, thus, infringement. In the court's view, once someone modifies a piece of artwork for any use other than that which the artist originally intended (e.g., for use as a trivet rather than as a notecard), the work has been sufficiently transformed or recast so as to constitute a derivative work.

Let's review section 101 and the definition of **derivative work** (above). If the definition ended after that first sentence, it would be much easier to defend the *Munoz* decision. The second sentence, however, states that a derivative (secondary) work consists of modifications *which, as a whole, represent an original work of authorship.* As later courts subsequently held, the changes or modifications must, themselves, qualify for copyright protection as "original works of authorship." If they do not, the secondary work is not a derivative of the original and, consequently, it does not infringe upon the original.

In 1996 ART defended another federal court action in which

the issues were substantially the same as they'd been in *Munoz*. This time, however, the presiding judge found for ART, holding that the tiles were not infringing (*Annie Lee v Deck the Walls*, 925 F Supp 576, affd 125 F3d 580 [7th Cir 1997]). In reaching this conclusion, the court found no legal distinction between displaying art in a frame or on a tile. In this court's view:

the court found no legal distinction between displaying art in a frame or on a tile

> *...the only relevant inquiry...is whether ART's ceramic tile process transforms, adapts or recasts [the artist's] original work into a new and different original work...[and] whether the new 'work,' the ceramic tile, contains sufficient originality, as required by the Constitution and the Copyright Act.*

Originality is a statutory and constitutional prerequisite for copyright protection (see Conversation #9). The United States Supreme Court has held consistently that while the threshold for originality is low, originality is the *sine qua non* of copyright. (Translation: ya gotta have it.)

> *The mundane act of placing notecards onto a ceramic tile falls into the narrow category of works in which no creative spark exists. Thus, the ceramic tiles are not a new and different original work, but the same exact work placed onto a different background. ART did not display any creativity in gluing [the artist's] work onto the separate surface....No intellectual effort or creativity was necessary to transfer the notecard to the tile.*

True derivative works are, themselves, subject to copyright protection (17 USC §103). After the *Munoz* determination (that ART's tiles were derivative works), ART attempted to register the tile design with the Copyright Office as a derivative work – and its application was rejected as not copyrightable because there was no original artistic expression. The *Annie Lee* court took note of this, in reaching its decision. The court further observed that the artist could have prevented ART from making and selling the tiles by refusing in the first instance to sell so many copies to ART. Finally, in response to the artist's argument that ART engaged in unfair competition by selling her work on their tiles, the court simply observed that nothing prevented the artist herself from doing the exact same thing.

Annie Lee was upheld on appeal by the Seventh Circuit Court of Appeals. In its decision the Seventh Circuit contributed these observations:

- If the framing process does not create a derivative work, then mounting art on a tile, which serves as a flush frame, does not create a derivative work.
- If mounting work on a tile amounts to "transfiguration" then so would changing a painting's frame or a photograph's mat – and clearly those actions do not constitute legal transfiguration.
- The artist's work, on ART's tiles, was not "recast, adapted or transformed" because the tiles still depicted exactly what the art depicted when it left the artist's studio.

At the time *Annie Lee* was decided, the federal circuit courts of appeal remained at odds over whether ART's tiling process constituted infringement. Some sided with the Seventh Circuit and some stuck with the reasoning of *Munoz*. Over time the Seventh Circuit's view came to prevail, however, and now most federal courts would adopt this approach when faced with similar facts. In the majority of circuits, therefore, artists should understand that when someone purchases a copy of your work, displays that copy in a manner you had not foreseen, and then sells it to someone else: it's not necessarily infringement.

artists should understand that when someone purchases a copy of your work, displays that copy in a manner you had not foreseen, and then sells it to someone else: it's not necessarily infringement

Conversation #26

You Can't Copyright a Jellyfish: Merger and Scenes a Faire

Ideas vs expression

Herbert Rosenthal Jewelry v Kalpakian

Satava v Lowry

Sometimes, phrases in foreign languages describe things more clearly than their English equivalents. And so it is, in this Conversation, that we consider two closely related copyright doctrines. One is known as the **merger** doctrine, and the other, ***scenes a faire***.

To start, let's review three basic concepts.

First: Facts and ideas are not copyrightable. Your original expression of a particular idea may be copyrightable. But the underlying idea itself, is not (see Conversation #8).

Second: Copyright only protects works of authorship that are "original" to the author. That means the author independently created the work and it has "at least some minimal degree of creativity" (see Conversation #9).

Third: It is possible (sometimes) to compile elements that are not, individually, copyrightable – and thereby create a copyrightable work of authorship (see Conversation #23).

The **merger** doctrine tells us that if there are only a limited number of ways a particular idea can logically be expressed, the idea and the expression merge and are inseparable, making the expression ineligible for copyright protection. One example: using an airplane icon to show an airport on a map.

Another example: using a trash bin as a symbol for deleted computer files.

Scenes a faire means "scenes that must be done" or "scenes to be made." In copyright law it refers to work that is standard to the treatment of a given topic. One example: depicting a clubhouse in a video game about golf. Another example: including the ocean in your beach scene. *Scenes a faire* is commonly used as a defense to copyright infringement, because no one can have a monopoly on such standard elements. In most jurisdictions you're not going to be liable for copyright infringement unless you made an absolutely identical copy of the material considered to be *scenes a faire*.

***scenes a faire* is commonly used as a defense to copyright infringement, because no one can have a monopoly on standard elements**

Theoretically, the merger and *scenes a faire* doctrines apply to all categories of copyrightable work. The problem, however, is that merger and *scenes a faire* make sense for certain works of authorship, but very little sense for others.

Think about your favorite slasher movies, romantic comedies, superhero adventures. They follow pretty standard formulas. (For example: boy meets girl; boy does something stupid; girl forgives; they all live happily ever after.) If it weren't for merger and *scenes a faire* the first person to come up with that formula would have a monopoly on the entire genre. That would be pretty stifling. So we apply merger and *scenes a faire*, and concern ourselves not with whether an alleged infringer expressed a particular idea (or formula), but whether she appropriated original, protectible elements of the manner in which the first author (the one alleging infringement) expressed that idea. (For example: the boy was from Hoboken and raced antique cars.) We throw out the stuff that's standard, and then see whether any truly original expression has been taken.

That's all fine when the work in question is literary work. Certain words, certain characters, certain settings are inevitable. They shouldn't be – and are not – protected by copyright. Visual art, though, is different. Most will agree: there are an infinite number of ways to depict nearly any image, visually.

Courts, however, don't always appreciate that there are many ways to depict something visually. In the context of infringement disputes, judges just apply merger and *scenes a faire* across the board to all types of authorship, including visual art. This can result in unjust treatment for visual artists.

courts don't always appreciate that there are many ways to depict something visually

Here are some examples.

The Jeweled Bee Pin. This is an old case. It was decided in 1971 by the Ninth Circuit Court of Appeals. The plaintiff held a copyright registration for a pin in the shape of a bee. The pin was made of gold and was encrusted with jewels. The defendants subsequently manufactured and sold their own line of jeweled bee pins, and plaintiff sued.

The lower court asked plaintiff's lawyer many questions about what, in plaintiff's view, defendants could have done differently so as not to infringe plaintiff's copyright. The lawyer responded, (this is the abridged version): *I don't know.* The lawyer was unable to offer any examples of possible ways in which different artists could originally express the idea of a jeweled bee. Not because there aren't any; just because the lawyer couldn't think of any. The court had no ideas of its own (and in fairness, the court is bound by the record before it), so the judges just applied the merger doctrine and that was that. The court held:

[O]n this record the 'idea' and its 'expression' appear to be indistinguishable. There is no greater similarity between the pins of plaintiff and defendants than is inevitable from the use of jewel-encrusted bee forms in both. When the 'idea' and its 'expression' are thus inseparable, copying the 'expression' will not be barred, since protecting the 'expression' in such circumstances would confer a monopoly of the 'idea' upon the copyright owner

(Herbert Rosenthal Jewelry Corp. v Kalpakian, 446 F2d 738 [9th Cir 1971]).

There are many different and original ways to depict a jeweled bee. (Take a moment and start sketching. See?) The plaintiffs lost this case, however, because the record did not contain evidence of artistic vision.

The Glass Jellyfish. Thirty years later, glass artist Richard Satava suffered the same result, from the same court. Mr. Satava produced lifelike sculptures of jellyfish in a glass-in-glass medium. A competitor later did the same, and Mr. Satava sued. The court held, *Satava may not prevent others from copying aspects of his sculptures resulting either from jellyfish physiology or from their depiction in the glass-in-glass medium* (Satava v Lowry, 323 F3d 805, cert denied 540 US 983, 124 S Ct 472, 157 L Ed 2d 374 [2003]) . OK, that's fair. But then the court started ticking off all the other elements it also found standard and subject to *scenes a faire*:

> *Satava may not prevent others from depicting jellyfish with tendril-like tentacles or rounded bells...He may not prevent others from depicting jellyfish in bright colors...He may not prevent others from depicting jellyfish swimming vertically...[nor] from depicting jellyfish within a clear layer of outer glass, because clear glass is the most appropriate setting for an aquatic animal...and he may not prevent others from tapering the shape of their shrouds, because that shape is standard in glass-in-glass sculpture.*

So...what was left? In the court's view, nothing. Does that mean Mr. Satava's work was unoriginal and thus ineligible for copyright protection? In this case, yes. That is exactly the effect of the court's decision. The court even acknowledged the well-established rule that a combination of separately unprotectible elements can be combined to create a copyrightable work: but in its view, *[t]he combination of unprotectable elements in Satava's sculpture falls short of this standard.*

Not all courts take such an expansive view of merger and

scenes a faire in visual art. Some do refrain from the 9th Circuit's "dissection" approach and instead consider the "total look and feel" of the work. In fact, our federal circuits are split in their approaches to this issue.

Someday, the US Supreme Court might speak on the proper role of merger and *scenes a faire* in visual art disputes. Until then (no matter what type of work you are creating), think carefully about whether your work has enough originality to sustain its copyright even after judicial elimination of the work's "standard" features. In plain English: just because it's cool doesn't mean it's legally original.

just because it's cool doesn't mean it's legally original

YOU TRY

As we have established, a combination of separately unprotectible elements can be combined to create a copyrightable work (see Conversation #23). We've also mentioned that things existing in nature cannot be copyrighted because they are not the result of the author's independent creation (see Conversation #9).

Centaurs are mythical creatures that do not exist in nature. (If you don't know what a centaur is, look it up now.) Suppose a sculptor combined real equine bones with real human bones to create the "skeleton" of a centaur. If you were the judge, would you find sufficient originality to support copyright?

CONVERSATION #27

Happily Ever After (Not): Copyright and Joint Authorship

COLLABORATION AGREEMENTS

JOINT AUTHORSHIP

When two or more authors collaborate on a work and each contributes material that, itself, would be separately eligible for copyright protection, the collaborators are joint authors and equal co-owners of copyright in the work (17 USC §201[a]). That's a valuable thing, because whoever owns the copyright controls the bundle of rights. Not surprisingly, therefore, an enormous body of case law has arisen from disputes over joint authorship.

Here's another conversation with Meg, the filmmaker from Conversation #13.

> Meg: So, if Jennifer and I make a documentary film together, we're automatically joint authors?
>
> TS: No, there are three specific requirements for joint authorship.
>
> Meg: What are they?
>
> TS: First, you and Jennifer must <u>intend</u> to be joint authors at the time you make your contributions to the work. To prove joint authorship there needs to be evidence that all joint authors had such prior intent <u>at the time they made their contributions to the work</u>. You can't just decide to be a joint author after-the-fact, when the work starts to make

money.

Meg: OK, so we should think this through and decide whether or not we're going to be joint authors, before we start working on the project.

TS: Exactly. And put your decision in writing so you have that dated evidence if you ever need it.

Meg: What's the second requirement for joint authorship?

TS: You need to have intent that the contributions of all joint authors will be merged with the contributions of all other joint authors, to create a single, unitary work.

Meg: OK. What's the third requirement?

TS: You need to show that each joint author's contribution was, itself, separately copyrightable.

Let's consider some scenarios.

Scenario #1. Meg and Jennifer talk about the film. Meg does all the work, but uses some of Jennifer's ideas. After the film achieves success, Jennifer claims that she is a joint author. Is she? No. Ideas are not copyrightable, so Jennifer flunks the third requirement.

Scenario #2. Meg and Jennifer each contribute elements that are, themselves, separately copyrightable. (For example: Jennifer wrote the script; Meg shot and edited the video.) It's pretty clear that their contributions were intended to merge and create a single, unitary work (the film). As for the first requirement, however, they disagree. Meg says she hired Jennifer to write the script and she (Meg) solely owns the copyright to the film. Jennifer says they are joint authors. Kaboom.

if you plan to collaborate don't make a move before examining the joint authorship issue

Scenario #2 is a disaster scenario, and it happens all the time. So if you plan to collaborate – ever – don't make a move before examining the joint authorship issue and committing your agreement to writing.

Oh, and there's something even worse than the disaster scenario.

Scenario #3. Meg and Jennifer disagree about being joint authors. Worse for Jennifer: Meg has the only copy of the film. So even if they are joint authors, Jennifer can't do anything with the film because she doesn't have a physical copy. (And now that they're enemies, the chances of Meg sending her one are pretty slim.)

> Meg: You said earlier that joint authors are *equal co-owners of copyright in the work*. What does that mean?
>
> TS: If you and Jennifer are joint authors, it means either one of you, individually, can exercise the film's bundle of rights. You can make and sell copies; you can enter it in festivals; you can grant licenses to others. Your only duty to the other joint author is one of financial accounting.
>
> Meg: So if I had the only copy and I withheld it from Jennifer, I'd be preventing her from making money on the film even though she's a joint author?
>
> TS: Correct. (And you'd never really do that, right?)
>
> Meg: Right. But what if Jennifer goes out and does something with the film I don't agree with?
>
> TS: Good point. That is another issue you need to think through and provide for in your written collaboration agreement.
>
> Meg: Is a collaboration agreement a contract?
>
> TS: Yes.
>
> Meg: If we have one, and Jennifer violates its terms, what do I do?
>
> TS: Well, hopefully you talk it through and work things out. If you can't, your remedy is for breach of contract.

Meg: Could I sue her for copyright infringement?

TS: No.

Meg: Why not?

TS: Because as joint authors you each acquired an "undivided ownership interest" in the entire work. This means that Jennifer, like you, owns the copyright. A person can't infringe her own copyright, so you can't sue a fellow joint author for infringement.

a person can't infringe her own copyright, so you can't sue a fellow joint author for infringement

Meg starts to recognize the importance of written collaboration agreements. What if a distributor approached her for "exclusive" rights to the film? Could Meg grant such rights without Jennifer's consent? What about non-copyright issues such as apportioning income other than equally; or requiring Jennifer's name to appear in a certain size in the credits; or prohibiting Meg from licensing the film for purposes to which Jennifer would normally object?

YOU TRY

Do some research on collaboration agreements in your field, and start a list of other issues that should be addressed up front, before any work begins.

Conversation #28

Copyright Ownership: Work Made for Hire

Community for Creative Non-Violence v Reid

Foraste v Brown University

Fig. 5: The Reid Factors

Another concept that complicates copyright ownership is the work made for hire (WMFH) doctrine. Authors and the public routinely misunderstand WMFH. So please read this entire Conversation and understand:

- Just because you paid somebody to create copyrightable work doesn't mean you own the copyright.
- Just because your contract says the work is to be "work made for hire" doesn't mean it really is.

There are two general rules of copyright ownership:

1. Whoever creates copyrightable work is its **author**.
2. The **author** of copyrightable work owns its copyright.

WMFH is an exception to those rules.

If copyrightable material is WMFH, someone other than the creator is the legal author of the work. There are two ways this can happen. Let's call these two ways the "Employment Scenario" and the "Nine Categories Scenario."

Employment. The first way work can be WMFH is if the creator is an actual employee and creates the work within the scope of his/her employment. If, for example, you are a graphic artist employed by an insurance company, copyright to your work on the company's annual report belongs to your employer and not to you.

Disputes often arise over whether an employer-employee relationship actually exists. A leading case on this point is *Community for Creative Non-Violence v Reid,* (490 US 730, 109 S Ct 2166, 104 L Ed 2d 811 [1989]). In *Reid* the United States Supreme Court set forth a long list of factors that figure into determining whether someone is or is not an employee for purposes of WMFH (see Figure 5). No single factor is determinative, and all

Figure 5

Factors to Consider in Determining Whether an Individual is an Employee or an Independent Contractor

The *Reid* Factors

- The hiring party's right to control the manner and means by which the product is accomplished
- The skill required to do the work
- The source of instrumentalities and tools used by the hired party
- Location: where the hired party performs the work
- The duration of the relationship between the parties
- Whether the hiring party has the right to assign additional projects to the hired party
- The extent of the hired party's discretion over when and how long to work
- The method of payment
- The hired party's role in hiring and paying assistants
- Whether the work is part of the regular business of the hiring party
- Whether the hiring party is in business at all
- The provision of employee benefits to the hired party
- The tax treatment of the hired party

No single factor is determinative!

situations are decided ultimately on a case-by-case basis. It's dangerous to make assumptions, so even if you think you know the answer, it would be wise to get a second opinion.

The Nine Categories. If there is no employment relationship, work is WMFH only if it was specially ordered or commissioned; and there is a written agreement to that effect signed by both parties; and the work falls within one of the following nine special categories[1]:

1. contributions to a collective work (e.g., a magazine, anthology, encyclopedia, etc.);
2. contributions to a motion picture or other audiovisual work;
3. translations;
4. supplementary works (e.g., introductions, forewords, illustrations, maps, charts, tables, editorial notes, bibliographies, appendices, indexes, etc.);
5. compilations (a work formed by the collection and assembly of pre-existing material);
6. instructional texts;
7. tests;
8. answer material for tests; or
9. an atlas

(17 USC §101)

If someone contracts with you to create copyrightable material and your work does not fall into one of those nine categories, the work cannot be WMFH. Period. Even if there's a written contract saying it's a work made for hire, it's not. If the contracting party wants to obtain copyright rights to the work and you agree, you, the author, must specifically trans-

[1]At one time, Congress tried to add "photographic or other portraits" to §101's list of works eligible for WMFH status. The Register of Copyrights successfully blocked this attempt, stating:

> *Artists and photographers are among the most vulnerable and poorly protected of all the beneficiaries of the copyright law, and it seems clear that, like serious composers and choreographers, they were not intended to be treated as 'employees' under the carefully negotiated definition [of WMFH] in section 101.* Reid, 490 US at 747, n 13

fer the copyright rights in a separate written **assignment** (see Conversation #29). Remember this:

1. If your work isn't in one of the nine categories it's not WMFH, no matter what anybody tries to tell you; and
2. If it is in one of the nine categories, it's only WMFH if you and the contracting party have a signed, written agreement to that effect.

Foraste v Brown University

if your work isn't in one of the nine categories it's not WMFH, no matter what anybody tries to tell you

In October 2003 the United States District Court for the District of Rhode Island decided a significant WMFH case involving a staff photographer at Brown University (*Foraste v Brown Univ.*, 290 F Supp 2d 234 [DRI 2003]). Before we discuss it, let's take a look at three specific sections of the copyright law.

17 USC **§201(b)** provides[2]:

In the case of a work made for hire, the employer or other person for whom the work was prepared is considered the author for purposes of [copyright law] and, unless the parties have expressly agreed otherwise in a written instrument signed by them, owns all of the rights comprised in the copyright.

17 USC **§201(d)** provides:

The ownership of a copyright may be transferred in whole or in part by any means of conveyance or by operation of law, and may be bequeathed by will or pass as personal property by the applicable laws of ***intestate succession****.*

In plain English: you can transfer or dispose of your copyright interests (that is, any one or more of the rights from the bundle) just as you would transfer or dispose of your car or your diamond ring or any of your other personal property.

[2]That big typeface is not a mistake. You'll be coming back to these provisions later in the Conversation. This will make them easier to find.

17 USC **§204(a)** provides:

> *A transfer of copyright ownership, other than by operation of law, is not valid unless an instrument of conveyance, or a note or memorandum of the transfer, is in writing and signed by the owner of the rights conveyed or such owner's duly authorized agent.*

If you transfer your copyright and the transfer is not by **operation of law**, <u>the transfer must be in writing and signed by you</u>.

Back to the Brown University case. Here's what happened.

John Foraste was a full-time photographer employed by Brown between 1975 and 1998. Brown was Mr. Foraste's employer and Mr. Foraste took photographs for Brown in the regular course of his employment. There is no question that the photographs Mr. Foraste took for Brown were WMFH, making Brown the legal **author** of the photographs.

In 1986 Brown adopted the following policy:

> *It is the University's position that, as a general premise, ownership of copyrightable property which results from performance of one's University duties and activities will belong to the author or originator. This applies to books, art works, software, etc.*

Quiz (and be honest): Do you think the policy changed anything? Were Mr. Foraste's photographs still considered WMFH or, after the policy, did copyright revert to Mr. Foraste?

We just established that Mr. Foraste's work was, in the first instance, WMFH. So at least initially, Brown held the copyright rights. However, Mr. Foraste alleged that through the policy Brown transferred its copyright interests in the photographs back to him. Upon that theory, he sued Brown for copyright infringement.

Look back at sections 201(b) and 201(d) of the copyright law. Mr. Foraste argued that section **201(d)** allows an owner to transfer copyright by <u>any means of conveyance</u>, and thus the policy was sufficient to transfer the photograph rights from Brown to him. Brown, however, contended that section **201(b)** creates an exception for WMFH requiring, for the transfer of rights to such work, a written instrument signed both by the creator and the employer or current owner of the rights.

Certainly, Brown's argument ran counter to the spirit of its own policy. But legally the argument prevailed. The court held that section 201(b) was intended to protect employers' interests and so, if the policy was going to alter WMFH ownership, it had to be written (which it was) *and* it had to be signed (which it was not). Because neither Brown nor Mr. Foraste had signed it, the policy did not comply with section 201(b); therefore Brown had not effectively transferred its ownership interests in the photographs to Mr. Foraste.

if you are the employer, and you truly wish to waive your WMFH rights, you need to do so in a written instrument signed by you and each individual employee

Brown won the case, based on the court's interpretation of section 201(b). However, the court went on to address "what if." What if Mr. Foraste had been correct, and a transfer could occur under section 201(d)? Even if that were possible, the court determined, the transfer would still be subject to section **204(a)**, which also requires a written signature in a transfer of copyright ownership. (Go look at the definition of "transfer of copyright ownership" in the law: 17 USC 101. Only transfers meeting that definition have to be in writing.)

Bottom line: WMFH is WMFH, and even if employers have policies supposedly waiving their copyright ownership rights, such policies might not be effective. If you are the employer, and you truly wish to waive your WMFH rights, you need to do so in a written instrument signed by you and each individual employee. If you are the employee and you want to acquire copyright ownership to work you created as WMFH, do not rely on an institutional policy like Brown's. Insist on an individualized written instrument, signed by you and the employer.

The Terminator:

Copyright Transfers Aren't Necessarily Forever

s we just learned in Conversation #28, copyright rights may be transferred by any "means of conveyance" (17 USC §201[d]). Two of the most common means of transfer are **licenses** and **assignments**.

COPYRIGHT TERMINATION RIGHTS

EFFECT ON ESTATE PLANNING

Licenses can transfer individual parts of the copyright (e.g., the right to reproduce the work; to create derivative works, etc.) or the entire bundle of rights. A license can be "exclusive," meaning that once you have granted it to one party, you cannot grant the same thing to anyone else. A license can also be "nonexclusive." In that case, you can authorize the same thing over and over, to as many parties as you wish. Licenses are often restricted to a specified period of time, after which all rights revert back to you.

An assignment transfers your entire copyright interest (the entire bundle of rights) to another party. After you execute an assignment, you no longer own any copyright interest in the work (unless you took a license back from the new owner). It's pretty extreme, so when you see the word "assignment" you should pause and make sure you know exactly what's happening.

Most people think that assignments are forever; that once executed, the copyright is irretrievably lost. Well, if we've learned anything from the previous Conversations, it's that there are exceptions to every rule. Please welcome...The Terminator.

TS: Welcome, Terminator. May I call you "Mr. T"?

TT: No (fool).

TS: What's your real name?

TT: I am a United States copyright statute, and my given name is "17 United States Code section 203." You may call me 203.

TS: Very well. What's your gig?

203: I protect the authors of copyrighted material against unremunerative transfers.

TS: *(Deciding already to wait until this one comes out on video)*: Huh?

203: Bad deals. I give copyright owners a second chance, after they've made bad deals.

TS: No kidding?

203: I do not kid.

TS: Why does the law give special protection for authors, but not for others who make bad deals?

203: My Congressional creators believe: *A provision of this sort is needed because of the unequal bargaining power of authors, resulting in part from the impossibility of determining a work's value until it has been exploited.*

TS: So if I write a novel or a song, and I transfer my copyright rights in the work to a publishing company for a very modest sum, and it later earns billions – you'll help me get my copyright back?

203: Yes.

TS: Cool! How does it work?

203: I am laden with rules, restrictions, and inscrutable procedures.

TS: Thanks for your candor. Can you offer anything more useful?

203: I am available for terminating the exclusive or non-exclusive grant of any right under a copyright (whether by license or assignment) that was executed by the author on or after January 1, 1978.

TS: Will you terminate such a grant if the author made it in her will?

203: No.

TS: Do you apply if the work was a **work made for hire**?

203: *(Short-circuiting, arms flailing wildly):* No! No! No work for hire!

TS: OK! OK! You do not apply to work made for hire....

TS: *(Following a suitable period of recovery)*: Who can use you to terminate a grant?

203: Only the author who made the grant.

TS: What if it's a joint work and there's more than one author?

203: I require a majority of the authors who executed the grant.

TS: What if the author is dead?

203: My creators vested me with explicit rules about who may seek a termination on behalf of a deceased author.

TS: May an author seek termination at any time?

203: No.

TS: When are you available?

203: Termination may be effected at any time during the five-year period beginning at the end of thirty-five years from the date of execution of the grant. If the grant covers the right of publication of the work, the five-year period begins either at the end of thirty-five years from the date of publication of the work under the grant, or at the end of forty years from the date of the execution of the grant, whichever term ends earlier.

TS: You're right. That's pretty technical. But the readers will understand if they go back and reread your answer a few times. Basically the author has to wait at least 35 years before terminating a grant, is that correct?

203: I dislike being so imprecise, but essentially...yes.

TS: Are there other deadlines?

203: Yes. You must serve a notice of termination not less than two nor more than ten years before your selected termination date.

TS: So, author chooses a termination date that falls within the applicable five-year window, and then serves notice of termination at least two but not more than ten years before that date?

203: Correct.

TS: Does the Copyright Office have forms for this?

203: No. You must create your own notice of termination and it must contain certain items in order to be valid.

TS: How would a person know what items it must contain?

203: You may consult my cousin, a federal regulation known as "37 Code of Federal Regulations section 201.10."

TS: Let me guess. I can call her 201.10?

203: We do in the 'hood.

TS: OK, so what happens once you terminate a grant?

203: All rights that were covered by the terminated grant revert to the author or authors.

TS: What if there were three joint authors and one did not participate in the termination. Does he get his rights back as well?

203: Yes.

TS: Suppose the original grant permitted the creation of a derivative work based on the copyrighted work. May the derivative work continue to be used under the terms of the grant after termination?

203: Yes, but no additional derivative works may be created.

the termination right can have serious, unforeseen effects on estate plans disposing of copyrightable assets

TS: Can an author waive his termination rights if someone asks him to?

203: No. The right to termination cannot be waived or contracted away. It is, as they say, **inalienable**.

TS: You mentioned that you apply to grants made by the author on or after January 1, 1978. What about grants made before that date?

203: Talk to my brother, "17 United States Code section 304."

TS: Will do. Well, thank you, 203, for taking time from your busy schedule to chat with the readers.

203: You're very welcome.

There's one final point about termination rights that authors and their estate planning attorneys should consider: the termination right can have serious, unforeseen effects on estate plans disposing of copyrightable assets. It would take a separate book to explain why, and only lawyers would have much interest in making it past the first page. But this is a big deal, and it's something with which most estate planning attorneys are unfamiliar. So write this down: if your estate contains copyrightable assets, *make sure* you consult with a copyright attorney as well as an estates attorney when preparing your estate documents.

CONVERSATION #30

Moral Rights: The Visual Artists Rights Act

ARA is an acronym for the Visual Artists Rights Act of 1990 (17 USC §106A), an amendment to the copyright law designed to protect artists' **moral rights**.

POLLARA V SEYMOUR

PHILLIPS V PEMBROKE REAL ESTATE

PUBLIC PRESENTATION EXCEPTION

MASSACHUSETTS MUSEUM OF CONTEMPORARY ART FOUNDATION, INC. V BÜCHEL

Moral rights (from the French *droit moral)* involve an artist's personal interest in receiving attribution and preserving the integrity of his/her work, even after the work has been sold.

VARA grants three rights: the right of attribution; the right of integrity; and, for works of recognized stature, the right to prevent destruction (17 USC §§ 106A[a][3]), [d)][3]). The right of **attribution** is the artist's right to be recognized as the author of the work, to prevent the work from being attributed to someone else, and to prevent use of the artist's name on works created by others – including distorted versions of the artist's original work. The right of **integrity** allows the artist to prevent mutilating changes to his/her work, even after title in the work has been transferred.

VARA suffers from significant limitations in its scope and application. The biggest limitation is the copyright law's definition of "work of visual art:"

(1) a painting, drawing, print or sculpture, existing in a single copy, in a limited edition of 200 copies or fewer that are signed and consecutively numbered by the author, or, in the case

of a sculpture, in multiple cast, carved, or fabricated sculptures of 200 or fewer that are consecutively numbered by the author and bear the signature or other identifying mark of the author; or

(2) a still photographic image produced for exhibition purposes only, existing in a single copy that is signed by the author, or in a limited edition of 200 copies or fewer that are signed and consecutively numbered by the author.

A work of visual art does not include —

(A)

(i) any poster, map, globe, chart, technical drawing, diagram, model, applied art, motion picture or other audiovisual work, book, magazine, newspaper, periodical, data base, electronic information service, electronic publication, or similar publication;

(ii) any merchandising item or advertising, promotional, descriptive, covering, or packaging material or container;

(iii) any portion or part of any item described in clause (i) or (ii);

(B) any work made for hire; or

(C) any work not subject to copyright protection under this title.

17 USC §101

Here are some other limitations.

Regarding distortion, mutilation, and modification: (a) the work has to fall within the definition of "work of visual art;" *and* (b) the distortion, mutilation, or modification has to be intentional; *and* (c) the distortion, mutilation, or modification has to be prejudicial to the artist's honor or reputation.

Regarding destruction: (a) the work has to fall within the definition of "work of visual art;" *and* (b) the work has to be of recognized stature; *and* (c) the destruction has to be intentional or grossly negligent.

VARA litigation is relatively rare, and court decisions few, because of these limitations. In the vast majority of cases VARA is simply unavailable or inapplicable to an artist's facts and circumstances. Consequently, when the federal courts do issue VARA decisions, they merit our attention.

Pollara v Seymour

In 2003 the United States Court of Appeals for the Second Circuit issued a VARA decision in the matter of *Pollara v Seymour* (344 F3d 265 [2d Cir 2003]), seriously restricting the scope of VARA and artists' moral rights.

VARA litigation is relatively rare, and court decisions few

Joanne Pollara was an artist from Albany, New York. The Gideon Coalition, a nonprofit group offering low-cost legal services, commissioned Pollara to create a large banner for Gideon's display table at a special event known as Lobbying Day. Pollara spent more than 100 hours creating the banner, which ended up being ten feet high by thirty feet long. Pollara applied latex paint to heavy-gauge photographer's paper and reinforced the edges with duct tape. According to the Second Circuit,

> *The completed banner, in three or four colors, depicts a tableau of two dozen stylized people, with few salient features, standing on line against a background of shut doors labeled "PUBLIC DEFENDER," "LEGAL AID," and "PRISONERS LEGAL SERVICES." They patiently await entry, at left, of an open door marked "LAWYER," inside which sits a person, wearing a jacket and tie.... Many of the people on line are depicted to suggest different ethnicities.... Large lettering across the top and left read: "EXECUTIVE BUDGET THREATENS RIGHT TO COUNSEL" and "PRESERVE THE RIGHT TO COUNSEL – NOW MORE THAN EVER!"*

Lobbying Day was scheduled to take place in Albany's Empire State Plaza, a complex of arguably distinctive buildings housing the New York State Legislature and other government offices. On Lobbying Day Eve, Pollara and several helpers erected the banner in an enclosed, indoor public space at the Plaza. Then they went home, leaving the banner unattended.

Here's the thing about Albany and, in fairness, most government hubs. They have a lot of rules. In order to place a banner in the Empire State Plaza one needs a certain type of permit; to leave it overnight yet another is required. Gideon had failed to obtain either. (Not the greatest endorsement for an organization offering to help others with their legal needs, but... we digress.)

in order to place a banner in the Empire State Plaza one needs a certain type of permit; to leave it overnight yet another is required

Later that evening a Plaza security person noticed the banner and alerted his supervisor. The supervisor made a personal inspection, determined that no permits were in place, and instructed his staff to remove the banner. They did so and, in the process, tore the banner vertically into three pieces. The next morning Pollara found her banner lying torn and crumpled in a corner of the supervisor's office. Long story short, she sued under VARA.

Defendants (the State of New York and the supervisor) argued that Pollara's banner wasn't entitled to VARA protection because, in their view, it was really a poster, and posters are not "works of visual art" under the statute. The district court disagreed, citing the dictionary definition of "poster:" *a large printed placard used for the purpose of advertising or publicity.* Pollara's banner was a single, hand-painted work and therefore not a "poster."

In its next breath, though, the district court dismissed Pollara's case. The court found the banner was not a "work of visual art" after all: not because it was a poster, but rather, because it contained "advertising or promotional material," and its purpose was to attract public attention to Gideon's table.

The district court further determined that even if the banner had been a "work of visual art," it wasn't of "recognized stature" and thus not entitled to VARA's protections. Pollara appealed to the Second Circuit Court of Appeals.

The Second Circuit found, first off, that the district court blew it on the "recognized stature" issue. According to VARA a work only needs to be of "recognized stature" if the issue is the work's destruction. The VARA section affording protection against mutilation or modification contains no such limitation. Pollara had sued under both sections: the one addressing destruction and the one addressing mutilation and modification – so the fact that her banner was not of recognized stature was no reason for throwing her out of court.

The Second Circuit agreed, however, that the banner contained advertising material, thus rendering it ineligible for classification as a "work of visual art." Pollara argued that the speech on the banner, though admittedly for promotional purposes, was noncommercial; in her view Congress only intended to exclude commercial advertising from VARA's scope. Pollara provided no evidence of such Congressional intent, however, and as the court observed, VARA on its face makes no distinction between commercial and noncommercial speech.

the banner contained advertising material, thus rendering it ineligible for classification as a "work of visual art"

The Second Circuit could have left it at that and dismissed the appeal. Instead, the court offered a lengthy explanation leaving no room for doubt or argument that VARA protects nothing that's used for advertising or promotion, regardless of the commercial or noncommercial nature of the cause or business the work of art promotes.

What, then, of a work (such as a painting commissioned to promote the Olympics or a sculpture to promote AIDS awareness) created originally for purposes of promotion that later in its life becomes a mainstream work of art? Can such a work ever acquire status as a "work of visual art" under VARA? One judge on the *Pollara* panel thought so; the rest disagreed. In the majority's view: once promotional, always promotional. To hold otherwise would require courts to become judges of a work's artistic merit. And that, held the court, would be a "dangerous undertaking."

Phillips v Pembroke Real Estate

Our next true story involves an artist named David Phillips, who sued the operators of a Boston sculpture park when they tried to remove his work.

As we shall see, VARA was ultimately unavailable to assist Mr. Phillips, not because his work didn't qualify as "visual art," but because the First Circuit Court of Appeals found that VARA does not apply to "site-specific" art at all.

Integrated and site-specific art. In a work of **integrated art**, two or more physical objects, together, comprise the work of art. Removing one of the component objects would destroy the work. An example is Marcel Duchamp's *Bicycle Wheel* consisting of a bicycle fork, a bicycle wheel, and a stool. Remove the stool (or either of the other two components) and you destroy the work.

Site-specific work is a subset of integrated art. A site-specific work *is* integrated art; it's just that one of the components is the work's location. Example: creating a bronze tributary in the ground so that, in sunlight, it glistens like a nearby stream. Remove the work from its location and that meaning is lost. Just like removing the bicycle fork or the stool, this would destroy the work.

Plop art. In the *Phillips* case the court referred to non-site-specific work, i.e., work that could be plopped down any old place, as, **plop art.** We might as well do the same.

Here's what happened. In 1999, Pembroke Real Estate set out to create a public sculpture park with a nautical theme, near Boston Harbor. Pembroke commissioned four artists to create art for the park, including David Phillips. Mr. Phillips executed two contracts in connection with the project: one for the creation of twenty-seven sculptures; and another for certain landscape design elements. Much of Mr. Phillips's sculptural work was organized along a diagonal axis running from the northeast to the southwest corner of the park. At the center of this axis was a large showcase sculpture called *Chords* which Mr. Phillips personally carved from granite.

The park was completed in 2000. In 2001, Pembroke realized that the park's original design had conceptual flaws, so Pembroke retained a new landscape architect to conduct a redesign. Pembroke wanted to simplify walkways, include more plants for better shade, and remove much of the original stone, which had caused maintenance problems. The redesign called for the removal and relocation of Mr. Phillips's sculptures. Phillips protested (to no avail) and ultimately sued under VARA.

a redesign called for the removal and relocation of Mr. Phillips's sculptures

VARA states that, with certain exceptions, the author of a work of visual art shall have the right:

To prevent any intentional distortion, mutilation, or other modification of that work which would be prejudicial to his or her honor or reputation... [and] *to prevent any destruction of a work of recognized stature....* (17 USC §106A[a][3][A] and [B]).

One of VARA's exceptions, however, says this:

The modification of a work of visual art which is the result of conservation, or of the public presentation, including lighting and placement, of the work is not a destruction, distortion, mutilation or other modification described in subsection (a)(3) unless the modification is caused by gross negligence. (17 USC §106A[c][2]).

This is called the **public presentation exception**.

Everyone agreed that Mr. Phillips's sculptures were site-specific. They were designed especially for Pembroke's sculpture park, and they incorporated elements of their natural surroundings.

Phillips argued that moving the sculptures would so modify

as to destroy them, and that VARA prohibited such action. Pembroke said it had every right to move the works, under the public presentation exception, which specifically refers to changes in "placement" as being OK. Phillips replied that the public presentation exception makes no sense when applied to site-specific work.

The court took a good look at Mr. Phillips' argument and realized he was asking for a dual regime under which the public presentation exception would apply to plop art but not to site-specific art. Unfortunately, VARA just doesn't say that. The court couldn't find any support in the statute for Mr. Phillips's reading. The court feared, too, that if it were to accept the Phillips interpretation, once a work of art were considered site-specific it could not be altered by a property owner – ever – without the consent of the artist. This, said the court, *could dramatically affect real property interests and laws.* If Congress intended to impose such radical restrictions on the ownership of land, merely being silent wasn't enough; Congress should have addressed the issue specifically. And because Congress had not, the court wasn't going to adopt an interpretation with such far-reaching implications.

the court concluded that VARA doesn't apply to site-specific art at all

OK, that was reasonable. But get this. Right after rejecting the "dual regime" theory, the court took things one step further and read something into VARA that also lacks support in the statute: the court concluded that VARA doesn't apply to site-specific art at all.

What this means for you

Scenario #1: You create a piece of plop art. Let's say it's a painting, and it qualifies as a "work of visual art" under VARA. Somebody defaces the painting. You can sue under VARA.

Scenario #2: Same as #1, except somebody totally destroys the painting. You can sue under VARA, but only if the work is of recognized stature.

Scenario #3: Same as #1, except the modification to which you object is that the gallery moved the painting from the sunny side of a room to a dark corner. You cannot sue under VARA, because the public presentation exception says this is OK and does not amount to actionable distortion or mutilation.

Scenario #4: You create a piece of site-specific art. Under *Phillips* the landowner can move the work, just as they could with your plop art. But they can also mutilate this work, deface it, or destroy it at will, because VARA doesn't apply to site-specific work <u>at all</u>. If you live in a state with a state-based moral rights law, you might have recourse under state law. But for site-specific work (at least in the First Circuit), VARA's not going to do you a bit of good.

So: what do you do to protect the integrity of your site-specific work?

Make sure you have a well-drafted, written contract spelling out the restrictions you wish to impose regarding subsequent use, maintenance, and ultimate disposition of your site-specific art. Then, when things go badly and VARA's not available, maybe you can sue for breach of contract.

Or, just make peace with the reality that as the site changes, so too will your work. And maybe that's OK. But think these issues through, at the beginning, so your decision is well informed.

MMoCA v Büchel

In 2010 the First Circuit Court of Appeals issued another rare VARA decision. This case involved a long-standing dispute between Swiss artist Christoph Büchel and the Massachusetts Museum of Contemporary Art ("MASS MoCA"). MASS MoCA strives to offer visual artists *the tools and time to create works of a scale and duration impossible to realize in the time and space-cramped conditions of most museums*, and prides itself on exposing its audiences to all stages of art production. Rehearsals, sculptural fabrication, and developmental workshops are frequently on view, as are finished works of art.

An area known as Building 5 was MASS MoCA's signature exhibition space, spanning the length of a football field. In 2006 Büchel conceived of an ambitious art installation titled *Training Ground for Democracy*, which was to be exhibited at MASS MoCA in Building 5. The project was to be Büchel's largest venture to date; he conceived of the exhibit as *essentially a village, ... contain[ing] several major architectural and structural elements integrated into a whole, through which a visitor could walk (and climb).* Major components were to include a movie theater, a house, a bar, a mobile home, various sea containers, a bomb carousel, and an aircraft fuselage.

the relationship deteriorated to the point where Büchel stated he would not allow the exhibit to open in his name

Büchel was not always on-site as the exhibit was being prepared. Instead, under Büchel's guidance from Switzerland, MASS MoCA was supposed to obtain and construct many of these components.

That didn't work out so well.

MASS MoCA watched its budget for the project soar out of control. Büchel became dissatisfied with the way in which MASS MoCA was implementing his instructions and procuring items necessary for the installation. The relationship deteriorated to the point where Büchel stated he would not allow the exhibit to open in his name, and he did not return to Massachusetts to complete the installation.

MASS MoCA finally announced the cancellation of *Training Ground*, and contemporaneously publicized the opening of a new exhibit entitled *Made at MASS MoCA*, which was to be *a documentary project exploring the issues raised in the course of complex collaborative projects between artists and institutions.* In order to enter *Made at MASS MoCA*, visitors would have to pass through Building 5, which still housed the materials and unfinished fabrications that were to have comprised elements of *Training Ground for Democracy*. MASS MoCA placed yellow tarpaulins over the unfinished *Training Ground* work. There was great dispute about whether the tarps actually concealed the individual components and design elements of *Training Ground*, or whether they simply "hid an elephant behind a napkin," effectively inviting individuals to peek behind the coverings and view Büchel's unfinished work.

In May 2007 MASS MoCA went to court seeking a **declaratory judgment** that it would be OK for the museum to display publicly the unfinished components of *Training Ground*. Mr. Büchel responded with claims that he was entitled to relief under VARA because MASS MoCA had intentionally distorted and modified his work. He also claimed that displaying the work publicly without his permission constituted copyright infringement. The First Circuit ultimately held as follows:

the right of integrity under VARA protects artists from distortions, mutilations, or modifications of their works that are prejudicial to their reputation or honor

1. VARA's protection of an artist's moral rights extends to unfinished creations.

2. The right of integrity under VARA protects artists from distortions, mutilations, or modifications of their works that are prejudicial to their reputation or honor.

3. Mr. Büchel raised a viable claim that MASS MoCA violated his VARA right of integrity by modifying *Training Ground* over his objections in a manner that harmed his honor or reputation.

4. Mr. Büchel raised a viable claim that MASS MoCA infringed his exclusive right under section 106(5) of the Copyright Act to display his work publicly.

YOU TRY

Often, when an appeals court (like the First Circuit) issues a decision, it sends the case back to the lower court for further proceedings consistent with the appeals court's ruling. Using Google Scholar, see if you can determine what happened in the MASS MoCA case after the First Circuit's decision.

CONVERSATION #31

Droit de Suite: Resale Royalties for Artists

With some exceptions, copyright law applies equally to all types of authors: visual artists, literary, dramatic, etc. When it comes to making money, though, the different **works of authorship** generate vastly different revenue streams for their creators.

RESALE ROYALTIES FOR ARTISTS

Typically, literary authors and musical work composers get paid (royalties) every time a **copy** of their work is sold. Visual artists, too, get paid every time a copy of their work is sold. But think about how often that actually happens. Songs and books, by their nature, get reproduced and sold in great quantities. Visual art, however, is often reproduced either in limited quantities or not at all. For the creator of a single visual work, therefore, payday might be limited to that one, single sale.

To generate an equitable financial return on a single piece of visual art, one of three things must occur: (a) the artist sets the right price for the work's initial sale; or (b) the artist plans in advance to generate income from licensing and the sale of reproductions; or (c) the artist receives royalties every time the work is resold.

Option "c," the concept of resale royalties for artists, is known as ***droit de suite***.

In Conversation #29 we talked about termination rights, i.e., provisions of law that allow artists to terminate lifetime copyright transfers after a certain period of time. Termination rights provide a second bite at the apple when (for example) significant appreciation in the value of a work renders the financial terms of its original transfer inequitable. More simply, termination rights afford artists and their heirs the benefit of hindsight, and the corresponding opportunity to renegotiate bad deals.

the theory of the *droit* is that artists should benefit from the increase in value of their work

Droit de suite stems from a similar concern: correcting for the artist's disadvantage at having to price a work at a time when its ultimate market value can't realistically be foreseen. The theory of the *droit* is that artists should benefit from the increase in value of their work. In jurisdictions recognizing *droit de suite*, resellers of artwork pay a sum of money (either a percentage of the selling price or a portion of the work's increase in value) to the artist who created the work. Read that again: if your work appreciates in value, you get paid every time the item is resold.

Don't get too excited, though. *Droit de suite* hasn't exactly caught on in the United States.

Although its history reaches back much further, *droit de suite* was first enacted in France in the 1920s, reportedly as a measure to assist the survivors of artists who were killed in World War I. Most European countries followed France's example with *droit* legislation of their own, although the United Kingdom was a notable holdout. In 2001 the European Union issued a harmonization directive regarding resale royalties; objections from British art dealers successfully blocked implementation of the directive in the UK until 2006.

In the United States, California is the only state to have enacted *droit* legislation. Governor Jerry Brown signed California's resale royalty act in 1977, at a ceremony attended by artist Robert Rauschenberg, state senator Alan Sieroty, and accountant Ruben Gorewitz (according to the caption of a photograph attributed to artist Harriet Zeitlin). The California *droit* statute stayed on the books and limped along in relative obscurity until May 17, 2012, when a district court declared the statute unconstitutional and struck it down in its entirety *(Estate of Robert Graham v Sotheby's Inc.*, CDCA, May 17, 2012, Nguyen, J.).

a district court declared the statute unconstitutional and struck it down in its entirety

Even though it has been struck down, let's take a quick look at California's statute just to illustrate how the scheme was supposed to work. The California Resale Royalties Act (Cal. Civil Code §986) stated, *whenever a work of fine art is sold and the seller resides in California or the sale takes place in California*, the seller is to pay the artist five percent of the sale. The right to receive this percentage lasted for the life of the artist and for twenty years following the artist's death. If the artist could not be located, the five percent was to be paid to California's Arts Council. The Arts Council would hold the money for the artist for seven years. If the artist did not claim the money within that period of time, the money passed to the Arts Council for use in acquiring fine art pursuant to California's "Art in Public Buildings" program.

The California Act did not apply:

- to the initial sale of the work;
- to a resale of the work for a gross sales price of less than $1,000;
- to a resale of the work for a gross sales price less than the purchase price paid by the seller;
- to a resale of the work by an art dealer to a purchaser within ten years of the initial sale of the work by the artist to an art dealer, providing all intervening resales were between art dealers; nor
- to a sale of a work of stained glass artistry where the work had been permanently attached to real property and was sold as part of the sale of the real property to which it was attached.

Efforts to enact *droit* legislation in New York failed, and as we discussed, British art dealers raised fervent objections in the UK. There have been efforts in Congress to enact federal *droit* legislation, but you'll have to use your skills with THOMAS to ascertain their status (see YOU TRY, below).

Why is *droit de suite* so controversial? Here's the other side of the coin, from the perspective of dealers and collectors:

- **We took the risk**. Art often declines in value, rather than appreciating. The initial purchaser took a risk that the work would increase in value, so that purchaser should benefit from any appreciation. Why should art be different than any other kind of investment?
- **This will decimate our business**. Major art markets (like London) argue that imposition of resale royalties will simply drive the major players to non-*droit* jurisdictions.

here's the perspective of dealers and collectors

- **Administrative costs**. Who's going to collect the royalties? A collection agency similar to **ASCAP** would have to be established, the cost of which might outweigh the benefits of the *droit*.
- **What a crock**. Arguments that *droit de suite* protects struggling artists are disingenuous. Resale royalties only protect affluent artists anyway, because less successful artists don't even have a resale market for their work.
- **What about the first sale doctrine**? Affording artists a royalty on resale goes directly against the copyright law's first sale doctrine (17 USC §109), which states that the owner of a particular copy of a work is entitled, without the authority of the copyright owner, to sell or otherwise dispose of that copy (see Conversation #25). If we are to modify the first sale rights of the public, why not extract a corresponding concession from artists by, for example, having them relinquish their exclusive rights to reproduction?
- **An exhibition royalty**? If we're going to provide artists with additional royalties, why not impose it on something already tied to one of their exclusive copyright rights: the

right of public display?

- **This is moral rights**. Critics go on to observe that *droit de suite* really has nothing to do with copyright law at all and that, rather, it is an extension of the artist's moral rights – something to which United States policy remains fundamentally opposed.

YOU TRY

1. Refresh your recollection about what it is that makes something "unconstitutional" (Conversation #1). Then read the decision striking down California's resale royalty act. On what basis did the court find California's statute unconstitutional?
2. Check the status of efforts in the United States Congress to enact federal *droit* legislation HINT: Start with the "Equity for Visual Artists Act of 2011."
3. See what you can find out about the "Projansky Contract."

Copyright's Architectural Exception

This Conversation looks at copyright protection for sculptural works that are permanent, integral components of buildings. In *Leicester v Warner Bros.* (232 F3d 1212 [9th Cir 2000]), a sculptor (The Artist) worked side-by-side with an architect to incorporate sculptural elements into the design of a building. Without a license from The Artist, Warner Brothers filmed the building and it appeared as the Second Bank of Gotham in the movie, *Batman Forever.* The Artist sued Warner Brothers for copyright infringement, and lost.

Leicester v Warner Brothers

Architectural Works Copyright Protection Act

Before diving in, let's review some basic concepts. Among other things, copyright protects pictorial, graphic, and sculptural (PGS) work (see Conversation #9). Copyright does not protect "useful articles," which, under the law, are defined as: *[articles] having an intrinsic utilitarian function that is not merely to portray the appearance of the article or to convey information* (17 USC §101; see Conversation #8).

We all know that art can be a component of useful articles. Jewelry, for example, is as much artistic expression as it is functional and useful. Sculpture can be useful too, as, for example, when it serves as the base of a lamp. Does such art lose its copyright protection because it is also functional? No. Copyright protection is available for PGS work if (and here is the test) it has *features that can be identified separately from, and are capable of exist-*

ing independently of, the utilitarian aspects of the article. Basically, if the art can stand on its own and the useful article can still function without it, the art is eligible for copyright protection (see Copyright Office Factsheet FL-103, http://www.copyright.gov/fls/fl103.pdf).

until 1990, buildings were "useful articles" and, once built, they were ineligible for copyright protection

Until 1990, buildings were "useful articles" and, once built, they were ineligible for copyright protection. The architect's plans were protectible as PGS work, but the buildings themselves were not copyrightable. In 1990 Congress passed the Architectural Works Copyright Protection Act (AWCPA) and buildings became eligible for copyright protection (see Copyright Office *Circular 41*, http://www.copyright.gov/circs/circ41.pdf).

Buildings did not, however, acquire the full bundle of copyright rights that PGS works enjoy. The AWCPA carved out a major exception for architectural works. The "architectural exception" states that, even though buildings have copyright protection, it's still OK (and not an infringement) for someone to make a *pictorial representation* of a building as long as the building is ordinarily visible from a public place (17 USC §120). In other words, you can paint a picture of the building, you can photograph the building, you can film it, and you can make any other kind of "pictorial representation" without infringing the building's copyright. The architectural exception also states that in addition to making your pictorial representation you can distribute it and/or display it publicly. Without a license, you can't do any of those things with copyrighted PGS work.

That's all very cool if you are an artist or a tourist and the building is your subject. Less so, if you are a sculptor who shares in the building's copyright.

Why would a sculptor share in the building's copyright? Joint authorship. When two or more people collaborate on a work and each contributes material that, itself, would be separately eligible for copyright protection, the collaborators might be **joint authors** (17 USC §201[a]; see Conversation #27). Unless there is a written agreement to the contrary, each joint author owns an equal share to the copyright of the work as a whole. In the Batman case, The Artist (the sculptor) and the architect were joint authors of the architectural work (the building).

Back to Gotham. The Artist said to Batman (Warner Brothers): *Sculpture is PGS work, not subject to the architectural exception. If you want to film my sculpture, you need a license!* Warner Brothers disagreed, so The Artist sued for copyright infringement. Here's what happened.

As his contribution to the building, The Artist had designed artistic elements of a courtyard, towers, and a street wall to convey an allegorical history of the City of Los Angeles and its vampire-like relationship with water. Warner Brothers' first legal hurdle was to establish that The Artist's work was "integrated" and "part of the design plan" of the building. The court found that it was.

Warner Brothers' first legal hurdle was to establish that The Artist's work was "integrated" and "part of the design plan" of the building

Next, the court had to determine whether, as an integral part of the building, The Artist's work was subject to the architectural exception – just like the building itself. If so, The Artist's work would lose a big chunk of its copyright protection, because people would be freely able to make and display pictorial representations of it, at will.

Warner Brothers argued that The Artist's sculpture, as an integral part of the building, was subject to the architectural exception. The Artist, on the other hand, argued that even if sculptural work is integrated into the design of the building, artists still have the right to protect such work separately, as PGS material.

The court sided with Batman. Finding for Warner Brothers, the court determined that once sculptural work is integrated into the design of a building, it becomes subject to the architectural exception. Said the court, *it would be counterintuitive to suppose that Congress (in the AWCPA) meant to restrict pictorial copying to some, but not all of, a unitary architectural work* (Leicester v Warner Brothers, supra, at 1220).

once sculptural work is integrated into the design of a building, it loses some of its PGS copyright protection

And you have to admit: if The Artist's argument had prevailed it would be nearly impossible for the public to know which part of a building is freely available because of the architectural exception, and which part is off-limits due to a sculptor's PGS copyright.

Here's the lesson, if you are The Artist. If you are creating sculpture that's to become an integral part of a building, negotiate a higher fee in anticipation of your work becoming subject to the architectural exception and its lesser measure of copyright protection.

The next Conversation goes into more detail about the workings and implications of the AWCPA.

CONVERSATION #33

More on Depicting Architectural Work

BUILDINGS
MONUMENTS
ORDINARILY VISIBLE
BUILDINGS AS TRADEMARKS

With passage of the Architectural Works Copyright Protection Act of 1990 (AWCPA), Congress made architectural work a new category eligible for copyright protection (17 USC §102 [a][8]). A congressional report supporting the AWCPA explains:

> *Architecture plays a central role in our daily lives, not only as a form of shelter or as an investment, but also as a work of art. It is an art form that performs a very public, social purpose....*
>
> *Architecture is not unlike poetry, a point made by renowned critic Ada Louise Huxtable, who wrote that architects can make "poetry out of visual devices, as a writer uses literary or aural devices. As words become symbols, so do objects; the architectural world is an endless source of symbols with unique ramifications in time and space."*
>
> *In short, the Committee concluded that the design of a work of architecture is a "writing" under the Constitution and fully deserves protection under the Copyright Act. Protection for works of architecture should stimulate excellence in design, thereby enriching our public environment in keeping with the constitutional goal.*
>
> *(H.R. 101-735; 1990 U.S.C.C.A.N. 6935, 6943–6944)*

The AWCPA defined "architectural work" as:

> *[T]he design of a building as embodied in any tangible medium of expression, including a building, architectural plans, or drawings. The work includes the overall form as well as the arrangement and composition of spaces and elements in the design, but does not include individual standard features.*
>
> (17 USC §101)

No one but the building's copyright owner may exercise any of the individual rights that come with owning a copyright. Architecture, however, doesn't get the full measure of copyright protection that other types of work enjoy. As we learned in Conversation #32, Congress included the following "architectural exception" in the AWCPA:

architecture doesn't get the full measure of copyright protection that other types of work enjoy

> *PICTORIAL REPRESENTATIONS PERMITTED. The copyright in an architectural work that has been constructed does not include the right to prevent the making, distributing or public display of pictures, paintings, photographs or other pictorial representations of the work, if the building in which the work is embodied is located in or ordinarily visible from a public place.*
>
> (17 USC §120 [a])

In support of this exception the congressional report states:

> *Architecture is a public art form and is enjoyed as such. Millions of people visit our cities every year and take back home photographs, posters and other pictorial representations of prominent works of architecture as a memory of their trip. Additionally, numerous scholarly books on architecture are based on the ability to use photographs of architectural works. These uses do not interfere with the normal exploitation of architectural works.*
>
> *(H.R. 101-735; 1990 U.S.C.C.A.N. 6935, 6953)*

With this background in mind, let's address some of the questions arts entrepreneurs raise in connection with the AWCPA.

What's a "building" for purposes of the architectural exception? Does it include other three-dimensional structures such as bridges, canals, dams, and pedestrian walkways? The congressional report says no, but suggests that the term does include structures used for shelter but not inhabited by human beings, such as pergolas, gazebos, and garden pavilions (H.R. 101-735; 1990 U.S.C.C.A.N. 6935, 6951).

What about monuments? This is a complicated question about which there is much debate. Many monuments, such as the Vietnam Veterans Memorial, are nonfunctional sculptural works that (one would think) should be entitled to the full measure of copyright protection – and not subject to the architectural exception. Others may indeed be "buildings" and, if constructed after 1990, subject to the exception's limitations. To answer this type of question one usually turns to the applicable statute's legislative history, i.e., the congressional report we've been discussing. As it turns out, there is an alleged typographical error in the congressional report. The report states:

> *Monumental, nonfunctional works of architecture are currently protected under section 102(a)(5) of title 17 as sculptural works. These works are, nevertheless, architectural works, and as such, will* ***[not]*** *be protected exclusively under section 102(a)(8) (H.R. Rep. No. 101-735, at 20 n.43).*

The debate is over the highlighted word: the report says "not" but some believe it was meant to be "now." Construed one way, all monuments would be characterized as architectural work subject to the architectural exception. Construed the other way, monuments could be eligible for protection either as sculptural or architectural work. (Intrigued? See YOU TRY, below).

What about the separate components of an architectural

work? Copyright does not extend to the "individual standard features" of an architectural work such as common windows, doors, and other staple building components. It does, however, protect *the overall form as well as the arrangement and composition of spaces and elements in the design* (17 USC §101).

In *Intervest Constr., Inc. v Canterbury Estate Homes, Inc.* (554 F3d 914 [11th Cir 2008]), the 11th Circuit Court of Appeals commented that the definition of an architectural work closely parallels that of a **compilation**: *[A] work formed by the collection and assembling of preexisting materials or of data that are selected, coordinated, or arranged in such a way that the resulting work as a whole constitutes an original work of authorship* (17 USC §101). And copyright protection for compilations is "thin." That means, it's more difficult to prove infringement when your work is a compilation than it is when your work consists of completely original material.

Intervest Construction was a dispute between the copyright owners of certain floor plans for single-family homes. Floor Plan #1 was entitled to copyright protection, but primarily as a compilation. Accordingly, when the owners of Floor Plan #1 complained that Floor Plan #2 infringed, they faced a very high burden of proof. Ultimately, it was a standard they could not achieve, and their infringement claim failed. Lesson: not all copyrights are created equal. If yours is "thin," as is the case with claims to compilation, your burden for establishing infringement against another will be more difficult than otherwise.

What's a "public place"? Does it have to be owned by the public? Or is it enough that the public simply has access, even though the property may be private? The congressional report observes that an earlier version of the AWCPA limited the exception to instances where the architectural work was "located in a public place." The report explains, *the Subcommittee added the phrase 'or ordinarily visible from' after the words 'located in' to broaden the exemption to include buildings located on private property but visible from a public place.* The report underscores, *nothing in this amendment permits or condones trespassing in order to make such pictorial representations* (H.R. 101-735; 1990 U.S.C.C.A.N. 6935, n48). The legislative history does not completely answer our questions. Based on the report, however, it seems reasonable to infer that if one is not trespassing, one's vantage point satisfies the "public place" requirement regardless of whether one is standing on public or private property. Again, it will be for the courts to decide this question definitively.

What's "ordinarily visible"? Is it OK to use special equipment to enhance one's ability to see the building? What about tethering a camera to a balloon? Again, there's no authority specifically addressing these questions. When that's the case, courts often take the extraordinary step of resorting to common sense. If you were the judge, would you find a building otherwise obscured from view to be "ordinarily visible" because an artist floated a balloon overhead?

Does the architectural exception permit the making of pictorial representations for commercial, as well as noncommercial, purposes? Yes, depriving architects of a potentially lucrative source of income. Now ask about trademark.

What about trademark? It's an increasingly important consideration. Even if you find a building subject to the architectural exception, it means only that you are free under copyright law to make a pictorial representation of the building. Buildings may also function as trademarks, and trademark law commands an entirely separate analysis (see Conversation #37). So do not be lulled into a false sense of security. If you are depicting a building in your work, understand that even if the architectural exception applies for copyright purposes, you may need to clear trademark rights before proceeding.

YOU TRY

For more on the "not - now" debate, read Judge Fisher's dissent in the *Leicester* case (232 F 3d 1212, 1225 n 10).

Conversation #34

International Copyright Issues

"All Rights Reserved." Sometimes we see it after copyright notices, as in: "Copyright © 2014 Maria A. Pallante. All Rights Reserved." But we don't see it all the time. So what does it mean, and when is it necessary?

Treaties and conventions

All Rights Reserved

Copyright circulars and factsheets

Intellectual property piracy

By and large, "All Rights Reserved" is a holdover from the past, with little remaining significance. Here's the story.

Copyright protection is not international. That is to say, if you obtain a copyright in the United States your work is not automatically protected in, for example, Nepal. Protection in a foreign country depends upon the laws of that country.

Does that mean you have to study the copyright laws of every single country in order to know your rights? Yes and no. Although the law of the country still controls, a number of international copyright treaties (called **conventions**) simplify things to some extent.

There are two main copyright treaties: the Berne Convention and the Universal Copyright Convention. If a particular country is a party (also called a **signatory**) to one or both conventions, you can predict with a certain degree of confidence what the copyright laws of that country might be. That's because the treaties set forth certain standards, and in order to be a party to the treaty, the signatory country must substantially adopt those standards as its own. (The United States joined the Universal Copyright Convention in 1955, and the Berne Convention in 1989.) For example, the laws of a signatory nation must recognize certain exclusive rights, including **moral rights**; they must grant protection for at least fifty years following the author's death; and they must grant protection to work originating in another signatory nation substantially as they would to work of the country's own nationals.

"Fascinating," you muse, "but what does this have to do with All Rights Reserved?" Thanks for asking.

Once upon a time, there was an international copyright treaty known as the Buenos Aires Convention of 1911. (And in case you're ever on a quiz show, you might want to know that President Woodrow Wilson officially proclaimed the United States' adherence to the Buenos Aires Convention on July 13, 1914.)

Aside from the United States, most signatories to the Buenos Aires Convention were Latin American countries. The Convention provided that work copyrighted in one signatory country received protection in all other signatory countries without the necessity of registration in the other countries. The catch, however, was that the work did need to contain a notice reserving these rights, and the most common phrase used for this purpose was...care to guess?... "All Rights Reserved."

as time marched on, bigger and better treaties pushed the Buenos Aires Convention into obscurity

As time marched on, bigger and better treaties pushed the Buenos Aires Convention into obscurity. The Berne Convention eliminated the requirement of affixing notice to a work in order to obtain copyright protection. That is why, in the United States and other Berne countries, placing a copyright notice on your work is now optional. Most Buenos Aires signatories eventually joined the Berne Convention, thus in most countries "All Rights Reserved" is no longer necessary.

The Copyright Office's *Circular 38a* has information on most of the major international copyright treaties. It also offers an alphabetical list of nations and the treaties to which each is a signatory.

YOU TRY

1. Why did we choose Nepal as an example, above?

2. Who is Maria A. Pallante?

   Hint: You'll find both answers in *Circular 38a*.

3. Don't know how to find *Circular 38a*? Go to the Copyright Office website: www.copyright.gov. Click on the "Publications" tab at the top of the home page. Then click on "Circulars and Brochures" and behold a treasure of free, easy-to-read copyright information on pretty much any topic you can think of.

4. Now scroll down to the "Factsheets" section, and click on *FL-100*: *International Copyright* (or, if you prefer, select the Spanish-language version: *Proteccion Internacional del Derecho De Autor*). The whole thing's only five paragraphs long, but it tells you what's what. For more links to international copyright resources, explore the Copyright Society of the U.S.A.'s website: http://media.csusa.org/links.html

5. There is a way to obtain information about which countries make good efforts to protect intellectual property rights, and which present problems for United States rights holders. Visit http://www.ustr.gov

6. Who currently serves as the United States Trade Representative?

7. Locate and read the current *Special 301 Report*. What countries are on the Priority Watch List? Why are they on the list?

Pseudonymity

Thinking about using a **pseudonym**? It makes a difference, in terms of how long your copyright is going to last.

Using pseudonyms
Effect on duration of copyright

Many artists figure: *I'm going to sell more art if I adopt a catchy name*. That catchy (fake) name is called a pseudonym. Other examples: Donatello (real name Donato di Niccolò di Betto Bardi), Il Sodoma (Giovanni Antonio Bazzi), El Greco (Doménicos Theotocópoulos), Grandma Moses (Anna Mary Robertson Moses) and Dr. Suess (Theodor Suess Geisel).

You don't have to change your legal name to produce and market copyrightable work under a pseudonym. The United States copyright registration process specifically provides for pseudonymous registration.

So using a pseudonym is fine, and you can keep your real name. But will you run into legal trouble? That depends on what pseudonym you choose and how you use it. For example, many states have statutes governing the authenticity of fine art; all states and the federal government have laws against fraud, trademark infringement, and unfair competition. If you choose the pseudonym "Pablo Picasso," therefore, and fashion your work after that of the famous Spanish artist, you may well get sued. Not because you adopted a pseudonym, but because the pseudonym you chose was designed to mislead (or actually misled) the art-consuming public. So if you're going to use a pseudonym, choose one that's uniquely your own.

The next thing to understand is that adopting a pseudonym can affect the duration of United States copyright protection for your work.

if you're going to use a pseudonym, choose one that's uniquely your own

TS recently had a debate with a writer named Mike, and it went something like this.

TS: Using a pseudonym affects the copyright duration of your work.

Mike: Why? I don't have to register to get a copyright, so the name I use should be irrelevant.

TS: True, you don't have to register to get your copyright. But that doesn't mean the copyright lasts forever. In general, copyright lasts for the life of the author plus 70 years. When one uses a pseudonym, however, the duration is different. Section 302(c) of the copyright law states:

> *In the case of an anonymous work, a pseudonymous work, or a work made for hire, the copyright endures for a term of 95 years from the year of its first publication, or a term of 120 years from the year of its creation, whichever expires first.*

Mike: Why is that?

TS: Because if the work is anonymous or pseudonymous, or if it's a work made for hire, there is no ascertainable life against which to measure [life + 70]. The law, therefore, arbitrarily applies a formula for such works. It's called the **95/120 rule**.

Mike: Who's to know if the name I use is real or not?

TS (quoting from 17 USC §101): *A "pseudonymous work" is a work on the copies or phonorecords of which the author is identified under a fictitious name.*

Mike: Like I said, who's to know?

TS: To some extent that's up to you and how much you choose to reveal. If a lot's at stake and the matter goes to court, it would be a question of evidence as to whether the name you used on your work was or was not your real legal name.

Mike (now reading the law itself, on the Copyright Office website): Look at the next sentence of Section 302(c). It says:

> *If, before the end of such term, the identity of one or more of the authors of an anonymous or pseudonymous work is revealed in the records of a registration made for that work ... or in the records provided by this subsection, the copyright in the work endures ... based on the life of the author or authors whose identity has been revealed.*

TS: That's right. You can get the benefit of [life + 70] if your true identity is revealed while the copyright is still in effect. Check this out, for more information: http://www.copyright.gov/fls/fl101.html

Mike: Which is better? A duration of [life + 70] or 95/120?

TS: You have to decide that for yourself. The 95/120 rule might afford longer protection if your remaining lifespan is short. If you're young and healthy, though, [life + 70] might yield a longer duration.

Mike: If I register under a pseudonym, can somebody else rat me out (i.e., reveal my true identity) to the Copyright Office?

TS: Yes, if they have an "interest" in the copyright. If that's the case, Section 302(c) provides:

> *Any person having an interest in the copyright in an anonymous or pseudonymous work may at any time*

record, in records to be maintained by the Copyright Office for that purpose, a statement identifying one or more authors of the work; the statement shall also identify the person filing it, the nature of that person's interest, the source of the information recorded, and the particular work affected, and shall comply in form and content with requirements that the Register of Copyrights shall prescribe by regulation.

Mike: Why would anyone do that?

TS: Probably because the copyright has become valuable; you're dead; and [life + 70] would extend the life of the copyright. Section 302(d) allows an interested person to file a statement regarding the date of death for a particular author or a statement that the author is still living.

Mike: What if nobody does that? How do you know if an author has died?

TS: Section 302(e) establishes a presumption of death:

> *After a period of 95 years from the year of first publication of a work, or a period of 120 years from the year of its creation, whichever expires first, any person who obtains from the Copyright Office a certified report that [Copyright Office] records ... disclose nothing to indicate that the author of the work is living, or died less than 70 years before, is entitled to the benefit of a presumption that the author has been dead for at least 70 years. Reliance in good faith upon this presumption shall be a complete defense to any action for infringement under this title.*

Pat: Interesting. I'll have to think about whether I'm going to keep using the name Mike.

Conversation #36

Listening In On a Trademark Workshop

Shortly after the copyright workshop in Conversation #9, TS conducted a companion session on trademark law. Not surprisingly, the first question was fairly basic.

Trademark basics

Choosing a strong trademark

Harry: What is a trademark, anyway?

TS: Harry! You're back!

Harry smirks at TS, implicitly encouraging her to keep this short.

A trademark identifies the source of goods and services. Words, slogans, logos, sounds, smells, and colors can all function as trademarks. When a consumer sees/hears/smells your trademark, *your* product comes to mind. The consumer doesn't think about a competitor's product. She thinks about yours. Why? Because an effective trademark sets your product apart from others and identifies you as the source of that product. Consider the following exchange:

Server: My name is Raymond and I'll be your server. May I bring you something to drink?

Julie: I'd like a Diet X, please.

Raymond: Is Diet Y OK?

Julie *(silently, to herself)*: No! I hate Diet Y!

Julie *(out loud, to Raymond)*: Yes.

Julie didn't ask for a cola. She asked for a particular

cola: Diet X. And she knows well enough that she'd rather have Diet X than Diet Y. Trademarks build brand loyalty and serve as representations of quality assurance. If Julie orders something called Diet X she can be pretty sure that she'll get the product with which she is familiar.

Harry: It sounds like trademarks exist more to help the consumer, than the brand owner.

TS: Exactly! But which brand owner is going to make more sales: the one that helps consumers distinguish among competing choices, or the one whose product blends in with all the others?

Harry: The one whose product stands out. But sales won't be strong for long if the product stinks.

if you've built goodwill in a superior product or service, a strong trademark distinguishes yours from inferior competitors

TS: Also true. And that's another function of trademarks. They become indicators of quality. If you've built goodwill in a superior product or service, a strong trademark distinguishes yours from inferior competitors. You can have many competitors; but with the combination of a superior product and a strong trademark, your product can become the "gold standard" in the eyes of consumers.

Harry seemed convinced that trademark issues were worthy of his attention, so TS moved on to the next big question: what makes a trademark "strong?"

G-D-S-A-F

Remember, the point of a trademark is to distinguish you as the source of your products. The strongest trademark, therefore, is the one that is most distinctive when used in connection with your goods or services. Consider a sliding scale consisting of the letters G-D-S-A-F where "G" is the weakest trademark and "F" is the strongest.

"G" stands for generic. The generic term for your product cannot serve as a trademark. Why? Because it does not identify you as the source of the product. Example: if you sell chairs, and you present them to the public as "Chairs," the consumer has no idea whether they are your chairs or those of your competitors.

"D" stands for descriptive, and this is almost as bad. Terms that merely describe your product are extremely weak trademarks. Example: "Pancake House." There are a million restaurants that serve pancakes, and "house" is a common term for a place of business. It is sometimes possible to secure trademark protection for descriptive marks, but it's very difficult and you'll always be in a weaker position, legally, than if you'd adopted a stronger mark.

"S" stands for suggestive. A suggestive term doesn't come right out and describe your product, but it plants the idea in your consumer's mind. Example: "Roach Motel." Suggestive terms aren't the strongest, but they can serve as trademarks.

"A" stands for arbitrary. An arbitrary trademark is a real word, but it has nothing to do with your goods or services. Example: "Apple" for computers; "Bicycle" for playing cards. As a trademark, Apple for apples would be useless. But in connection with computers it's very strong because it immediately identifies the source of the computers.

"F" stands for fanciful. This is the strongest possible trademark. A fanciful trademark is a made-up word that does not otherwise exist except in connection with your product. Examples: "Exxon" and "Kodak."

> Harry: That all makes sense, but my marketing people told me I should pick a trademark that clearly conveys what my product does. They're saying, "Be as descriptive as possible," and now you're saying the exact opposite.
>
> TS: I know. There's tension between what works legally and what works from a marketing perspective. The trick is to have your marketing people and your trademark

lawyer work together – from the beginning – so your branding accomplishes both objectives. One way to do this is by adopting a fanciful trademark and then using it together with a descriptive slogan or design.

Harry: OK. I'll choose a strong trademark. Then am I good to go?

As TS shook her head, Harry texted Kay to say he might be stuck here forever.

TS: Choosing a "strong" trademark is only the first step. If you're planning to apply for US trademark registration you need to consider the many (many!) bases upon which an application for registration can be refused. Here are some situations that could pose problems:

- The trademark is primarily a surname.
- The trademark includes a geographic indicator.
- The trademark identifies a living person or any deceased US President.
- The trademark has any meaning in a foreign language.
- The trademark depicts the flag or coat of arms of any government.
- The trademark is merely ornamental.
- The trademark is functional.
- The trademark is a single literary title.
- The trademark could be considered immoral, scandalous, or disparaging.

Sensing a brewing storm (named Harry), TS suggested a short break.

YOU TRY

What do the words Aspirin, Escalator, Bikini, Kerosene, Thermos, and Yo-Yo have in common?

CONVERSATION #37

The Trademark Workshop Continues

ully refreshed, Harry returned to the trademark session ready to tackle the next big question:

TRADEMARK SEARCHING
PROTECTING TRADEMARKS
REGISTRATION
TRADEMARK SYMBOLS
TRADE DRESS
USING TRADEMARKS IN ARTISTIC WORK

How do I protect my trademark?

TS surprised the room with a two-word answer:

Use it.

Harry: *Use it?* That's it?

TS: There's more to it, of course. But trademark rights arise from actual use, not registration. So actually using the trademark is very important.

Harry: I get trademark rights just by using the mark? Without registration?

TS: You get some, yes.

Harry: What if somebody else used the trademark before me?

TS: It depends on how and where they used the mark, but the short answer is that their rights might be superior to yours.

Harry: So I should get out there and start using my trademarks right away!

TS: That's basically true, but give your trademark lawyer a chance to chime in, before you launch.

Harry: Why?

TS: You have to make sure your use doesn't infringe on somebody else's superior rights.

Harry: I don't need a lawyer for that. I'll just look on the Trademark Office website.

TS: Bad idea, Harry. You're not alone in this thinking; some lawyers even believe it's that simple. But you're not OK just because you don't find an application or registration for your exact trademark listed on the **USPTO** website. Marks that sound like yours, look like yours, and even those with similar meaning or translations can be conflicts, causing your junior use to constitute infringement. Remember, too, that registration is not required. So a senior user might be out there and you'd have no idea, if all you're looking at is the USPTO website.

you're not OK just because you don't find an application or registration for your exact trademark on the USPTO website

Harry: So what do I do?

TS: You work with your trademark lawyer, who will order and analyze a comprehensive search report.

Harry: Why else would I need a lawyer at this stage?

TS: Well, you have to analyze all those causes for refusal we talked about in Conversation #36. Also, how you actually use and depict your trademark can affect your rights and your ability ultimately to obtain a federal registration. If you make mistakes you might have to start all over later on.

Harry: OK. I'll use a trademark lawyer. But I'm still not clear on the registration thing. If I don't have to register, why should I?

TS expected this question, and was already writing a few reasons on the whiteboard.

- Registration is a public record of your claim to ownership of the mark.
- Registration precludes others from registering the same or similar marks in connection with the same or similar goods/services listed in your registration.
- You can sue in federal court, you enjoy a legal presumption that you are the owner of the mark, and you become eligible to recover higher damages and attorney fees.
- You can use your registration as a basis for obtaining registration in foreign countries.
- You can record your registration with US Customs and Border Protection (see Conversation #15) to help prevent the importation of infringing goods.
- You won't be looking over your shoulder all the time, wondering if some other user is going to shut you down and make you start all over.
- You can use the federal registration symbol: ®

A lively discussion ensued, particularly in connection with the ® symbol.

TS: Using the ® symbol means, *I hold a federal registration for this trademark*. Don't ever use the ® symbol if you do not, in fact, have a federal registration. It's fraud.

Greg: Really? Man, I slap that ® symbol on everything, figuring it will scare people away from using my mark.

TS: You might want to stop doing that. Remember, though, that even if you don't have a federal registration you still acquire common law rights in a mark, just by using it. When you see the symbols TM or SM after a mark, it means that the owner doesn't have a federal registration, but still intends to protect those common law trademark rights.

Greg: So it's OK to use TM and SM without a registration, but not the ® symbol.

TS: Correct.

Greg: What does SM mean?

TS: Service mark. It's the same as TM except it's used in connection with services rather than goods.

Greg: Are trademark owners required to use the ®, TM, or SM symbols?

TS: No. (Though failing to use the ® symbol, if you do hold a registration, can cause you to lose certain advantages.)

Greg: You mean, someone can be claiming trademark rights and I might not even know it?

TM and SM are general indicators that a mark owner is hoping to preserve common law rights in the mark

TS (Somewhat sheepishly): I'm afraid so.

Greg: Well, how can I determine whether someone's claiming rights to a particular mark?

TS: That's why your lawyer will order that comprehensive search report.

Greg: Can you register trademarks with the states, as well as federally?

TS: Yes.

Greg: Is there any particular symbol that serves as an indicator of state registration?

TS: You're starting to sound like a lawyer, Greg.

Greg: Very funny. What's the answer?

TS: No. TM and SM are general indicators that a mark owner is hoping to preserve all common law rights in the mark – including those arising under state law.

Greg: So if I see ®, TM, or SM, it's a signal to me that I can't use the mark?

TS: Not necessarily. You can't use the mark in connection with providing the same or similar goods or services as the owner of the mark, and you can't trade on the business goodwill of the mark. But if (for example) you're using the mark for purposes of artistic expression, that can be OK. For example, if your photograph of a kitchen includes a canister of Lipton® tea, you aren't infringing on the Lipton® mark unless (a) you're using your artwork to sell tea, or (b) the public would be confused into thinking that your work was created by or on behalf of the company that owns Lipton, or (c) you are trading on the goodwill of the trademark more than making an artistic statement.

Greg: So I can use other people's trademarks in my work?

TS: Often, yes. And many trademark owners don't understand this concept. It's very common for trademark owners to say, I own the trademark so you can't use it for anything, no matter what. That's simply not true.

Greg: Can you give another example?

TS: Sure. Consider our friend Spofford, a photographer. He was hired to photograph the construction process of a new insurance company building. The shape of the building is very distinctive, and it has come to serve as an indicator of source for the insurance company's services and business goodwill. So the insurance company obtained trademark protection for the design of the building. That's fine. But their protection only extends to the goods and services in their "channels of trade," i.e., insurance services, maybe other financial services, and maybe even merchandise they distribute to promote the business.

Greg: I don't see the problem.

TS: Spofford?

Spofford: Well, I own the copyright to my photos, and I make the photos available for licensing. A textbook company asked to license one of my photos of the insurance company building, for use on the cover of a textbook. That was fine with me, but then the insurance company made noise saying the textbook company couldn't use the photo, because the building design was its trademark.

Greg: And that was improper?

Spofford: You bet. As TS just explained, the insurance company's trademark protection is limited in scope. If the textbook company wanted to use my photo to provide insurance services, or similar types of promotional merchandise, then the insurance company would have a valid concern. But the insurance company is not in the business of publishing textbooks, and the textbook company has nothing to do with insurance. Furthermore, the textbook company isn't going to sell more books, or sell them for more money, because a photo of the building appears on the cover.

there are special rules for famous trademarks, so you have to be more careful about using them

TS: Well said, Spofford. The textbook company was not using the insurance company's trademark as an indicator of source, and so there was no likelihood that consumers would be confused into thinking the insurance company was the source of the textbooks.

Greg: That's interesting. But I'm still not clear. Are you saying I can use somebody else's trademark in my artwork whenever I want?

TS: No, I'm not saying that. You can cross the line. For one thing, there are special rules for famous trademarks, so you have to be more careful about using them. Generally, though, the issue is whether your use of the trademark is likely to cause consumer confusion regarding the source of goods. If the mark appears so prominently in your work, or in such a manner that a reasonable consumer might believe the work was created by or on behalf of the company that owns the mark, there might be a case for trademark infringement. Similarly, if your work is more likely to sell, or to sell at a higher price, solely because it includes the mark, then you're no longer using the mark for purposes of artistic expression. You're trading on the business goodwill of the trademark, and that could subject you to liability.

YOU TRY

1. A product's overall packaging and appearance is known as **trade dress**. In Spofford's example, above, the insurance company in claiming trademark protection for the building's design was really protecting trade dress. Trade dress is a type of trademark and can be registered as such, so long as it is sufficiently distinctive and serves no functional purpose. Trade dress is subject to the same rules regarding use and infringement as are other types of trademarks. Examples of trade dress include the shape of a Coca-Cola® bottle and the yellow McDonald's® arches. Can you think of others?
2. Those special rules for famous trademarks are legal concepts known as **dilution** and **tarnishment**. To learn more, do some general research on the "Federal Trademark Dilution Act" and the "Trademark Dilution Revision Act of 2006."
3. It's also OK to use other people's trademarks for purposes of **comparative advertising**. Look it up!
4. How does this Conversation shed light on Andy Warhol and the Campbell's soup can?

How to Get Sued for Using People in Your Art

Right of publicity
Invasions of privacy
Defamation
Post-mortem rights
Showler v Harper's Magazine

There is considerable tension between an individual's right to control the use of her identity, and an artist's constitutional right to freedom of speech. **When is it OK to use another person's likeness in your work, without first obtaining the subject's consent?**

When you want to use someone's likeness in your work, you need to ask some threshold questions, the most important of which is, *Why don't I just get a release from the subject?!*

That would be best.

But if you can't – or didn't – get a release, you and your lawyer will need to conduct a thorough analysis of the situation. You'll need to assess whether the subject is a public figure. You'll need to identify whether the nature of your work is commercial or noncommercial, and you'll need to know how to tell the difference[1]. You may need to consider whether your work is a conventional portrait of the subject, or whether you have added "transformative" artistic elements to the depiction[2]. You'll also need to know that this question raises issues of both state and federal law and that as to both, a lot

[1]*Hoffman v Capital Cities/ABC, Inc.*, 33 F Supp 2d 867, revd 255 F3d 1180 (9th Cir 2001)

[2]*Comedy III Productions, Inc. v Gary Saderup, Inc.*, 25 Cal 4th 387, 106 Cal Rptr 2d 126, 21 P 3d 797, cert denied 534 US 1078, 122 S Ct 806, 151 L Ed 2d 692 (2002); see also Estate of Presley v Russen, 513 F Supp 1339 (DNJ 1981])

depends on the jurisdiction in question. State laws vary dramatically, as can the federal courts' analyses on seemingly similar sets of facts.

We'll sort this out by looking at five important concepts you'll have to consider (the "Big Five"). First, though, some caveats.

- The Big Five are primarily creatures of state law. Not every state recognizes each of the Big Five as actionable, and among those that do, there can be significant differences in how a state interprets and applies each theory.

use our discussion of the Big Five as an initial checklist when you're thinking about using a real person in your work

- Use our discussion of the Big Five as an initial checklist when you're thinking about using a real person in your work. If your gut tells you there's likely to be a problem, and you can live without using this person in the work: don't use the person.
- If using the person is really important and you want to move forward, you're going to need legal advice. Call an attorney. To help streamline your consultation, bring along your list of the Big Five. Tell the attorney that you're aware of these potential issues, and start by asking the attorney to answer two questions: (a) how, if at all, might the Big Five create liability for me in this state? and (b) what issues *other* than the Big Five (including copyright and trademark) might be a problem?
- You might have to consult more than one attorney, since you could potentially be sued in a state other than your own. In such case, assuming you have "minimum contacts" with the other state (see Conversation #2) the law of that state might apply. So before committing to using a real person in your work, you and your attorney should think about which other states are likely to be of concern – and you should then get "Big Five" advice specific to those other states.

The Big Five

#1: The Right of Publicity. Worry about this one, generally, if the person you're intending to use is a celebrity. As we shall see, the other four theories involve right of privacy laws, which are available to celebrities and noncelebrities alike. In many states, however, right-of-publicity laws apply only to the famous[3]. They exist to protect people whose identities already have commercial value from the financial loss that occurs when someone uses their name or likeness without first obtaining a release.

Actors from the TV show *Cheers* prevailed on a right of publicity claim, for example, when a string of airport taverns produced life-sized robots modeled on the actors' images. The actors in question (George Wendt and John Ratzenberger) played characters in *Cheers* named Norm and Cliff. The taverns were properly authorized, by the *Cheers* copyright owners, to re-create Norm and Cliff. But nobody asked George and John, the actors, if it would be OK to use their personal images. And because the actors were celebrities (whose identities had commercial value), using their images without permission was like stealing. The airport taverns rode the wave of their well-known faces, for free. That violated the actors' rights of publicity under California law[4].

Now. Don't think you can't ever use a famous person's image. The First Amendment does protect artistic expression. And though it would take volumes to explain this in detail, the general concept is this: if you depict a famous person for purposes of your own expression or commentary, you're likely to be OK. If you include a famous golfer in your painting expressing the history of the Masters golf tournament– the law is likely to be on your side[5]. In the *Cheers* case, on the other hand, using the actors' images served an exclusively commer-

[3]See, e.g., *Landham v Lewis Galoob Toys, Inc.*, 227 F3d 619 (6th Cir 2000)

[4]*Wendt v Host International*, 125 F3d 806, cert denied 531 US 811, 121 S Ct 33, 148 L Ed 2d 13 (2000)

[5]*ETW Corp. v Jireh Publishing, Inc.*, 99 F Supp 2d 829, affd 332 F3d 915 (6th Cir 2003)

cial purpose: to attract travelers to the bar. That crossed the line.

Let's move on. Our next four theories involve different claims for invasion of privacy. (That's right: there isn't just one potential claim for invasion of privacy, there are four; and you could be sued separately on any or all of them.)

there isn't just one potential claim for invasion of privacy, there are four

#2: Appropriation Invasion of Privacy. This theory prohibits the unauthorized use of a person's identity for purposes of advertising or trade. It's similar to the right of publicity, except it applies also to noncelebrities, and it involves injury to the person's psyche as opposed to the person's pocketbook. To prevail under **common law**, a victim must show measurable damage to her peace of mind or dignity.

Often, this type of claim will also appear in a state's **statutory** law, and when that's the case it's typically easier to prove. Under many statutory provisions, the actual unauthorized use of a person's identity for purposes of advertising or trade is enough to state a claim; the victim doesn't necessarily have to show damage to her peace of mind. So make sure you know if your state has such a statutory provision.

#3: Intrusion Invasion of Privacy. This one involves the *manner* in which you obtain the image or information you subsequently disclose. In order to win on a claim for intrusion invasion of privacy, the plaintiff usually must establish that:

a.) You intentionally intruded into their seclusion without permission (e.g., you broke into their house; you crashed their party; you spied through their bedroom window);

b.) They had a reasonable expectation of privacy;

c.) Your actions were offensive or objectionable to a reasonable person;

d.) The matter at issue involved something private; and

e.) The plaintiff suffered emotional anguish.

#4: Defamation and False Light Invasion of Privacy. Defamation and false light invasion of privacy are technically two separate theories. They're very similar, though, so we'll discuss them together.

You've probably heard about **libel** and **slander**, two types of the wrong known as **defamation**. Libel refers to defamatory statements that are written; slander refers to such statements made verbally. To prevail in a defamation action, the plaintiff usually must establish that:

a.) You made a false statement about him or her;

b.) You made the statement to at least one person other than the plaintiff;

c.) The statement was understood by others as being about the plaintiff; and

d.) The statement caused injury to the plaintiff's reputation.

You've probably also heard this, about defamation: the truth is an absolute defense. If the statement you made was actually true, the plaintiff loses.

Now let's consider false light invasion of privacy. Some states don't even recognize this as an actionable theory, because it's so similar to defamation. The only real difference is that, in a false light claim, the plaintiff need not establish injury to reputation. Instead, the plaintiff must show that your statement, placing him or her in a false light, would be highly offensive to a reasonable person. Otherwise, the elements of proof in a false light claim are substantially the same as in a defamation claim.

you've probably heard this, about defamation: the truth is an absolute defense

#5: Disclosure Invasion of Privacy. We just observed that the truth is an absolute defense to a defamation claim. Not so, with this next theory. In a disclosure invasion of privacy action, the plaintiff is complaining that you disclosed something private about him or her that might actually *be* true; and that the disclosure would be considered highly offensive to a reasonable person. In this case, if you disclose something private and embarrassing about a person, the fact that it's true actually makes things worse because the plaintiff is all the more embarrassed!

Let's look at some examples.

Intrusion invasion of privacy. When is it an "intrusion" to photograph a person in a public place? Here's a random sampling of what some state courts have decided, on the facts before them:

- Alabama: Observing someone else's activities when they are exposed to the public view is not actionable as intrusion invasion of privacy. On the other hand, publishing a picture showing plaintiff with her dress blown up as she was leaving the fun house at a county fair was intrusion invasion, because even though the plaintiff was part of a public scene, she neither caused nor expected her dress to blow up. When it did, exposing her in public, she was in a situation that an ordinary person would consider embarrassing. Taking advantage of that situation constituted invasion.
- California: Videotaping and broadcasting actions someone voluntarily performs in public is not intrusion.
- Florida: Intrusion requires a trespass or intrusion upon physical solitude, as by invading one's home.
- Georgia: A teacher who photographed a student did not commit intrusion invasion of privacy, where: photographs were taken in the school building during regular school hours; other students were present; and the photographs did not reveal any aspect of the student that was not readily visible to anyone else who saw her during the school day.
- Iowa: If a person is dining in a restaurant where anyone can see him/her, there likely is no intrusion invasion. On the other hand, to film a person in a private dining room might be an actionable intrusion upon that person's

seclusion. The mere fact a person can be seen by others does not mean that person cannot legally be secluded, nor does the person's visibility to some people strip him/her of the right to remain secluded from others.

Dead or Alive? It Matters. There's a big difference between the right of publicity, which is a **property right**, and the various rights of privacy – which are **personal rights**. The difference is this: a property right can be passed to one's heirs, but a personal right is extinguished at death. In states that recognize a postmortem right of publicity, therefore, the heirs can enforce a celebrity's right of publicity even after the celebrity has passed away. Not so, with rights of privacy. There is no postmortem right to privacy.

Example. A filmmaker depicted a well-known boxer in an unfavorable light. If the boxer were living, the filmmaker's depiction may well have constituted false light invasion of privacy. Believing the boxer to be dead, however, the filmmaker took liberties. Well, wouldn't you know, the boxer turned out to be alive. The boxer sued, and the filmmaker settled the case. Moral of the story: if you're going to take liberties with the reputation of a dead person, make sure they're really dead!

if you're going to take liberties with the reputation of a dead person, make sure they're really dead

Showler v Harper's Magazine. This case, decided in Oklahoma, helps to illustrate our Conversation.

Sgt. Kyle Brinlee was killed in action in Iraq on May 11, 2004. He was the first member of the Oklahoma National Guard to be killed in action since the Korean War. As such, his death and funeral were the subject of intense media coverage. The funeral was open to the media. More than twelve hundred people attended, including the governor of Oklahoma. Sgt. Brinlee's family decided to open his casket at the funeral, but requested that no one take photographs.

Peter Turnley was a photojournalist working on assignment for *Harper's*. He took photographs of Sgt. Brinlee in the open casket. The photographs were published in the August 2004 edition of *Harper's*; they were also sold and published in the French magazine, *Le Monde 2*. In addition to other claims, Sgt. Brinlee's family sued under three of the privacy causes of action we just discussed: appropriation, disclosure, and invasion. They lost on all three.

The astute reader might suggest: *We just learned there's no postmortem right of privacy. Is that why they lost?*

Good thinking, but no.

In Oklahoma, as in many states, the cause of action for appropriation is codified in a statute that prohibits the use of one's name, portrait, or picture for purposes of advertising. As it happens, the Oklahoma statute actually permits a deceased's heirs to pursue an appropriation claim. That's why the family could bring the appropriation claim at all. They lost, though, because in Oklahoma an appropriation claim won't succeed if the use (of the person's name, portrait, or picture) was, essentially, to report on a newsworthy event. Sgt. Brinlee's death and funeral were unquestionably newsworthy; and even though *Harper's* used the photographs to increase its circulation, that didn't rise to the level of "advertising."

On the disclosure claim, the family contended that publication of the photographs disclosed private facts about their *own* lives, namely, their mourning process. They lost because they themselves had chosen to make the funeral public, and the photographs revealed no information that was private.

the photographs accurately depicted a funeral that the plaintiffs themselves had opened to the public

The family also complained that the photographs were obtained by a nonconsensual intrusion that should be considered highly offensive to a reasonable person. The intrusion claim failed for the same reasons as the disclosure claim: the photographs accurately depicted a funeral that the plaintiffs themselves had opened to the public. Mr. Turnley took the photographs from an area that was specifically designated for the press, and other photographers were present. Taking photographs of the casket may have disrespected the family's request, but it did not constitute intrusion invasion of privacy.

YOU TRY

Some states recognize a postmortem right of publicity, and some do not. The law keeps changing, so when you're ready to learn more, do a search for "right of publicity" and "postmortem" – and see what's new! (If you're really interested, add "Marilyn Monroe" to your search terms.)

CONVERSATION 39

Art and Uncle Sam

In this Conversation we will discuss three related issues: using work that *belongs to* the United States government; creating work *for* the government; and types of work the government (by law) says you can't use.

WORK OF GOVERNMENT EMPLOYEES

WORK OF THE US POSTAL SERVICE

CREATING WORK FOR THE GOVERNMENT

USING NATIONAL INSIGNIA

Using Government Works

Section 105 of the copyright law (17 USC §105) states:

> *Copyright protection…is not available for any work of the United States Government….*

We read that first sentence and think, "Great! We can use any work that belongs to the US government!" Then we read the second sentence:

> *…but the United States Government is not precluded from receiving and holding copyrights transferred to it by assignment, bequest, or otherwise.*

Well, shoot. How are we supposed to know if something is a work *of* the government, or if it's something for which the government *received* copyright rights?

If you're short on time, here's a quick answer: "Ask."

Here's a longer answer.

It's a work *of* the US government if a government

official or employee created the work as part of his or her official duties. (We know this, because section 101 of the copyright law [17 USC §101] states: *A "work of the United States Government" is a work prepared by an officer or employee of the United States Government as part of that person's official duties.*) Such work is, by virtue of section 105, in the **public domain** and free to use.

But what if the government employee created the work after hours, for fun?

The law itself doesn't address this, but congressional notes to the statute do shed some light. The notes state: ... *[A] Governmental official or employee would not be prevented from securing copyright in a work written at that person's own volition and outside his or her duties, even though the subject matter involves the Government work or professional field of the official or employee.*

don't let the name fool you: the US Postal Service is not, actually, the "government"

So let's say, for example, an off-duty Secret Service agent sketches zombie-themed caricatures of the First Family and posts the sketches on a website. Are the sketches public domain because the agent is a government employee? No. The agent is entitled to the full protections of US copyright law – even though the subject matter involved her line of work – because (presumably) she made the sketches on her own time and was not required to do so as a part of her official duties.

Next example: Work of the US Postal Service.

Don't let the name fool you: the US Postal Service is not, actually, the "government." The US Postal Service is an *independent establishment of the executive branch of the Government of the United States* (39 USC §201).

Huh?

Maybe this would be clearer; it's paraphrased from a court decision: *Congress' purpose in establishing the US Postal Ser-*

vice was to permit the Service to operate in a 'business-like' fashion; to such end, Congress removed the Service from the political sphere and authorized it to act as an independent establishment with powers equivalent to a private business enterprise, such as the power to make contracts, keep accounts and to acquire and lease property.

Huh?

Whatever. Here's what matters: US postage stamps are copyrightable.

The congressional notes to section 105 state: *In accordance with the Postal Reorganization Act of 1970...[section 105] does not apply to works created by employees of the United States Postal Service. In addition to enforcing the criminal statutes proscribing the forgery or counterfeiting of postage stamps, the Postal Service could, if it chooses, use the copyright law to prevent the reproduction of postage stamp designs for private or commercial non-postal services (for example, in philatelic publications and catalogs, in general advertising, in art reproductions, in textile designs, and so forth.)*

So. If a postage stamp was designed by a Postal Service employee, it's subject to copyright because of the Postal Reorganization Act of 1970. If the stamp was designed by an independent artist, the artist almost certainly **assigned** his or her copyright to the Service; and if not, the artist retained his or her copyright. Either way, the stamp is not in the public domain.

The US Postal Service has a licensing division to control the use of USPS intellectual property. Do generally accepted standards of fair use apply? Yes. But take note: the USPS's view of fair use is not expansive. Consider this warning from the USPS website:

> *The U.S. Postal Service has a statutory obligation to operate as a business and so vigorously defends its intellectual property rights. If you are uncertain about whether or not*

your intended use falls within [fair use] (or if it simply does not), we strongly recommend that you contact the Rights and Permissions office before proceeding to use the U.S. Postal Service's property.

(http://about.usps.com/doing-business/rights-permissions/fair-use-exceptions.htm)

Creating Work for the Government

What if you are commissioned by the US government to create a work of art? Do you automatically lose your copyright?

No, but you don't automatically get a copyright, either.

The leading case on this point is *Schnapper v Foley* (667 F2d 102, cert denied 455 US 948, 102 S Ct 1448, 71 L Ed 2d 661 [1982]). *Schnapper* confirms that US copyright law "does not prohibit" copyright protection for work that is produced pursuant to a government commission. But that doesn't mean copyright protection is automatically conferred.

Citing more of those congressional notes to section 105, the *Schnapper* court clarified that sometimes the government may withhold copyright protection from the author of a commissioned work, *if it would be in the public interest to do so or if the commission is merely an alternative to producing the work in-house.*

On the other hand (said the court), *[Section 105] deliberately avoids making any sort of outright, unqualified prohibition against copyright in works prepared under Government contract or grant. There may well be cases where it would be in the public interest to deny copyright....However, there are almost certainly many other cases where the denial of copyright protection would be unfair or would hamper the production and publication of important works.*

Bottom line: Whether you may or may not claim copyright protection for works commissioned by the government depends on what, exactly, you are creating. Is it sensitive material? Could the government just as easily have created the work in-house? If so, you're not likely to have any claim to copyright protection. On the other hand, if the work has no particular security issues and could not be created by a government employee, copyright protection might be available.

even if copyright is available, the government might require you to assign your copyright as a condition of the commission

Remember, though, that even if copyright is available, the government might (and likely will) require you to **assign** your copyright as a condition of the commission. And once you've done that, the government holds the copyright anyway. Still, it's important to understand your rights when you're negotiating the commission, as assigning the copyright is additional value for which you should be fairly compensated.

Using National Insignia

The provisions that follow summarize provisions of chapter 33 of title 18 of the United States Code. Title 18 is entitled, "Crimes and Criminal Procedure." Chapter 33 is entitled, "Emblems, Insignia and Names." Violations of these provisions can result in fines, imprisonment, or both.

§701: Official badges, identification cards, other insignia

The heads of United States departments and agencies prescribe the design for badges, identification cards, and other insignia used by their officers and employees. If, without authority, you manufacture, sell, or possess any badge or ID card bearing such a design, or if you make any engraving, photograph, print, or impression in the likeness of any such badge or ID card, you go directly to jail. (OK, you might just get a fine, but imprisonment is a possibility.)

§702: Uniform of armed forces and Public Health Service

You can't wear the uniform or anything similar to a "distinctive part of the uniform" of the armed forces of the United States anywhere within the jurisdiction of the United States or the Canal Zone, without authority to do so. If you do: see ya in six months. And note, intent to violate the provision is not a prerequisite for conviction.

In 1944 a 74-year-old man proudly wore the uniform of a captain in the United States Army to a social dinner. He honestly believed he was entitled to wear the uniform, but in fact he was not. A United States federal court found him guilty, notwithstanding his belief in the propriety of his conduct. The courts have upheld exceptions to this provision for actors wearing military uniforms in theatrical productions, so it bears observing that if a protected First Amendment interest is involved, there can be exceptions to this restriction. Artists would be well advised to seek counsel on this issue before taking the risk.

if you wear the uniform or regalia of a foreign nation with which the United States is at peace and you do so "with intent to deceive or mislead," you violate the law

<u>§703: Uniform of friendly nation</u>

Unlike §702, noble intent can save you from prosecution under this provision. Inadvertent behavior won't get you in trouble. However, if you wear the uniform or regalia of a foreign nation with which the United States is at peace and you do so "with intent to deceive or mislead," you violate the law. Curiously, the statute says nothing about wearing the uniform of an unfriendly nation. (If you're dumb enough to do that, though, you'd likely be arrested on other grounds altogether!)

<u>§704: Military medals or decorations</u>

You may not wear, manufacture, or sell any decoration or medal authorized by Congress for the armed forces of the United States. Six months in the slammer. And if that decoration or medal happens to be the Congressional Medal of Honor: you go away for a full year.

<u>§705: Badge or medal of veterans' organizations</u>

This provision involves badges, medals, emblems, and other insignia of veterans' organizations and their auxiliaries. If you knowingly manufacture, reproduce, sell, or purchase such items for resale, you break the law. Imprisonment looms if, without authority, you knowingly print, lithograph, engrave, or otherwise reproduce the designs on any poster, circular, periodical, magazine, newspaper, or other publication. You also risk prosecution if you circulate or distribute any printed matter bearing a reproduction of such badge, medal, emblem, or other insignia.

§706: Red Cross

You may not wear or display the sign of the Red Cross for the fraudulent purpose of inducing the belief that you are a member of or agent for the American National Red Cross; nor may you use the emblem of the Greek red cross on a white ground, or the words "Red Cross" or "Geneva Cross" or any combination of those words.

§707: 4-H club emblem fraudulently used

It's a fine and/or prison if, with intent to defraud, you wear or display the sign or emblem of the 4-H clubs, consisting of a green four-leaf clover with stem, and the letter H in white or gold on each leaflet. It's also a crime to use any such sign or emblem or the words "4-H Club" or "4-H Clubs" or any combination of those words or characters. The only people authorized to use these words and emblems are 4-H clubs, representatives of the United States Department of Agriculture land grant colleges, and persons authorized by the Secretary of Agriculture.

§708: Swiss Confederation coat of arms

No person or entity may use the coat of arms of the Swiss Confederation, consisting of an upright white cross with equal arms and lines on a red ground, as a trademark or commercial label or as an advertisement or insignia for any business or organization or for any trade or commercial purpose.

§711: "Smokey Bear" character or name

Do not even think about using the name or character "Smokey Bear" before consulting the rules and regulations of the Secretary of Agriculture, the Association of State Foresters (http://www.stateforesters.org), and the Advertising Council (http://www.adcouncil.org).

§711a: "Woodsy Owl" character, name or slogan

Same goes for "Woodsy Owl" and Woodsy's famous slogan, "Give a Hoot, Don't Pollute."

§713: Use of likenesses of the great seal of the United States, the seals of the President and Vice President, the seal of the United States Senate, the seal of the United States House of Representatives, and the seal of the United States Congress

You can't display or print any of these seals in or in connection with any advertisement, poster, circular, book, pamphlet, or other publication, public meeting, play, motion picture, telecast, or other production, or on any building, monument, or stationery for the purpose of conveying a false impression of sponsorship or approval by the Government of the United States. Nor may you manufacture, reproduce, sell, or purchase for resale any likeness of such seals.

§715: "The Golden Eagle Insignia"

The Golden Eagle Insignia is defined in the United States Code as the representation of an American Golden Eagle (colored gold) and a family group (colored midnight blue) enclosed within a circle (colored white with a midnight blue border) framed by a rounded triangle (colored gold with a midnight blue border). Except as authorized under the rules and regulations of the Secretary of the Interior, anyone who knowingly manufacturers, reproduces, or uses the Golden Eagle Insignia is subject to prosecution, fine, and/or imprisonment.

§716: Police badges

You may not transfer, transport, or receive a counterfeit police badge, nor may you transfer a genuine police badge to an individual, knowing that such individual is not authorized to possess it. It is a defense to prosecution under this section, though, if the badge is used or is intended to be used exclusively as a memento, in a collection or exhibit, for decorative purposes, for a dramatic presentation such as a theatrical, film or television production, or for any other recreational purpose.

The Flag

That leaves the most controversial symbol of all, the flag. Section 700 of Chapter 33 is entitled, "Desecration of the flag of the United States; penalties." Flag desecration statutes have been held unconstitutional by the United States Supreme Court (see *Texas v Johnson,* 491 US 397, 109 S Ct 2533, 105 L Ed 2d 342 [1989]; *United States v Eichman*, 496 US 310, 110 S Ct 2404, 110 L Ed 2d 287 [1990]). The flag plays a prominent role in contemporary art and its use as a medium of expression has sparked heated constitutional debate. Entering "flag desecration" into any major search engine will yield a plethora of resources to inform this ongoing discussion.

the flag plays a prominent role in contemporary art and its use as a medium of expression has sparked heated constitutional debate

YOU TRY

1. For an interesting account of copyright litigation involving a US postage stamp: *Gaylord v United States,* 678 F3d 1339 (Fed Cir 2012).
2. Using United States currency is another interesting issue. Visit the United States Mint's website for information: http://www.usmint.gov/consumer/?action=FAQ
3. For a pop culture explanation about why flag desecration statutes are unconstitutional (and for a bit of comic relief) listen to "The Amendment Song" by Alf Clausen and John Swartzwelder. Yes, this is the one from *The Simpsons*.

Doing Business Online

Customers expect you to have a presence on whatever communications platform happens, at the moment, to be "it." They want to find you using the devices of their choosing, not yours. They expect to use these devices to learn more about you, to assess whether you present yourself professionally, to see samples of your work, to obtain your contact information and – most importantly – to purchase your goods and retain your services.

Trademarks
Domains
Copyright ownership
Royalty free materials
Creative Commons
DMCA safe harbors
Website policies
Hosting considerations

If you want to do business, you will accommodate these expectations. In doing so, you will encounter legal issues.

Here are some tips.

Don't identify yourself using somebody else's trademark. One of your first steps will be to select the various names and addresses that others will use to communicate with you and your business. Today, you acquire **domain names** and **short codes** and you create **QR codes**. You choose user, page and group names on social media platforms. As technology evolves, different means for identifying yourself will emerge. Whatever they may be, remember this: do not identify your business using somebody else's trademark.

People often think that if they are first to register a given domain name (or other type of identifier) they are free to use it. Not true. If your identifier happens to be another company's trademark (or is confusingly similar to another company's trademark), that company could shut you down. It is very important to clear your proposed identifiers, early on.

Don't let a web designer hold your domain name hostage. In the hierarchical domain name system, a **top level domain** (TLD) is the last part of the name. For example, in the domain name *xyz.com* the TLD is "com." When you go to acquire your domain, you typically are reserving the part that comes before the dot, known as the **second level domain** (SLD). In our former example, the SLD is "xyz." You reserve SLDs by registering with an **accredited registrar** (http://www.icann.org/en/about/learning/faqs).

Sometimes, if you've retained a web designer or developer to create your internet presence, that person (or company) will register the SLD for you. And sometimes they'll register the SLD in their name, rather than yours.

Engaging in this practice doesn't necessarily mean the designer is dishonest. Sometimes it's part of their service to manage renewals, and having the SLD in their name makes things easier from an administrative point of view. Bottom line, though, it's your domain, and if your relationship with the designer sours, you need assurance that the registration will be transferred to you. The best way to deal with this issue is (a) ask the designer to register all domains in your name and never in their own; and/or (b) have a written contract with the designer requiring, upon your request, the immediate transfer of any domains not registered in your name.

ask the designer to register all domains in your name and never in his own

If you're a designer, you're probably thinking: *Hey. This is the only power I have over the client, to make sure I get paid.* Tread carefully. Of course you are entitled to be paid. And for that reason you, too, should insist on a well-drafted contract with your clients. But the mere fact that a client owes you money does not entitle you to retain a domain that rightfully belongs to someone else, and holding it hostage can subject you to liability.

Understand who owns what. Here's another reason to have a good contract with your designers. Just because you paid the designer doesn't mean you acquired any copyright interest in the designer's work. Unless the designer **assigns** his/her work to you, the designer retains all copyright rights and your use of the work requires appropriate licenses. For maximum flexibility it's best to negotiate a complete copyright assignment (see Conversation #29). Most designers will agree to assign the copyright, once they have been paid.

Don't commit copyright infringement. Copyrightable work does not lose its protection just because it appears online. Unless some legal exception applies, material you find on the internet is not free to use. Get permission. And if a designer is obtaining this material for you: make sure the designer obtains appropriate licenses that specifically name you as the licensee.

unless some legal exception applies, material you find on the internet is not free to use

"Royalty Free" doesn't mean "Restriction Free." There is plenty of royalty free material online. When material is "royalty" free, though, it just means you don't have to pay money for using it (as in, "free beer!"). It doesn't mean there aren't restrictions on how you can use the material. (For example: the beer might have been free, but the law says you can't drink too much and then drive. So it was not "restriction free.")

Almost all stock music and photography sites impose extensive licensing terms and conditions. You are contractually subject to those terms, regardless of whether you are being charged a fee. So be sure to find and read the fine print before using stock or "royalty free" material. (Tip: even **Creative Commons** licenses are far more extensive than most people realize. Visit http://creativecommons.org/licenses, and click on "View Licenses.")

Don't be held liable when *others* commit copyright infringement. If you have features on your platforms that permit third parties to post material, and it turns out the material they post is infringing, you are potentially just as liable for copyright infringement as they are. Does your website have a chat room, forum, or blog? Do you provide others with email accounts or web space? Do you, yourself, provide search capabilities or links to other material? If so, you are very likely an **online service provider** and that means you're on the hook for the infringement of others. Why? Because you provided access (the "on ramp") to the infringing material.

if you have features on your platforms that permit third parties to post material, and it turns out the material they post is infringing, you may be just as liable for copyright infringement as they are

Fortunately, there are steps you can take to protect yourself. The Digital Millennium Copyright Act (DMCA) sets forth procedures that can provide "safe harbor" for online service providers. To qualify for safe harbor you must post a policy that contains specified elements; you must implement a "notice and takedown" procedure in the event someone makes an infringement complaint; you must designate an agent to receive infringement complaints; and you must register your agent with the Copyright Office. Follow these procedures, properly, and you may be eligible for safe harbor. Fail to follow these procedures, and you're a potential defendant. Consult your attorney to make sure you comply fully with the DMCA's current requirements.

Recognize a DMCA attack when you see one. The flip side of DMCA protection is that sometimes companies use notice and takedown procedures inappropriately to shut down their competitors' websites. This is not OK! If your hosting service says they're going to remove material or take down your site because someone submitted an infringement notice, call a copyright attorney right away. A practitioner familiar with the

DMCA will know what to do to protect your rights and fend off an inappropriate attack.

Don't abuse the DMCA. You should also consult a copyright attorney before you submit a DMCA takedown request against somebody else. If it turns out the alleged infringer actually has a legal right to post your work (as, for example, if their use qualifies as fair use), you could be held liable for damages.

Register your website. You can register many copyrightable elements of your website together in a single application. To learn more, check out the Copyright Office's *Circular 66: Copyright Registration for Online Works* (http://www.copyright.gov/circs/circ66.pdf). Once registered, you will enjoy a superior negotiating position in the event an infringer copies your site. (And don't forget to include a claim for your **compilation** of the materials on your site.)

place a copyright notice on every page of your website, in your metatags and, if feasible, on or near images of your work

Use the copyright notice. You don't have to use the familiar © indicia, but you should. Place a copyright notice on every page of your website, in your **metatags** and, if feasible, on or near images of your work. Doing so announces to the world that you are protecting your rights and, in the event of litigation, helps prevent an infringing party from claiming **innocent infringement** as a defense. (For more about the copyright notice, see Copyright Office *Circular 3* [http://www.copyright.gov/circs/circ03.pdf] and Conversation #14.)

Have the right kind of website policies (and follow them).

- A **browse wrap** terms of use agreement states, without requiring any affirmative action, that a website user's mere use of a site binds the user to the terms and conditions of the agreement. Browse wrap agreements are not always enforceable. To increase the likelihood of enforceability you are better advised to adopt a **click wrap** agreement, i.e., one requiring the user to click his/her affirmative acceptance.

- If you collect personally identifying information from website users under the age of 13, you must adopt policies and procedures that comply with the federal **Children's Online Privacy Protection Act** and its corresponding regulations. This is just one example of an ever-expanding net of privacy laws and regulations. An increasing number of states have statutes that regulate online privacy. Also know that the European Union's privacy regulations are extremely strict. (See generally: (http://business.ftc.gov/privacy-and-security.)
- Website privacy policies create the "law of the site." That is to say, you are bound by all representations you make in your policy. Often, carelessly drafted policies make representations that are difficult, if not impossible, to uphold. One very common error is stating: *We will never share your information with anyone, ever.* That's almost never true. You will share that data when you sell your business; when you engage contract vendors to fix problems; when software developers work on new builds for your site. Don't cut and paste something as important as your privacy policy from somebody else's site. Get advice.

you are bound by all representations you make in your privacy policy

Take technical measures. It's a good idea to post visual images as low resolution files, if possible. Digital watermarking is also a common technique. Instead of just plastering the watermark over your image, though, consider disguising it in the work itself. That helps to preserve the aesthetic presentation of your work; plus, if the infringers don't notice the watermark they won't try to defeat it. Disabling the "right-click" option (which otherwise allows users to capture images from your site) is another protective measure to consider.

Have a good contract with your hosting service. Unless you have your own servers, you are at the mercy of your hosting service. They could pull the plug and make your website disappear, at any time. So make sure, contractually, that the hosting service is held to acceptable standards of performance and that it's required to provide you with reasonable notice before disabling your site for any reason. Even if the hosting service provides you with a "standard" form contract (which most will do) – read it, and object to portions that seem unreasonable.

YOU TRY

Why do you think browse wrap agreements are not always enforceable? (Hint: come back to this question after you've read Conversation #41)

· PART III ·

Contracts

CONVERSATION #41

Contract Basics

This book is not a treatise. It's just a starting point. We could fill volumes with conversations about contracts. Learn what you can, and then please: work with a lawyer.

USING FORMS AND TEMPLATES
MORE ABOUT WORKING WITH LAWYERS
THOUGHTS ABOUT KEEPING IT SHORT
"TOO SCARY" IS A RED FLAG
CONTRACT FORMATION
STATUTES OF FRAUDS

Let's chat about why.

Rule number one. Forms and templates can be a starting point for your contract, but do not trust them. No two transactions will ever be the same; so no sample form will ever provide adequate protection for you or the person with whom you are doing business. Don't copy other people's contracts and don't lift language from the internet.

Rule number two. You get what you pay for. Entrepreneurs often wonder whether doing legal work themselves will save on expenses. After all: you're smart, capable and genetically engineered to do things your own way. But doing your own legal work is a bad idea. Long term, you'll pay more rather than less.

This is a "big picture" issue. You might draft your own contract; submit your own application for copyright or trademark registration; form your own business entity. And things might go just fine, thereby proving your point that lawyers are irrelevant and overpaid. But here's the thing. The deficiencies in your do-it-yourself legal work most likely won't become apparent until months, years, or decades down the road when you need to rely on what you drafted. By that time, it will be too late to remedy your errors and you will suffer the consequences of having placed your business in a vulnerable legal position. So use a qualified attorney. It's good business.

Most attorneys would prefer to be involved in your matter from the beginning, and see it through to conclusion. When there are background tasks you can do yourself, great. But you will achieve greatest efficiency and best results if you authorize the lawyer to perform all of the services your matter requires. If not, the lawyer will spend even more billable time coordinating efforts and verifying your work. And quite honestly, the lawyer will not enjoy working with you.

you will achieve greatest efficiency and best results if you authorize the lawyer to perform all of the services your matter requires

Rule number three. Short is nice, but usually not better. When drafting contracts, lawyers hear the same thing over and over: *Keep it short*. Clients don't say, *Make sure it protects my interests* or *Be thorough* or *Be accurate*. They expect those things, surely. But when they see a well-drafted contract their comments are more along the lines of, *It's too many pages* or *It looks too scary* or *What can we cut?*

Short is great, but only if it does the job. Think about it. If your skirt is too short it doesn't cover...what it needs to. Same with your contracts. It's not about length. It's about doing the job. If all you want is short, the response has to be: *OK, fine. What part of your @$$ do you not want to cover?*

If you want to be protected in a transaction, there are certain concepts that must be addressed in the agreement. Period. Often, too, they have to be stated in a certain way. That's just the way it is. Should you insist on clarity? Absolutely. But do not sacrifice accuracy or effectiveness just because you want the entire contract on a single page.

Rule number four. As for scary: get over it. If the other side walks on your deal because the contract "looks too scary," they're either trying to get away with something or they're too lazy (or too cheap) to seek qualified advice. Either way, it's a red flag. You shouldn't hear such things from true professionals.

If you're concerned that the "other side" means your customers, who might be less sophisticated than a business associate, look at it as a question of communication. If you can explain in plain English what every section of your contract means, and why it's there, you're going to appear more professional by using a well-drafted contract. Look in the mirror. Is it really the customers who think your contract is too scary – or are the fears your own?

Is it really the customers who think your contract is too scary – or are the fears your own?

With these rules in mind, let's chat about what contracts are, and how they work.

What is a contract?

A contract is an agreement:

- between two or more people (who must be of legal age and otherwise competent to contract)
- that creates an obligation
- requiring each of the parties to do or not to do a particular thing.

Generally speaking, when a party fails to deliver on its obligation, that's called a **breach of contract**, and it causes the other party to become eligible for legal **remedies**. We'll talk about remedies, later. But first:

How do you form an enforceable contract?

An enforceable contract requires all three of the following elements:

- A valid **offer**
- A valid **acceptance** of the offer
- An exchange of **consideration**

Offer. The first step in contract formation occurs when one party makes a valid offer. The party making the offer is called the **offeror.** The **offer** is the offeror's expression of willingness to contract, on a specific set of terms, with the intention that if the offer is accepted, the offeror will be bound by the contract. Consider these examples.

- Frank owns a nightclub called the Lavner Lounge. Tony, a singer of questionable abilities, is a lounge singer. Frank says to Tony, "You should perform at the Lavner Lounge sometime." Is this a valid offer? No. Why? Because the offer has to be specific enough so that, if the other party accepts, each party's obligations are clear and capable of being enforced.
- Frank says to Tony, "I'd like to hire you to sing at the Lavner Lounge next Friday at 8pm." Is this a valid offer? No. It's not a valid offer because the offer must recite the **consideration** that is to be exchanged. This offer is not valid because it doesn't state what Frank has to do.
- Frank says to Tony, "I'd like to hire you to sing at the Lavner Lounge next Friday at 8pm and I will pay you $500." Is this a valid offer? Yes!

Acceptance. Once there's been a valid offer, the other party has to accept it in such a manner that there is clearly a "meeting of the minds." A valid acceptance is an expression of absolute and unconditional agreement to all the terms set out in the offer. The acceptance must exactly mirror the original offer. Consider these examples.

a valid acceptance is an expression of absolute and unconditional agreement to all the terms set out in the offer

- Tony responds to Frank, "I wouldn't play the Lavner Lounge if my life depended on it." Obviously, this is not an acceptance. It's a flat out rejection. Game over; no contract.
- Tony responds to Frank, "I have received your offer to sing at the Lavner Lounge." Is this a valid acceptance? No. Merely acknowledging the offer doesn't convey that you agree to its terms. There's no meeting of the minds, so no contract.

- Tony responds to Frank, "Sure. I'll sing at the Lavner Lounge next Saturday at 8pm for $750." Is this a valid acceptance? No. It's a **counteroffer**. By changing the terms Tony has rejected Frank's offer and made a new offer of his own. Frank's offer is no longer valid and cannot be accepted. Now, if there's to be a contract, Frank must accept Tony's new offer.
- Tony is silent. He does not respond to the offer. But he does show up; he plays the gig; and he takes home his $500. Later on, there's some kind of dispute and Tony tries to weasel out by saying there was no contract because he never accepted Frank's offer. Can he do that? No. It is possible to accept an offer by one's actions. In this case both parties performed their obligations and both received the "benefit of their bargain." The contract is enforceable.

a bad deal isn't unenforceable just because you were dumb enough to accept it

Consideration. Consideration is the act of doing something or promising to do something that a person is not otherwise legally required to do; or the forbearance or the promise to forbear from doing something that he or she has the legal right to do. Consider these examples.

- Tony and Frank agree that Tony will play the four-hour gig for $1.50. Is this valid consideration? Yes! So long as Tony is **competent** and not under any kind of duress or undue influence, i.e., if he agrees of his own free will to play the gig for $1.50, that's fine. A bad deal isn't unenforceable just because you were dumb enough to accept it. So long as the consideration creates an obligation for both parties, that's good enough.
- Tony agrees to play the gig in exchange for Frank's promise to provide Tony's mother with unlimited food and drink during Tony's performance. Is this valid consideration? Yes. It creates an obligation that Frank must fulfill. And it's OK to have your benefit flow to a third party.

- Tony agrees to play the gig in exchange for Frank's promise to pay the $500 he already owes Tony. Is this valid consideration? No. To support a contract, consideration must be "present," i.e., new. A previous obligation cannot support a new contract.

Does all of this have to be in writing? No. Certain types of contracts have to be in writing, and we'll talk about them later. But many do not, and you can form such contracts verbally or by your actions. So don't make the mistake of assuming there's no contract just because you never signed on the dotted line.

don't make the mistake of assuming there's no contract just because you never signed on the dotted line

How do we know which types of contracts have to be in writing? The good news is, we have statutes that come right out and tell us. These are called **statutes of frauds**. They exist to discourage fraud in contracts for the types of transactions where fraud is common. The bad news is, statutes of frauds are spread out all over the place, in state and federal **codes**. Bottom line: they're almost impossible to find. That's why best practice is to do your contracting in writing, whether or not it's legally required.

Here's a fine point about statutes of frauds. If there *is* such a statute, and you did *not* get your agreement in writing, that doesn't mean your transaction cannot move forward. If you and the other party both choose to fulfill your obligations, the transaction will be complete and you can go on with your lives. If, however, the other party decides to renege before the transaction is complete – and you never obtained his written agreement to the bargain – he might be able to walk away without consequence.

YOU TRY

1. There are statutes of frauds in the copyright law. Use your legal research skills to review 17 USC §§201(b) and 204(a).

2. Contracts that typically require a written agreement, under state law, include those involving real estate; wills; marriage; insurance; those that cannot be performed within one year; and those where the amount of money involved exceeds a stated amount. Every state's laws are different. See what you can find, in your state.
3. Does your state permit electronic contracting? Check to see if your state has adopted a version of the Uniform Electronic Transactions Act. (Hint: you might find what you're looking for on the website of the National Conference of State Legislatures. Enter "UETA" in the search box.)

Contracts: There's a Reason for the Legalese

There aren't any rules about what a contract has to look like. The point is to make sure the contracting parties have been properly identified and that their respective obligations have been made clear. This sounds simple. Unfortunately, an endless universe of "what ifs" quickly derails simplicity.

CAPTIONS
IDENTIFYING THE CONTRACTING PARTIES
SUCCESSORS
COLLECTIONS
SURVIVAL

Let's face it. The reason you want a contract at all is to be protected in case the other party breaches its obligations. You don't want to be left holding the bag, when one of the "what ifs" comes to pass. In this Conversation we'll look at some of those "what ifs."

As we've discussed, drafting your own contract is a bad idea. Accordingly, the comments that follow are intended not for you as a drafter, but to help you spot issues if you're taking the first look at a contract drafted by somebody else. More than anything, this Conversation is intended to convince you that there's a reason for all that "legalese" you want to cut. This is just a sampling of the "what ifs." There are many more! DO NOT RELY on these examples and always get qualified legal advice.

What if the title is not accurate? Contracts can have titles, but they don't have to. If there is a title, (a) make sure it's accurate; and/or (b) request a captions clause (see below). Why? Because you don't want to give the other party grounds for interpreting the agreement against your interests. For example: if the title of the contract is "Publishing Agreement" and it's really just a record deal with no publishing component, that inaccurate title opens the door for the other side to say, "well, it's plainly called a Publishing Agreement, so you must have intended to grant me publishing rights for your compositions."

A *captions clause* would provide clarity. Here's an example:

> *Captions and headings used in this Agreement are for purposes of convenience only and shall not be deemed to limit, affect the scope, meaning or intent of this Agreement, nor shall they otherwise be given any legal effect.*

What if the contract names the wrong party? The contract must accurately identify the parties to be bound. If either party operates as a corporation, a limited liability company, or other type of legal entity, the contract must express that entity's full and correct legal name. If you're not entirely sure what that is, take the time to find out (see YOU TRY, below). Your contract with Bear Claw, Inc. isn't much good if you really needed to contract with Bear Claw Enterprises, LLC. By the same token, if you created an LLC for your business, yet you allowed yourself personally to be named as a party, you just defeated the purpose of having the LLC.

if you created an LLC for your business, yet you allowed yourself personally to be named as a party, you just defeated the purpose of having the LLC

What if one party dies or sells its business? If you want the contract to be binding on whoever steps into the departing party's shoes, the contract had better make that clear. Here's an example:

> *This Agreement will be binding upon the heirs, executors, administrators and other legal representatives of the Parties and will be for the benefit of the Parties' successors and assigns.*

What if the other side doesn't pay? There are many ways to address the other side's failure to meet their contractual obligations. If it's a question merely of collecting money they owe, and you intend to recoup your costs of collection, the contract needs specifically to provide for that.

> *Customer agrees to pay Company all reasonable collection and related attorney fees incurred by the Company whether incurred prior to or after the commencement of formal legal action.*

In addition: procedures for collecting debts are highly regulated in most states. Do not attempt collections without consulting qualified counsel.

do not attempt collections without consulting qualified counsel

What if the other side breaches the contract, but the contract has terminated or expired? There's likely nothing you can do about it, unless your contract had a "survivals" clause.

> *The rights and obligations of the parties, which by intent or meaning have validity beyond the termination of this Agreement shall survive the termination of this Agreement.*

These examples represent the tiniest tip of the iceberg. If there's more at stake than you can afford to lose, take the time and spend the money to have your contract properly and thoroughly drafted.

YOU TRY

To verify the correct legal name of an entity with which you are contracting, go to the website of the Secretary of State where the entity was organized. Look for a link that says "Search Corporations" or something similar. (Tip for Wisconsin: this information resides on the website of the Department of Financial Institutions.)

CONVERSATION #43

Contracts: More Tips

DEFINITIONS
CHOICE OF LAW
CONSTRUCTION
BREACH
REMEDIES

This Conversation discusses some additional contract-related concepts. They are no more or less important than other concepts that didn't make it into this Conversation. So please remember the most important concept of all: your lawyer is there for a reason.

Understand Every Word. Most contracts will contain a "definitions of terms" section. This is an extremely important section of the contract. If there is any word in the contract you do not understand, look for it in this section. If it's not there, either consult an attorney or insist that the word and your understanding of its definition be spelled out in the contract. (Hint: if you can't articulate a word or phrase's definition to a fifth-grader, you don't really understand it. Do not proceed until you have obtained clarification.)

Don't Blindly Accept Choice-of-Law Provisions. What does it mean when the contract says it will be governed by the law of a particular state? It probably means you don't know what you're getting into. Every state does things differently and every state has provisions of law that surprise the unsuspecting. For example. There's this one state that fancies itself a leader in the entertainment industry. It has a law that says no personal service contract can last for more than seven years. Well, one particular segment of the entertainment industry (the one that used to make records) found this to be inconvenient because they wanted artists to remain bound to record deals for way longer than seven years. So this industry successfully lobbied for an exception. The exception allows record labels to sue recording artists for damages if they don't deliver their contracted number of records within seven years. An uninformed artist could find herself facing this pretty drastic consequence, all because of the seemingly innocuous phrase, "governed by the law of the state of California."

an uninformed artist could find herself facing this pretty drastic consequence, all because of the seemingly innocuous phrase, "governed by the law of the state of California"

Learn the Rules of Construction. When we're talking about contracts, the word **construction** means interpretation. It refers to how the contract will be...that's right... *construed.* There are variations from state to state, but here are some general rules of contract construction.

- The cornerstone of contract construction is to ascertain the true intentions of the parties.
- The best indication of the parties' intent is the language of the contract itself. So say what you really mean.
- Plain and ordinary meanings of words will prevail.
- Courts will presume that all parties were aware of laws in effect at the time of agreement. It's up to you to be fully informed.
- Courts will give meaning and effect to all of the contract's provisions. In other words, if it's in the contract the court will figure it's there for a reason. So don't try later to say, "That part isn't important."
- Courts will give greater weight to specific language (rather than general).
- Courts will construe ambiguities against the party that drafted the contract.

There Are Different Types of Breach. Here are some fundamental concepts about breach of contract.

- All parties have a duty to act in good faith. Failure to do so can be a breach, even if the party *technically* complies with the terms of the contract.
- A **material** breach is one that harms the other party in a significant way. When there's a material breach, the non-breaching party has the right to seek **remedies.** On the other hand, a **technical** breach is harmless – as, for example, when the contract requires delivery to the stage door but actual delivery is made through the front entrance. Yes, technically that is a breach, but if the non-breaching party was not harmed in a meaningful way, that party has no viable claim for remedies.

all parties have a duty to act in good faith

- Good idea: have the contract define what constitutes a material breach. (Because maybe delivery through the front entrance *would* result in real damage! If that's a possibility, spell it out as grounds for material breach.)
- A **time is of the essence** clause is important if on-time delivery of the other party's obligations is important. Otherwise, delay in a party's performance is not necessarily a breach.

Remedies. Once the other party's material breach has been established, the non-breaching party is entitled to remedies. There are several different types of remedies for breach of contract:

- Money damages.
- Injunctive relief. An injunction is a court order that halts the offending behavior immediately (before the dispute is finally decided) in order to prevent irreparable harm.
- Specific performance. When money damages aren't adequate or appropriate, specific performance makes the breaching party do what they'd promised to do.
- Reformation. This corrects good faith mistakes and mutual misunderstandings in the contract. The contract still exists.

- Recission. This will nullify the contract so that it no longer exists.
- Restitution. This will nullify the contract and the breaching party (who did something pretty bad) will have to make the non-breaching party whole.

there are several different types of remedies for breach of contract

YOU TRY

See what you can find about California's "DeHaviland Rule." It will make you think twice about blindly accepting a choice of law provision.

Agreements with Independent Contractors

As an entrepreneur you will probably retain independent contractors to provide services. It is also likely that others will retain *your* services. So read this Conversation from both points of view.

Importance of Proper Classification

Let's start from scratch. What is an independent contractor?

You might think this an easy question to answer, but it isn't. In fact, it might be the most difficult question in this entire book, as well as one of the most misunderstood. It's simpler to begin with what an independent contractor is not: in short, a person is not an independent contractor just because you say so in a contract.

Often, businesses try to avoid the paperwork and expense of having employees merely by designating their service providers as independent contractors. (Filmmakers are especially prone to this mistake.) What you choose to call someone, however, is all but irrelevant. It's what you do, and how you actually structure the working relationship, that counts.

The law itself prescribes certain factors for determining whether a particular individual, in a particular situation, is an employee or an independent contractor. If you don't satisfy the required factors, the individual is an employee – whether you like it or not, and regardless of what your agreement says.

"OK, that comes as a surprise, but good to know. Where's the list of factors?"

Well, here's the thing. There isn't one list. There are many different lists, for different circumstances. For example, the IRS has a list. If you satisfy its test the person can be treated as an independent contractor for purposes of federal income taxation. Your state has other lists, each with slightly different factors, for determining whether exemptions are available from unemployment and workers compensation insurance obligations. The US Supreme Court hammered out yet another list, for making the employee versus contractor determination when **work made for hire** is the issue in copyright disputes (see Conversation #28). If a business misclassifies an individual as an independent contractor, when really (because of the lists) the person is an employee, both the business and the individual are at risk for financial penalties.

YOU TRY

The lists of requirements, for different purposes, can vary. Here is a link to the criteria for classification as an independent contractor, for purposes of federal income taxation:

http://www.irs.gov/Businesses/Small-Businesses-&-Self-Employed/Independent-Contractor-%28Self-Employed%29-or-Employee%3F

Do searches in your state, to find the criteria for unemployment compensation and workers compensation. As examples, here are lists for the state of Wisconsin:

Unemployment Compensation:
http://dwd.wisconsin.gov/ui201/t2201.htm

Workers Compensation:
http://dwd.wisconsin.gov/wc/employers/independent_contractors.htm

CONVERSATION #45

Commissioning Agreements

This Conversation applies to any sort of commissioning agreement. For convenience, however, let's assume you are being commissioned to paint a portrait, and that your commissioning party is named Jim.

OWNERSHIP
NEGOTIATING APPROPRIATE FEES
MODEL RELEASES
LIMITING CHANGE REQUESTS
CHARGING INTEREST
MORAL RIGHTS
TIME IS OF THE ESSENCE

Have a written contract. In many states, a statute of frauds might render your agreement unenforceable if it is not in writing. A **statute of frauds** is a type of law that requires the contract for a particular sort of transaction to be in writing. For more on this, review our discussion in Conversation #41. It can be difficult to identify when (or whether) statutes of frauds might be lurking, so best practice is just to use written agreements.

Educate Jim about copyright law. The vast majority of commissioning parties believe they own the copyright to your work, just because they paid you to create it. You know (from Conversation #28) this isn't true. It's important that they understand, as well. Consider the following conversation with Jim.

> You: Once I've delivered the work, Jim, do you intend to do anything with it that might require a copyright license from me?
>
> Jim: Once you deliver the work I own it, so why would I need any kind of license from you?

You: As the author of the work I retain the copyright to the work. That means I continue to control the exclusive bundle of rights that every copyright includes. You will exclusively own the physical work itself, but you will not own the copyright. If you want to exercise any copyright rights you will need a license from me.

Jim: Like what, for example?

You: The copyright bundle of rights includes the exclusive rights to reproduce the work in copies; to prepare derivative works based on the work; to distribute copies of the work; to publicly perform the work; and to publicly display the work.

are you telling me I pay seven million dollars for this portrait and I can't hang it in my office?

Jim: *Publicly display*? Are you telling me I pay seven million dollars for this portrait and I can't hang it in my office?

You: Actually, there's an exception for that. You can publicly display the work without my consent, but only to viewers who are physically present in the same location as the work. So you can hang it in your office, but you can't display it, for example, on the Internet or TV. (See Conversation #24.)

Jim: Back to the part about me paying seven million dollars. Isn't this a work made for hire? If so, I'm the employer for hire, which means I *do* own the copyright as well as the work itself.

You: No, this is not a work made for hire. I am not your employee. And although certain types of commissioned work can qualify as work made for hire, the work has to fall into one of nine specific categories in the copyright law. The work I am doing for you does not fall into any of those categories. (See Conversation #28.)

Jim: Alright, then. I am most grateful to you for providing me with this information. I shall pass it on to other commissioning parties so they, too, can be gracious, informed consumers.

If Jim really wants the copyright, raise your fee. If Jim wants to control the copyright, and you agree, you must negotiate either a **license** that accomplishes your mutual objectives, or a complete **assignment** of your copyright to Jim. Both must be crafted very carefully to be effective under United States copyright law, so you'll almost certainly need an attorney. That's one reason, right there, for raising your fee. The other reason is that once you assign your copyright, Jim – not you – will own the entire bundle of rights (see Conversation #29). You need to make sure your fee provides adequate compensation for relinquishing your rights and delivering such additional value to Jim.

Obtain a model release from the subject(s) of your portrait. If you retain copyright, you might want to make other use(s) of the portrait, in the future. Remember, though, that owning the copyright is not the only issue to consider. Make sure your written agreement grants you whatever authority you might need, under state **right of privacy** and **right of publicity** laws, to make subsequent use of the commissioned work (see Conversation #38). If you fail to do so, the bundle of rights you so carefully retained won't be worth a whole lot. And please note: if Jim is not the subject, Jim may not have authority to grant the release you need. You'll either need a written agreement with the subject, or you'll need a **warranty and representation** from Jim that Jim has legal authority to act on behalf of the subject.

define any words or terms of art that could be open to differing interpretations

Define, define, define. Define any words or terms of art that could be open to differing interpretations. Add a definitions section to your contract and capitalize all words that are specifically defined in that section or elsewhere in the contract.

Clarify the extent to which Jim can request changes or reject the work altogether. Preferably, make it say this: "Jim cannot request changes or reject the work." OK, seriously. If there are any circumstances under which Jim will be permitted to request changes, additions, or deletions, make sure the procedure for doing so is clearly defined in the contract. Impose reasonable limits, and get paid for your time.

Prescribe a specific payment schedule. If you intend to charge interest for late payments, you must in writing specify the rate and method for calculating such interest. Make it clear that payments will not be refundable and the work you deliver will not be returnable.

if you intend to charge interest for late payments, you must in writing specify the rate and method for calculating such interest

Moral rights. Do you expect to receive credit when Jim displays the portrait? Put it in the contract. What's going to happen to the work when Jim grows tired of it? The Visual Artists Rights Act (17 USC 106A) and corresponding state **moral rights** statutes might apply – and they might not (see Conversation #30). If you're concerned about destruction, mutilation, attribution, and the ultimate disposition of the work, address those issues now, in your written agreement.

Time is of the essence. In general, if it's really important that one party perform its contractual obligations precisely on the date specified in the contract, it's best to include a clause stating that "time is of the essence." If there is no such clause and there's no indication that one party has been substantially harmed by the other party's delay, courts are likely to apply the rule of reason and excuse minor delays.

Good faith goes a long way. The parties to a contract have an obligation to act in good faith. They are expected to act in the best interest of accomplishing the expressed goals of the agreement, and not to take advantage of one another by invoking legal technicalities. The party that can demonstrate good faith has a significant advantage in court.

YOU TRY

1. Research the highly publicized debacle involving the late Dennis Oppenheim and his commission from the county of Milwaukee, Wisconsin, to create a large-scale sculpture at Mitchell International Airport.
2. Review Conversation #28 and the types of work that can qualify as work made for hire. Jim's portrait doesn't count. Make a list, though, of commission situations that might, indeed, qualify as work made for hire.

Fine Art Consignment Agreements

What happens to my art if it's hanging in a restaurant and the restaurant goes bankrupt?

Can a gallery's creditors seize art that's being held on consignment?

Consignment statutes
Uniform Commercial Code

In a worst case scenario, yes. It surprises many (including lawyers) to learn that a gallery's creditors can seize **consignment** pieces and/or the proceeds from such pieces, even though title to the art never passed to the gallery.

Happily, there are ways to protect against this odious consequence. Some states (but not all) have pro-artist consignment laws that shield the art from a gallery's creditors. And in most states without art consignment laws, there are affirmative steps artists can take to protect themselves. But you have to learn about them.

The first thing to do is find out if your state has a consignment law that applies specifically to art and artists. Use your research skills from Conversation #4 and navigate to your state's legislative website. Most offer a user-friendly search function. Enter a few good keywords (such as "artist," "fine art," "dealer," and "consignment" in various combinations) and soon you'll have a list of interesting statutes.

If your state's site does not have a workable search

function, you'll probably need to consult an attorney to find out whether your state has an art consignment law. There are books you can consult on this topic, but remember that the law changes constantly – and books become outdated very quickly. It's better practice to consult an official source with the most up-to-date version of your state's statutes. If doing so is not within your interests or abilities, hire a lawyer – or at least ask a law librarian for the most up-to-date sources.

What if your state either doesn't have a consignment law, or it doesn't apply to you, or its provisions don't cover your particular set of facts?

If your state has an art consignment law, read it very carefully. They vary considerably from state to state. As a threshold matter, you and your attorney will want to clarify whether the law applies to you at all, based on the statute's definitions of (for example) "art," "artist," and "consignment."

What if your state either doesn't have a consignment law, or it doesn't apply to you, or its provisions don't cover your particular set of facts?

Then you need to find out whether your state has adopted a version of the Uniform Commercial Code, or "UCC" (this is pronounced, "you-see-see;" it does not rhyme with "yuck"). The UCC governs commercial transactions. (See YOU TRY, below, if you're wondering what makes it "Uniform.") Most states have adopted some version of the UCC: http://www.law.cornell.edu/uniform/ucc.html (Note to Louisianans: No offense, but your laws are just plain weird. You might want to consider moving.)

UCC Article 2 covers the sale of goods, and **consignment** relationships. If your state does have a version of UCC Article 2, chances are good that (in the absence of an art consignment law) its provisions will govern when a gallery's creditors attempt to seize your art. This is not good news!

The UCC favors good faith creditors. Our first clue in this regard is the caption of the applicable provision, UCC §2-326:

"Consignment Sales and Rights of Creditors." Section 2-326 defines two categories of transactions in which the "buyer" can return goods to the "seller." The transaction is a **sale or return** if the goods are delivered primarily for resale. The transaction is a **sale on approval** if the goods are delivered primarily for the buyer's own use.

Let's pause for clarification. In an artist-gallery consignment situation, the "buyer" is the gallery and the "seller" is the artist. The gallery is also known as the "consignee" and the artist is the "consignor." So:

Gallery = buyer, consignee

Artist = seller, consignor

When an artist delivers art to a gallery "on consignment," the idea is for the gallery to sell the art to a third party. Consequently, since the "goods" (i.e., the pieces of art) were delivered primarily for resale, the transaction is a **sale or return** transaction rather than a **sale on approval** transaction. This is where things turn nasty, because UCC §2-326(2) states that although goods held on **approval** are not subject to the claims of the buyer's (i.e., the gallery's) creditors, goods held on **sale or return** *are* subject to such claims while they are in the buyer's possession.

when an artist delivers art to a gallery "on consignment," the idea is for the gallery to sell the art to a third party

The UCC provides three ways to protect one's art from claims of the gallery's creditors.

1. The first method only works in states that have **sign laws** (and not too many states have them). If your state happens to have a sign law, you can insist that the gallery position a sign by your art, placing the world on notice that the art is being held on consignment and that you, the consignor, have a superior interest in it.
2. Under the second method, you can protect your work by establishing that the person conducting the business (i.e., the gallery) *is generally known by his creditors to be*

substantially engaged in selling the goods of others. This means you'll have to prove (probably in court) that the gallery's creditors actually knew that the gallery regularly sold consignment work rather than work the gallery owned outright. It's something of a crapshoot as to whether you'll be successful in meeting your burden of proof. If the "gallery" is a restaurant, for example, the restaurant is probably not known to its creditors as being substantially engaged in the business of selling the goods (artwork) of others. This method, therefore, is far from foolproof.

3. The third method is much more reliable, but it's complicated. To protect your work under the third method, you need to file a **security interest** in the art. You do this (or more accurately, your attorney does this) by complying with your state's version of UCC Article 9.

And that's it. If there's no consignment statute you either have a sign law (and use it); or you gamble on meeting the burden of proof; or you hire an attorney to file a security interest under UCC Article 9.

OK. You've protected your art from the gallery's creditors. Now what happens if the gallery burns down with your work inside?

As an example, let's say Margaret received a contract with the following clause:

> *The Gallery assumes no responsibility for any consigned work lost, stolen or damaged while in the Gallery's possession.*

Margaret called them out, and this is how the gallery owner replied:

> *Insurance costs have skyrocketed. We are one of many galleries that no longer assume any liability for work left at the gallery. Most artists who have been exhibiting a long time are used to this. As an emerging artist you need to*

weigh showing your work at your own risk or not showing it. The decision is yours.

That didn't set right with Margaret, so she decided to look at her state's fine art consignment laws. Margaret lives in Alaska and her research proved fruitful. Here's what she found:

what happens if the gallery burns down with your work inside?

(a) When an artist delivers or causes to be delivered a work of art of the artist's own creation to an art dealer for the purpose of sale, or exhibition and sale, on a commission, fee, or other basis of compensation, the acceptance of the work of art by the art dealer is a consignment, and

... (5) the art dealer is strictly liable for loss or damage to a work of art while the work of art is in the possession of the art dealer; the value of a lost or damaged work of art is the value established by written agreement between the artist and art dealer before the loss or damage of the work of art; if no written agreement establishing the value of the work of art exists, the value is the fair market value of the work of art less the art dealer's commission or fee....

Alaska Statutes §45.65.200, emphasis supplied.

So, Margaret concluded, the Alaskan gallery owner was **strictly liable** for loss or damage to art in her possession and the "take-it-or-leave-it" position she so confidently espoused was illegal and unenforceable.

Or was it?

As it turns out, Alaska has another statute that allows artists to waive their protections:

A provision of a contract or agreement whereby the artist waives a provision of AS 45.65.200 is void except as provided in this subsection. An artist may waive the provisions of AS 45.65.200 if the waiver is clear, conspicuous, and agreed to in writing by the artist....

Alaska Statutes § 45.65.210, emphasis supplied.

The Alaskan gallery owner could present Margaret with "take-it-or-leave-it" after all: either sign this clear, conspicuous waiver saying my gallery has no liability, or don't exhibit your work.

Wisconsin has a provision similar to Alaska's:

> *The art dealer is strictly liable for the loss of or damage to the work of fine art while it is in the art dealer's possession....*
>
> Wisconsin Statutes § 129.02.

In Wisconsin, however, the corresponding waiver statute is short and sweet:

> *Waiver voided. Any portion of an agreement which waives any provision of this chapter is void.*
>
> Wisconsin Statutes § 129.07.

In Wisconsin, then, "take-it-or-leave-it" won't fly. The gallery is liable, period. Here, of course, is where the artist needs to be savvy about her rights. If Margaret were dealing with a gallery in Wisconsin and she didn't know about the "no waiver" law, Margaret might have signed an unscrupulous gallery's "take-it-or-leave-it" waiver not realizing it violates the law.

In Wisconsin, "take-it-or-leave-it" won't fly. The gallery is liable, period.

Other states have lesser measures of protection. In Maryland, art on consignment is **bailment** property in the hands of the gallery (Maryland Statutes §11-8A-02). Bailment is a legal term referring to the standard of care one party must exercise when lawfully holding the property of another. In general, bailment imposes less liability on a gallery than, for example, the strict liability standard found in the Alaska and Wisconsin statutes. Minnesota's standard is vaguer still. In that state a gallery "*is responsible for* the loss of, or damage to the work of art" held on consignment (Minnesota Statutes §324.03). Just how far the gallery's liability extends, we can't tell from the face of the Minnesota statute.

The point, of course, is that you need to know the law. A gallery owner in one state might be totally within her rights to disclaim liability for Margaret's art. In a different jurisdiction, her disclaimer would have been unenforceable.

If your state does not have art consignment laws, or if your laws do not impose liability upon the galleries, the game isn't necessarily over. Revisit the Uniform Commercial Code. In addition to governing the rights of creditors, most states' versions of the UCC also address liability for damage to consigned goods. Artists should explore this avenue before submitting blindly to a gallery's waiver of liability.

even though galleries can be held liable – sometimes – for damage to your work, you still need to be insured

Even though galleries can be held liable – sometimes – for damage to your work, you still need to be insured. Artists should take care to obtain coverage for their work while it's still in the studio, while it's in transit and, if necessary, while it's on display. If the work itself could cause injury to others, insurance for that purpose is also a good idea. For more information, check out the resources at Fractured Atlas: http://www.fracturedatlas.org/site/liability/

YOU TRY

Back in 1892 the American Bar Association (ABA) recognized that sometimes it's valuable to have uniformity among state laws. So the ABA convened the first National Conference of Commissioners on Uniform State Laws (NCCUSL), which set to work drafting "uniform" laws on various topics that states were then encouraged (but not required) to adopt. NCCUSL continues its work today; you can learn more at: http://www.uniformlaws.org

· PART IV ·

Business Issues You Might Have Overlooked

Organizing Your Business: What Are the Options?

Entity choices
Piercing the corporate veil
Capital contributions
L3Cs
B Corps

It's important to organize your business and choose the legal structure that's right for you. Don't ignore this aspect of entrepreneurship, as your choices early on will affect your success later. This Conversation will get you started and, ideally, motivate you to consult qualified legal and tax professionals. (Note: This Conversation sticks with for-profit models. We'll discuss nonprofits in Conversation #52.)

Many entrepreneurs conduct business as sole proprietors. **Sole proprietorship** is the default business structure for a single owner. That is to say: if you do business alone, and you have not officially formed any other type of recognized business entity, your business is – by default – a sole proprietorship.

There are advantages to doing business as a sole proprietor. For one, it is very easy to manage. You alone make all decisions, and you don't have to account to partners or shareholders or the public. You don't have to take any particular action to form the business (although in some locales it is wise to file a "doing business as" designation with the county or other branch of local government). You alone own all assets of the business, and all profits flow to you personally.

There are also disadvantages to this model. As a

sole proprietor you are solely and personally responsible for all debts and all liabilities of the business. You and the business are, legally, one and the same. So if you default on a business loan, or someone trips and falls in your studio, your personal assets are on the line.

Things aren't much different if you operate as a **partnership**. A partnership is the default structure when two or more people carry on a business together, for profit. (Note: you don't actually have to be *making* a profit, to satisfy this definition!)

Partnership is risky business. As with sole proprietorship, you don't have to do anything official to form the partnership. All you have to do is start conducting business together with another person or persons. This happens all the time, and it is exceedingly dangerous.

That's right. If your partnership owes $1 million and your partner flees, you alone remain liable for the full $1 million.

Too often, entrepreneurs find themselves in "accidental" partnerships. (Bands are particularly susceptible to this mistake.) They never even knew they'd entered into a legal partnership, and they find themselves facing ramifications they'd never – ever – intended. For one, just like sole proprietorships, there is no legal distinction between the business and its owners. This leaves the personal assets of all partners, individually, at risk for 100% of all debts and liabilities of the partnership. That's right. If your partnership owes $1 million and your partner flees, you alone remain liable for the full $1 million.

Once you decide to conduct business with another person or persons, STOP. Be proactive. Don't move ahead until you've made a conscious, informed choice regarding the legal nature of your business relationship. Then, if you really want to form a partnership, obtain competent advice and enter into a formal written partnership agreement.

(Have you noticed how freely people throw around the word, "partner"? It's oh-so-vogue for businesses to say, "We're going to partner with X," or to list "our partners." Don't do it! In fact, unless you really, really mean it: banish this word entirely. Intent plays an important role in proving the existence of a legal partnership. If you proclaim to the world that someone is your "partner," well...good luck when it comes time to prove otherwise.)

Those who consider these issues often choose to structure their businesses more formally, usually as **business corporations** or **limited liability companies** (LLCs). Although there are many factors driving a business owner's choice of entity (e.g., taxation, succession, ease of administration), the overriding motivator for selecting the corporate or LLC form is to limit the entrepreneur's personal liability.

Unfortunately, that's where the thinking often ends. Many a small business owner creates a business corporation or an LLC, and then essentially forgets about it. They figure, "I *have* an LLC" or, "I *am* a corporation," and they conclude (erroneously) that that's all it takes to shield their personal assets.

forming a limited liability entity is merely the first step toward limiting your personal liability

Don't let this happen to you.

There is no "easy button" in business. Forming a limited liability entity is merely the first step toward limiting your personal liability. You must adhere to strict procedural and recordkeeping requirements – forever – if you truly intend to reap the benefits of limited liability. Failing to do so can trigger a legal phenomenon known as **piercing the corporate veil**. In plain English, this means: run your business like a real business, or else *no protection for you!* You don't get a free pass just by filling out a form and paying a nominal fee.

If you've been sleeping soundly but now anticipate a restless night, here's a tip: invest in an hour or two of an accountant's or a business attorney's time, to make sure you're running your business in accordance with your state's requirements. Recordkeeping is a good place to start. In Wisconsin, for example, section 183.0405 of the Wisconsin Statutes tells us what records a limited liability company must keep at its principal place of business. This isn't a suggestion; it's the law.

Do you have a corporate record book? Do you maintain it properly? Did you issue yourself actual, physical shares of stock (if you're a corporation)? If not, your protection is questionable. If you fail to observe the required formalities, you run the risk of a court finding your limited liability entity to be a sham and "piercing the corporate veil" to reach your personal assets.

even if you are the only member of the LLC, or the only shareholder of the corporation, you may not treat the business account as your personal checkbook

Handling the money is another big deal. Even if you are the only member of the LLC, or the only shareholder of the corporation, you may not treat the business account as your personal checkbook. If the company needs cash and you (or a co-owner) are going to supply the funds, you must review the proposed transaction with your accountant or attorney, and prepare appropriate documentation and resolutions. Contributing cash can be structured as a loan; it can also constitute a **capital contribution** increasing your percentage of ownership in the company. Either way, there are serious tax and ownership consequences. You must consider and document them thoroughly before making the contribution.

You must also understand that, unless your contribution is structured properly as a loan, you are not necessarily entitled to repayment of the contribution. When you put money into your corporation or LLC, it's an investment. Sometimes investments pay off, and sometimes they don't. So if you put $50,000 into the company and it doesn't make a profit, you lose your $50,000. Period.

Oh, and don't just pay yourself random amounts of cash for no apparent reason. Payments to LLC members and corporate shareholders have to be declared and voted on by the owners or managers. If you're the only owner, so be it. You still have to go through the motions of declaring a distribution and approving it in a formal resolution, before writing yourself a check. If you don't, once again: you're supplying the court (and your creditors) with evidence that the company is a sham.

Is your entity in good standing with your state? Check your secretary of state's website to make sure. Almost certainly, you have to file annual reports and pay annual fees to maintain your entity's good status. If this doesn't ring a bell, your entity might not even exist anymore!

Do you have an operating agreement for your LLC? Bylaws for your corporation? A formal partnership agreement? If you treat yourself as an employee of the company, do you have supporting documentation? Do you file state and federal employment taxes on a regular basis?

Do you do business in states other than your home state? If so, get advice regarding your obligation to file in such other states as a "foreign" corporation or LLC. Are business assets such as vehicles and real/intellectual property properly titled to the entity?

Sometimes, no matter how good your business practices, personal liability may attach. There is no completely bulletproof solution.

Sometimes, no matter how good your business practices, personal liability may attach. There is no completely bulletproof solution. Attending to the details we've just discussed, however, will at least strengthen your position.

If any of this sounds startling: good. You still have time to get things in order and start running your limited liability entity properly. You'll need to invest time, and probably some money to run things properly. Is it worth it? That's your call.

It's your house.

YOU TRY

1. If your business plan is to promote socially beneficial objectives (rather than maximizing profit), but you still

want to organize as a for-profit entity: start researching the "low profit limited liability company," or **L3C**.

2. If you already operate a business and you want to bake a commitment to sustainability into its legal structure, consider pursuing certification as a **B Corp**. B Corps are certified by a nonprofit organization (B Lab) to meet rigorous standards of social and environmental performance, accountability, and transparency (http://www.bcorporation.net).
3. One form of business organization that artists sometime explore is the **cooperative**. This Conversation doesn't discuss cooperatives (intentionally) because they are highly regulated and far more complicated than most entrepreneurs fully appreciate. If you are part of a group seeking to organize as a cooperative, there is no alternative to retaining the counsel of an attorney with specific experience in this branch of the law, in your state.
3. There is great information about business entity options on the website of the US Small Business Administration: http://www.sba.gov/category/navigation-structure/starting-managing-business/starting-business/choose-your-business-stru

CONVERSATION #48

Buy-Sell Agreements

HOW NOT TO END UP IN BUSINESS WITH STRANGERS

ENTITY-PURCHASE BUYBACKS

CROSS-PURCHASE BUYBACKS

FUNDING PURCHASES WITH INSURANCE

Do others own a stake in your business? If so, it's important to ensure that when ownership interests in the business are transferred – and inevitably they will be – they don't pass to strangers. You want to see ownership interests pass back to the company or to individuals with whom you know you can do business. Buy-sell agreements are the way to make this happen. No matter the size of your business, overlooking the importance of a buy-sell agreement can be a painful, expensive mistake.

Tammy, Russ, and Herb are all visual artists. They retained a lawyer to create a business entity through which they would open a gallery to sell their own work and the work of others. At first they wanted to organize as a nonprofit corporation and seek **tax-exempt status**. Their lawyer advised against this because their primary objectives were neither charitable nor educational and thus the likelihood of obtaining tax-exempt status was slim (see Conversation #52).

These artists wanted to sell art. Period. That's a for-profit business mission. In terms of choosing an appropriate business entity, therefore, they could organize their business as a **partnership**, a **business corporation,** or a **limited liability company** (see Conversation #47). Tammy, Russ, and Herb chose the LLC.

Once the lawyer formed the LLC, Tammy, Russ, and Herb were all **members** of the limited liability company. Each made an initial **capital contribution**, determining the percentage of their ownership interests. Let's say that Tammy contributed cash, Russ contributed more cash, and Herb contributed services but no cash. The members agreed that the value of Herb's services was equal to the amount of cash that Tammy contributed. That being the case, Tammy and Herb each acquired a 30% interest in the LLC, and Russ acquired a 40% interest.

They thought everything was settled until their lawyer started asking a few questions:

- What happens when Tammy wants to retire?
- What happens if Herb becomes disabled?
- What happens if Russ goes bankrupt?
- What happens if Herb gets divorced?
- What happens when a member dies?

Horrific possibilities started to form in their minds. In the absence of a **buy-sell agreement** any of the members could simply transfer their ownership interests in the company to anyone they wished: Tammy could sell out to a random purchaser; Russ could transfer his interest to a trustee in bankruptcy; Herb's interest could be awarded to his former spouse; any of the members' interests could pass to heirs upon their deaths. Should such transfers occur, the remaining members would find themselves in business with strangers. Imagine the fun Tammy and Russ would have sharing the gallery with Herb's former wife. Or suppose Russ died and his wayward nephew Ron inherited his controlling interest in the company.

any of the members could simply transfer their ownership interests in the company to anyone they wished

A buy-sell agreement is a contract among those with ownership interests in a business. It can be a stand-alone contract or it can be part of the business's governing documents (e.g., an LLC's operating agreement; a partnership agreement; or the by-laws of a corporation). Buy-sell agreements can determine, in advance of controversy, when an owner may sell his or her interest in the business; who may purchase the interest; what price will be paid for the interest; and how the seller of the interest will be paid.

buy-sell agreements can have significant income and estate tax implications for those with ownership interests in the business

Structuring the buy-sell agreement is not a do-it-yourself task. Buy-sell agreements can have significant income and estate tax implications for those with ownership interests in the business. A critical player in this process, therefore, is your tax professional. Ideally you should retain an attorney and an accountant, both of whom are familiar with your business and with the individual owners. Even more ideally, the accountant and attorney should consult with one another as your buy-sell agreement is being developed.

There are two basic ways that buy-sell agreements can be structured. In the first, the company itself buys the departing owner's interest. This is called an **entity-purchase buyback**. In the second, the remaining owners purchase the departing owner's interest. This is called a **cross-purchase buyback**. Either way, strangers are effectively prevented from acquiring ownership interests in your business.

Let's go back to Tammy, Russ, and Herb. The lawyer drafted their LLC operating agreement to include buy-sell provisions. Herb, whose contributions to the gallery consist entirely of services, noticed that the agreement authorized the company first, and if the company passed then Tammy and Russ individually, to purchase his membership interest in the event he became totally disabled. Herb had no objection to this, but he wondered how either the company, or Tammy or Russ individually, would be able to afford the purchase, should his disability occur.

The answer: disability insurance. The LLC and/or Tammy or

Russ personally, could take out disability insurance on Herb. Then, in the event of his disability, the insurance proceeds would provide funds for purchasing his membership interest. It would work the same way, with death. The company and/or the individual members could take out life insurance on the lives of the other members and, in the event of death, the proceeds would provide funds for purchasing the deceased member's interest.

Insurance works for death and disability, but not for other transfer events such as retirement, discord, divorce, or bankruptcy. In those cases the company and individual owners need to pursue alternative financing options such as borrowing and installment payment plans. An important thing to remember is that most states require organized business entities to remain solvent after a buy-sell event. Buying out the departing owner's interest, in other words, can't bankrupt the company.

one way or another, the agreement needs to specify either a fixed dollar amount for each owner's interest, or a formula for determining such values

Another important buy-sell issue is valuation. One way or another, the agreement needs to specify either a fixed dollar amount for each owner's interest, or a formula for determining such values. And the valuation needs to be reasonable. If you fix the value of each owner's interest at $5.00 and the company is making millions in profits, the IRS will bellow and you will be made to suffer. So don't undervalue or overvalue the ownership interests. Again, obtain advice on this issue from a good accountant or business valuation specialist before finalizing your buy-sell agreement.

CONVERSATION #49

Why Plastic Is Good: Installment Payment Pitfalls

ou want to make the sale. So when a hot prospect asks to pay in installments, it's tempting to say OK.

Not so fast.

DEBT COLLECTION PERILS

PASSING TITLE TO GOOD FAITH PURCHASERS

When your business permits buyers to pay over time, you are engaging in the highly regulated practice of extending credit to consumers. You shouldn't even consider the possibility if you aren't prepared to engage competent counsel to guide you through the process.

Skeptical? Let's look at some hypothetical scenarios.

(By the way. If you're pressed for time and want to get on with your life, here's a solution: take credit cards. If your buyers want to pay over time, fine. Let 'em use their plastic.)

OK, let's look at those scenarios.

Kim strolls into your studio wishing to purchase five of your most expensive works. You know Kim; everyone does. She's a revered entertainment industry icon. You maintain a professional demeanor, all the while thinking to yourself, "Ka-CHING!"

The limo is outside and her driver is loading up all five pieces, when Kim asks whether she can pay over time. Not wishing to appear un-hip (or desperate), you say yes. You strike an agreement and pat yourself on the back for remembering to put it in writing. Kim drives away with the art...and our camera pans to your empty cash register.

Next scenario. Same thing, the following day (what luck!), except Karl drives himself to your door in a Ford Pinto patched together with duct tape. When Karl asks to pay over time you refuse, and he goes away.

Shortly, you're in a heap of trouble.

Karl belongs to a protected class and sues you for discrimination. (And as it turns out: he's rich.) Kim's personal debt exceeds that of a small country. You had no idea, because you didn't want to offend her by running a credit check.

Oh, and she's got your work.

Well, at least your agreement with Kim is in writing, so you set about collecting what she owes. But you employ methods that inadvertently violate state and federal debt collection acts and now you have fines to pay. Plus: you failed to provide Kim with legally required disclosures and disclaimers; your interest rate exceeded the legal maximum; and you didn't adhere to consumer privacy requirements.

On the one hand: she hasn't paid you in full. On the other: it's in her possession. Who owns the work?

Oh, and she's still got your work.

Let's focus our attention on the artwork Kim took back to her mansion. On the one hand: she hasn't paid you in full. On the other: it's in her possession. Who owns the work? Worse yet: what happens if she sells it to her neighbor?

Chances are: you lose.

Well, you lose if you haven't taken proper precautions. And for purposes of this Conversation, you haven't.

Many states (but not all) have statutes that require art merchants to treat your work as trust property while it's in their possession and/or until you have been paid in full. If Kim were an art merchant, and your state had such a statute, you might have a basis for relief and recovery. But let's assume that Kim is not in the business of buying and selling art. She's not a merchant; she's just a famous person who likes art. Where does that leave you?

That leaves you with the body of law that applies to commercial transactions generally: your state's version of the Uniform Commercial Code (see Conversation #46). "Uniform" laws, remember, are suggested statutes on various topics that states are free to adopt in whole or in part, or not at all. Because the state legislatures can modify these suggested statutes however they please, the UCC isn't as "uniform" from state to state as its name suggests. Still, nearly every state has adopted some version.

Back to the Kim debacle. Unfortunately, UCC section 2-403(1) leaves you high and dry. It provides:

> *(1) A purchaser of goods acquires all title which his transferor had or had power to transfer .... A person with voidable title has power to transfer a good title to a good faith purchaser for value. When goods have been delivered under a transaction of purchase the purchaser has such power even though*
>
> > *(a) the transferor was deceived as to the identity of the purchaser, or*
> >
> > *(b) the delivery was in exchange for a check which is later dishonored, or*
> >
> > *(c) it was agreed that the transaction was to be a "cash sale", or*
> >
> > *(d) the delivery was procured through fraud punishable as larcenous under the criminal law.*

Almost every word you read in the UCC has a definition that appears somewhere *else* in the UCC – so if you really want to know what a section means, you spend most of your time hunting for those definitions. Here's a plain English translation of section 2-403(1):

1. If you voluntarily delivered the art to Kim – even if she fraudulently induced you to do so! – Kim can pass good title to the work to a "good faith purchaser for value." So if Kim sells the work to David, David gets good title even though you never got paid.
2. The term "good faith purchaser for value" includes creditors, so if Kim's creditors come and take the work to satisfy Kim's debts, they also get good title – even though you never got paid.
3. If Kim broke into your studio and physically stole the work, Kim would *not* be able to pass good title to others. But that's pretty much the only scenario under which you would prevail over David, if you hadn't taken those "proper precautions" we discussed earlier.

Taking proper precautions means perfecting a **security interest** by filing a financing statement with your state (see Conversation #46). Usually, you file financing statements with the secretary of state or similar office in your state. Although this requires some effort on your part, the UCC figures it's more reasonable for you to perfect your security interest than it is for David to fully research the work's chain of title; that's why section 2-403(1) is so slanted against you and in favor of David. Remember this: the UCC will almost always favor an innocent purchaser over an unpaid seller.

the UCC will almost always favor an innocent purchaser over an unpaid seller

You will need an attorney's assistance to perfect your security interests. If work of substantial value is in someone else's hands, though, and you haven't yet been paid – make the effort and file a financing statement to protect your interests. If you don't, David will walk away with legal title to your work.

No Contest! (The Problems with Promotions)

Contest. Competition. Sweepstakes. Lottery. In a nonlegal sense they're all promotions. That is to say, they wouldn't exist if the sponsor didn't have something to gain. Legally, though, each of those terms has a different meaning, and very different rules apply.

Lotteries
Skill contests
Sweepstakes

Please. Pay more attention to promotions.

Participants: This is a business transaction. You don't do business with just anyone...do you? (The correct answer is, "No.") Whether it's a distributor or a vendor or the woman who fixes your car, you base your business decisions on many different factors. Take a moment to identify a few. (We'll wait.)

What did you come up with? One factor, most likely, is the appearance of professionalism. In the context of promotions: how professionally does the sponsor present itself? If you're looking at terms and conditions that contain grammatical errors, missing text, broken hyperlinks, slang – those are red flags. If the sponsor can't get it together to present the promotion in a professional manner, do you really think they're going to administer the promotion any differently? When deciding whether or not to participate in a promotion, exercise the same degree of care as you would with any other business decision.

Sponsors: Get legal advice. Running a promotion

is a legal minefield. Too often, sponsors just slap together some rules (and, indeed, the promotion itself) without consulting legal counsel. That's a huge mistake. Every state has a body of law governing and restricting the sponsorship of promotions. And get this: if you conduct the promotion online you must comply with the laws of each and every state. Failure to do so can result in civil and criminal liability – which far outweighs the cost of seeking legal advice at the outset.

Participants: Guard your copyrights. If you're entering your work in a promotion (e.g., your art, song, photograph, screenplay, etc.), an issue that frequently arises is the extent to which the sponsor acquires copyright rights to your entry. If you see words like, "assign," "sell," or "transfer" in connection with copyright: watch out. Chances are the sponsor is requiring you to surrender copyright. This is bad. Is it illegal, or unenforceable? No. It's just unfavorable to you. Contest terms and conditions are a contract. If that contract is properly formed and you agree to its terms... you're bound.

Contest terms and conditions are a contract. If that contract is properly formed and you agree to its terms... you're bound.

In certain circumstances you might have grounds for challenging the contract's enforceability, as, for example, if your state does not permit electronic contracting; if the contract is unsupported by consideration; if you are a minor, etc. In general, however, it's best to live by this rule: if the terms and conditions use the words, "assign," "sell," or "transfer" and you do not wish to part with your copyright, do not participate in the promotion.

Sponsors: You probably don't need to own the copyright. You don't need to strip the participant of his/her copyright to accomplish your objectives. Perhaps you wish to display the entries publicly; or to reproduce, sell, and distribute copies of the winning entries for a period of time (or even forever). Maybe you wish to sell the original entries on commission; or use the entries for other promotional purposes. You can do any of this with properly drafted licensing agreements. In most cases, it is simply unnecessary to require a complete assignment of the participant's copyright rights. This is bad for the participants and it's bad for you. Savvy participants aren't going to stand for this practice, and they will choose not to participate in your promotion. It's good for everyone, though, if you draft promotion documents to provide only the authority you need to carry out your intended activities.

Promotion Fundamentals

Every state prohibits the sponsoring of a **lottery** except by the government. If your promotion qualifies as a lottery, therefore, you're in trouble. There are three elements of a lottery: (a) prizes are awarded; (b) participants must furnish **consideration** to enter[1]; and (c) winners are selected by chance. If all three of these elements are found to exist, your promotion is an illegal lottery. To avoid running afoul of the lottery laws, you must eliminate one of the three elements from your promotion.

to avoid running afoul of the lottery laws, you must eliminate one of the three elements from your promotion

In a legitimate **sweepstakes**, prizes are awarded and winners are selected by chance. However, participants need not furnish consideration to enter. By eliminating the element of consideration, sweepstakes are not illegal lotteries.

Art, music, film, and writing competitions are examples of **skill contests.** Prizes are awarded, and often, consideration is required to enter. Winners, however, are not selected by chance; they are selected based upon their skill as determined by qualified judges. By eliminating the element of chance, skill contests are not illegal lotteries.

Sponsoring a skill contest, though, is nonetheless an endeavor fraught with peril. This is especially so, if the contest is conducted on a nationwide basis.

[1] Consideration can be anything of value, such as an entry fee, consent to be on a mailing list, or even making multiple visits to a store.

- At least eight states prohibit consideration in skill contests.

  Sponsors: Do you know which states are on this list? If not, and your contest-with-an-entry-fee is open to contestants nationwide – you could be in serious trouble.

  Contestants: Do you live in one of these states? If so, you have grounds for challenging the legality of the contest.
- At least eleven states permit consideration for skill contests, but require specified disclosures.
- At least two states require sponsors to register with the state and post a bond.

YOU TRY

It has become common and convenient to run promotions on social media platforms such as Facebook®. When you do this, you must comply not only with applicable law, but with the terms and conditions of the platform. Facebook's promotion rules are complex, and if you violate them Facebook will at a minimum terminate your account.

Good Gifts for Arts Entrepreneurs

In this Conversation we will chat about tax. Just generally, of course, because for specific advice you must consult your tax professional. But we'll chat about gifts and taxes. And we'll explore the notion that the best gift for an arts entrepreneur might be … cash.

Gifting
Taxation
Why cash is good

Whether you operate your business as a sole proprietorship, a partnership, an LLC, or a corporation, there is generally some kind of tax benefit associated with expenditures made for business-related purposes. Some business expenses are outright deductible. Others (such as expenditures for tools and equipment) have to be **capitalized**, which spreads your cost recovery over a period of time. Either way, you benefit. See http://www.irs.gov/publications/p535/ch01.html#d0e414

If (for example) you're planning to purchase a new camera for use in your business and somebody instead gives it to you as a gift: hooray! You have the camera. But you might not get a tax benefit because you didn't make the purchase. If your benefactor had simply given you cash to fund the purchase, you'd have the camera and a tax benefit as well.

Sure, if the camera is expensive enough and you transfer it to the business you might be able to capitalize it. But receiving cash is far less complicated, and it eliminates tax-related disputes regarding valuation. For tax purposes, physical things have to be valued. Cash speaks for itself.

Warning. If someone is going to give you cash for your business, make sure they give the cash to you – the individual – and not to the business itself. For one thing, doing it this way affords you and your tax planning professional more flexibility in terms of deciding when you will funnel the cash (or what you buy with the cash) into the business. Timing can be everything, in tax planning.

if someone is going to give you cash for your business, make sure they give the cash to you – the individual – and not to the business itself

Another reason to make sure the cash goes to you personally is that if it goes to your actual business entity, the gift might be considered a **capital contribution** which could give the donor a potential claim to an ownership interest in your business. Even though it was very generous of Aunt Sally to give you $5,000, you probably don't want her as co-owner of your business.

Let's answer some additional questions you might have about gifting.

Q: If I don't get a tax deduction because I didn't make the purchase, does that mean the giver gets a tax deduction?

A: No. It's not their business.

Q: Do I have to pay tax on the value of gifts I receive?

A: Not to the IRS, but check with your tax advisor regarding any state taxes that might apply to you.

Q: Does the donor have to pay tax on the value of gifts he or she makes?

A: We do have a federal **gift tax** in the United States. Under the current scheme, every person may gift up to a certain amount per year, per **donee**, without incurring gift tax liability. The Yearly Amount (YA) is set by law and often changes. So this means each of us can give up to $YA per year to an unlimited number of recipients. For example: in the same year you can give $YA to your sister, $YA to your neighbor, $YA to Chuck the mailman and anyone else you choose, without having to worry about gift tax.

If the donor does happen to give more than $YA to the same person in the same year, the donor becomes liable for the payment of federal gift tax. In many cases actual payment of this tax is deferred until after the donor's death; but the donor still has to file a gift tax return. So whenever a donor makes such a gift (i.e., more than $YA to the same donee in the same year), the donor should seek counsel from a qualified tax professional. Also see http://www.irs.gov/businesses/small/article/0,,id=98968,00.html

if the donor does happen to give more than $YA to the same person in the same year, the donor becomes liable for the payment of federal gift tax

Q: Is there any way for the donor to gift more than $YA to the same donee in the same year, and avoid gift tax liability?

A: Yes. The donor might avoid gift tax liability by making the gift directly to an educational institution for the donee's tuition or to a medical provider for the donee's care. Other gifts that do not count for gift tax purposes are gifts to one's spouse; gifts to a political organization for its use; and gifts to charity. Of course, these rules all have restrictions, and are subject to change.

Q: If somebody gives me cash, can he/she place restrictions on how I use the money?

A: This is one of those issues that vary from state to state. In general, though, there are three elements to a completed gift: (a) the donor has to have a present intent to make the gift; (b) the donor has to actually deliver the property to the donee; and (c) the donee has to accept the gift. When those three elements are present, generally, the gift is completed and considered irrevocable. Presumably, if the donor imposed restrictions on the gift and you violated those restrictions, the donor would have a right to revoke the gift and take back the property. If that's the case, there was no legal gift in the first place.

if the donor imposed restrictions on the gift and you violated those restrictions, the donor would have a right to revoke the gift and take back the property

Q: I'm fascinated! What else can you tell me about completed gifts?

A: In one case, a ridiculously wealthy individual made a "gift" to a university to establish and fund a research institute. The donor attached a number of strings, however, and the IRS determined that the gift was not completed until the donor was actually obligated to provide an ascertainable amount.

Q: Why did it matter if the gift was completed or not?

A: If the gift isn't considered "completed," the donor doesn't get to take advantage of the $YA-per-donee gift tax exclusion; and if the gift is made to charity the donor won't get an income tax deduction for a charitable donation.

Q: Ouch. Say, what are the rules if I give "business" gifts to others?

A: According to the IRS: *If you give business gifts in the course of your trade or business, you can deduct the cost subject to special limits and rules. In general, you can deduct no more than $25 for business gifts you give directly or indirectly to any one person during your tax year.* For more information on business entertainment expenses: http://www.irs.gov/taxtopics/tc512.html

Q: I heard the IRS is cracking down on stars who receive gift bags at the Academy Awards ceremony. Really?

A: The IRS doesn't call it a crackdown; they call it an "outreach campaign to the entertainment industry." But, yes. The IRS and the Academy reached an agreement confirming that the content of gift baskets, for stars appearing on award programs, is taxable income. In a press release, the IRS Commissioner said he "appreciated the Academy's leadership on this issue."

Q: Is that the same as "thanking the Academy?"

Nonprofit Doesn't Mean Tax Exempt

In Conversation #47 we looked at various for-profit options for organizing business entities. Now let's talk about nonprofits.

Nonprofit does not mean tax-exempt.

REQUIREMENTS FOR OBTAINING FEDERAL TAX EXEMPT STATUS

In most states, **nonprofit** is a type of corporation. You can organize as a "business corporation" or a "nonprofit corporation" – but they're both corporations. The difference, generally, lies in the applicable rules of governance (i.e., the statutes that govern that type of corporation). But it has nothing to do with federal taxation. If your objective is to become exempt from federal income taxation, you must separately apply for and obtain tax-exempt status from the Internal Revenue Service (IRS). Until that happens, your nonprofit corporation is not tax exempt.

There are many types of tax-exempt status.

The term, "501(c)(3)" is tossed about rather freely. (If you've never heard this term, hang on. We'll explain it shortly.) It has wrongly become a noun rather than an adjective (as in, "they're a 501[c][3]"). Most unfortunately, it has become a designation to which many organizations consider themselves unconditionally entitled. The prevailing notion is that all one needs to do is fill out a form and ... *voila!*... the organization is tax exempt. Not so.

"501(c)(3)" refers to section 501, subdivision (c)(3) of the **Internal Revenue Code**. Organizations existing for the purposes set forth in subdivision (c)(3) may qualify for federal tax-exempt status, and with certain restrictions donations to such organizations are tax-deductible to the donors. What many people don't realize is that section 501(c) has 27 subdivisions *other than* (c)(3), each requiring totally different criteria for qualification (see *IRS Publication 557*, pages 60-61). Consequently, any organization applying to the IRS for tax-exempt status must first identify the appropriate subdivision of section 501(c) under which to apply. The appropriate subdivision might or might not be subdivision (c)(3), depending on the primary purposes and activities of the organization (http://www.irs.gov/pub/irs-pdf/p557.pdf)

Section 501(c) (3) applies to organizations that exist for *religious, educational, charitable, scientific or literary purposes*; that *provide testing for public safety*; or that exist *to foster national or international amateur sports competition and/or the prevention of cruelty to children or animals.*

TS: What's wrong with this picture?

TS (answering her own question): The term "artistic" does not appear anywhere on that list of qualifying purposes.

Lucy: So how does an arts organization acquire 501(c)(3) status?

TS: It must demonstrate that although its activities are artistic in nature, the organization nonetheless exists for one or more of the purposes that do appear on the list.

Lucy: So our orchestra has to provide testing for public safety?

TS: Very funny, Lucille. Not specifically that, no. But more realistically it would have to highlight educational or literary purposes. For musical and visual arts organizations it is more difficult to obtain 501(c)(3) status than it is for organizations whose primary activities correspond directly with the purposes set forth in subdivision (c)(3).

The application process for obtaining 501(c)(3) status is formidable. Your group should exist, in a well-organized manner, for a reasonable period of time before you begin the process of applying for tax-exempt status. This is not a legal requirement, but it's good practice that will increase the likelihood of your application's success. The IRS wants to see that you've actually started the process of accomplishing the tax-exempt purposes you'll be claiming.

your group should exist, in a well-organized manner, for a reasonable period of time before you begin the process of applying for tax-exempt status

Don't overlook the importance of selecting your name. Is the **domain name** available? An organization's online presence is vital. If you invest time and money in a name for which you cannot obtain an identical or intuitively similar domain name, you're at a disadvantage. More critically, you need to make sure that neither your organizational name nor your domain name is somebody else's trademark. Getting sued for trademark infringement can seriously interfere with accomplishing your mission.

Then you need to incorporate in your state. We'll use New York as an example, but you must get individualized advice regarding proper procedure for incorporating in your own state. In New York, there are four different types of nonprofit corporations: Types A, B, C, and D (very creative, New Yorkers!) You need to identify which type you are. Then you need to draft your corporate purposes. Doing this properly is enormously important, because when ultimately you apply for 501(c)(3) status, the IRS will closely examine the purposes stated in your certificate of incorporation.

Do you anticipate that your organization will ever own real property? In New York you'll want to know about specific language that will help you acquire property tax exemption when the time comes.

You must select three people to serve as your initial directors and you must draft, finalize, and notarize your certificate of incorporation. In New York most cultural organizations need to have their certificates of incorporation approved by the State Education Department – so if you skip that step your application for incorporation will be rejected.

Once you've submitted the application for incorporation it's time to recruit your full board of directors. Do not make the mistake of filling your board with artists. Your organization is as much a business as the local laundromat, and your board must include representatives from all walks of business life. Your first recruit should probably be an accountant. When the IRS is scrutinizing your 501(c) (3) application, your organization's financial house must be in order. Make it clear to the accountant on your board that his or her job is to make sure the board establishes sound financial policies for the organization and that staff is properly trained and instructed to implement those policies.

do not make the mistake of filling your board with artists

Continue board development by recruiting representatives from your community's primary employers, persons skilled in your organizational mission, an attorney skilled in nonprofit and arts law (the personal injury lawyer won't do much good), and of course – people who can raise money, donate money, and/or lead your organization to sustainability through earned income.

When recruiting is complete, hold your first board meeting. At that meeting you will elect officers of the board, adopt bylaws, adopt your mission and vision statements, adopt board policies, and map out your fundraising plan. If that sounds like a tall order, it is. But if you don't do all those things – properly – you won't obtain 501(c)(3) status.

After the state confers corporate status, you must obtain an **Employer Identification Number** (EIN) for the organization, and open a bank account using the EIN (don't forget to establish board policies regarding check-signing procedures). Pay close attention to your budget: it's got to be detailed and realistic. Establish your accounting, financial, and internal control systems; analyze and execute your staffing and volunteer needs; and set up a reliable record-keeping system. Analyze your insurance needs in areas such as workers' compensation, unemployment, disability, general property and liability, auto liability, and directors' and officers' liability. How is that budget coming along? You need accurate income and expense forecasts for at least two years. Have you secured office space and necessary equipment? Do you have a gift receipt and acknowledgement system? In most states, being a nonprofit corporation means having to file a lot of reports. Make sure you've got systems in place to ensure these reports get filed accurately and on time.

pay close attention to your budget: it's got to be detailed and realistic

Now – and only now – you might be ready to apply for 501(c)(3) status. You need a track record, proving that you have successfully accomplished the items outlined above. You need concrete examples of services you've provided, consistent with the corporate purposes set forth in your articles of incorporation and bylaws. You must demonstrate that volunteers contribute in meaningful ways to the organization's mission and that you have significant expectations of public support. You'll be asked to write detailed narratives, and to submit financial records and realistic projected budgets. In short, you've got to be a real business with your act together.

The benefits of 501(c)(3) status are significant and if your organization realistically has a chance of qualifying for such status, go for it. Understand, however, that even after you achieve 501(c)(3) status, your work is not done. In order to maintain tax-exempt status the organization must file annual returns with the IRS; comply with the fundraising registration laws of each state in which it solicits support; generate enough income to support its budget; and (oh yeah) do the work it organized to do in the first place!

A successful tax-exempt organization needs a broad base of human and financial support. All too often, one dedicated founder and a handful of friends decide to take this on, alone. They have noble intentions but almost always underestimate what's really involved. Over time, after achieving a measure of success, they become overwhelmed and burn out. The founder doesn't want to cede control; the handful of friends can't manage all the work on their own; there's not enough money to hire staff; and the volunteers become loose cannons. Kaboom. End of organization.

Make sure you're prepared for all that tax-exempt status requires, before jumping in. If it's not quite time for a standalone organization, consider **fiscal sponsorship** as an alternative. Either way, analyze carefully and make your choice as an informed businessperson with eyes wide open.

YOU TRY

1. It costs almost as much to shut down a nonprofit, tax-exempt organization as it does to establish the organization in the first place. If closing the doors is imminent, be prepared: there will be legal fees, and it will take more time than you expected.
2. Most states require nonprofits that conduct fundraising activities within their borders to register with the state. "Within a state's borders" can be very easy to achieve, if your organization uses its website or social media to solicit contributions. Do not overlook this very important step. For more information: http://www.multistatefiling.org

APPENDIX 1

Bill of Rights

Amendment I

Congress shall make no law respecting an establishment of religion, or prohibiting the free exercise thereof; or abridging the freedom of speech, or of the press; or the right of the people peaceably to assemble, and to petition the Government for a redress of grievances.

Amendment II

A well regulated Militia, being necessary to the security of a free State, the right of the people to keep and bear Arms, shall not be infringed.

Amendment III

No Soldier shall, in time of peace be quartered in any house, without the consent of the Owner, nor in time of war, but in a manner to be prescribed by law.

Amendment IV

The right of the people to be secure in their persons, houses, papers, and effects, against unreasonable searches and seizures, shall not be violated, and no Warrants shall issue, but upon probable cause, supported by Oath or affirmation, and particularly describing the place to be searched, and the persons or things to be seized.

Amendment V

No person shall be held to answer for a capital, or otherwise infamous crime, unless on a presentment or indictment of a Grand Jury, except in cases arising in the land or naval forces, or in the Militia, when in actual service in time of War or public danger; nor shall any person be subject for the same offence to be twice put in jeopardy of life or limb; nor shall be compelled in any criminal case to be a witness against himself, nor be deprived of life, liberty, or property, without due process of law; nor shall private property be taken for public use, without just compensation.

Amendment VI

In all criminal prosecutions, the accused shall enjoy the right to a speedy and public trial, by an impartial jury of the State and district wherein the crime shall have been committed, which district shall have been previously ascertained by law, and to be informed of the nature and cause of the accusation; to be confronted with the witnesses against him; to have compulsory process for obtaining witnesses in his favor, and to have the Assistance of Counsel for his defence.

Amendment VII

In Suits at common law, where the value in controversy shall exceed twenty dollars, the right of trial by jury shall be preserved, and no fact tried by a jury, shall be otherwise re-examined in any Court of the United States, than according to the rules of the common law.

Amendment VIII

Excessive bail shall not be required, nor excessive fines imposed, nor cruel and unusual punishments inflicted.

Amendment IX

The enumeration in the Constitution, of certain rights, shall not be construed to deny or disparage others retained by the people.

Amendment X

The powers not delegated to the United States by the Constitution, nor prohibited by it to the States, are reserved to the States respectively, or to the people.

APPENDIX 2

Table of Cases

ADA v Delta Dental Plans Ass'n, 126 F3d 977 (7th Cir 1997)

Billy-Bob Teeth, Inc. v Novelty, Inc., 329 F3d 586 (7th Cir 2003)

Bouchat v Baltimore Ravens, Inc., 215 F Supp 2d 611, affd 346 F3d 514, cert denied 541 US 1042, 124 S Ct 2171, 158 L Ed 2d 732 (2004)

Campbell v Acuff-Rose Music, Inc., 510 US 569, 114 S Ct 1164, 127 L Ed 2d 500 (1994)

Cariou v Prince, Docket No. 11-1197-cv (2d Cir April 25, 2013)

Comedy III Productions, Inc. v Gary Saderup, Inc., 25 Cal 4th 387, 106 Cal Rptr 2d 126, 21 P 3d 797, cert denied 534 US 1078, 122 S Ct 806, 151 L Ed 2d 692 (2002)

Community for Creative Non-Violence v Reid, 490 US 730, 109 S Ct 2166, 104 L Ed 2d 811 (1989)

Dr. Seuss Enters., L.P. v Penguin Books USA, Inc., 109 F3d 1394 (9th Cir 1997)

Eldred v Ashcroft, 537 US 186, 123 S Ct 769, 154 L Ed 2d 683 (2003)

Estate of Presley v Russen, 513 F Supp 1339 (D NJ 1981)

ETW Corp. v Jireh Publishing, Inc., 99 F Supp 2d 829, affd 332 F3d 915 (6th Cir 2003)

Feist Publications, Inc. v Rural Telephone Service Co., Inc., 499 US 340, 111 S Ct 1282, 113 L Ed 2d 358 (1991)

Gaylord v United States, 678 F3d 1339 (Fed Cir 2012)

Gregerson v Vilana Financial, Inc., 446 F Supp 2d 1053 (D Minn 2006)

Herbert Rosenthal Jewelry Corp. v Kalpakian, 446 F2d 738 (9th Cir 1971)

Hoffman v Capital Cities/ABC, Inc., 33 F Supp 2d 867, revd 255 F3d 1180 (9th Cir 2001)

Intervest Constr., Inc. v Canterbury Estate Homes, Inc., 554 F3d 914 (11th Cir 2008)

Landham v Lewis Galoob Toys, Inc., 227 F3d 619 (6th Cir 2000)

Lee v Deck the Walls, 925 F Supp 576, affd 125 F3d 580 (7th Cir 1997)

Leibovitz v Paramount Pictures Corp., 137 F3d 109 (2d Cir 1998)

Leicester v Warner Bros., 232 F3d 1212 (9th Cir 2000)

Levine v McDonald's Corp., 735 F Supp 92 (SDNY 1990)

Lucky Break Wishbone Corp. v Sears Roebuck & Co., 373 Fed Appx 752 (9th Cir 2010)

Mackie v Rieser, 296 F3d 909, cert denied 537 US 1189, 123 S Ct 1259, 154 L Ed 2d 1022 (2003)

Massachusetts Museum of Contemporary Art Foundation, Inc. v Büchel, 593 F3d 38 (1st Cir 2010)

Munoz v Albuquerque A.R.T. Co., 829 F Supp 309, affd 38 F3d 1218 (9th Cir 1994)

Phillips v Pembroke Real Estate, Inc., 459 F3d 128 (1st Cir 2006)

Pollara v Seymour, 344 F3d 265 (2d Cir 2003)

Rogers v Koons, 751 F Supp 474, affd 960 F2d 301, cert denied 506 US 934, 113 S Ct 365, 121 L Ed 2d 278 (1992)

Satava v Lowry, 323 F3d 805, cert denied 540 US 983, 124 S Ct 472, 157 L Ed 2d 374 (2003)

Schnapper v Foley, 667 F2d 102, cert denied 455 US 948, 102 S Ct 1448, 71 L Ed 2d 661 (1982)

Showler v Harper's Magazine Found., 222 Fed Appx 755 (10th Cir 2007), cert denied 128 S Ct 196, 169 L Ed 2d 37 (2007)

Smith v George E. Muehlebach Brewing Co., 140 F Supp 729 (D Mo 1956)

Sony Corp. of America v Universal City Studios, Inc., 464 US 417, 104 S Ct 774, 78 L Ed 2d 574 (1984)

Texas v Johnson, 491 US 397, 109 S Ct 2533, 105 L Ed 2d 342 (1989)

United States v Eichman, 496 US 310, 110 S Ct 2404, 110 L Ed 2d 287 (1990)

Wendt v Host International, 125 F3d 806, cert denied 531 US 811, 121 S Ct 33, 148 L Ed 2d 13 (2000)

Glossary

A

acceptance

In contract law, words or actions signifying consent to the terms of an offer

act

A bill that has been passed by a legislature

administrative agency

An official governmental body empowered with the authority to direct and supervise the implementation of particular legislative acts

alternative dispute resolution

Methods, other than litigation in the courts, by which conflicts and disputes are resolved privately. ADR usually takes one of two forms: mediation or arbitration. It typically involves a process much less formal than traditional court procedure and includes the appointment of a third-party to preside over a hearing between the parties. ADR is quicker and less expensive than court litigation. Usually, however, it does require compromise.

appropriation invasion of privacy

Using the name or likeness of another person for personal gain or commercial advantage

article of manufacture

US patent law states: *Whoever invents or discovers any new and useful process, machine,* manufacture, *or composition of matter, or any new and useful improvement thereof, may obtain a patent therefor* (35 USC §101). For purposes of this definition, "manufacture" means any useful product made from raw materials directly by human labor or by machines controlled by humans.

Articles of Confederation and Perpetual Union

The first constitution of the United States of America

ASCAP

The American Society of Composers, Authors and Publishers (www.ascap.com)

assignment

The transfer of any property right, claim or interest, in its entirety, to another person or entity

attribution (right of)

Under the Visual Artists Rights Act, the right of an author of a work of visual art to claim authorship of the work and to prevent the use of his/her name as the author of any work of visual art which he/she did not create

author

In copyright law, the person who created copyrightable material

B

B Corp

A business entity certified by a nonprofit organization (B Lab) to meet rigorous standards of social and environmental performance, accountability, and transparency (www.bcorporation.net)

bailment

A legal relationship created when one party gives property to another for safekeeping

bill

A proposed law

Bill of Rights

The first ten amendments to the United States Constitution

breach of contract

Failing to perform a contractual obligation, without a legal excuse

browse wrap

The terms and conditions of use for a website or other downloadable product that are posted on the website, but do not require the user's express manifestation of assent

bundle of rights

In copyright law, the exclusive rights in copyrighted works (17 USC §106)

buy-sell agreement

A binding contract among co-owners of a business that controls who can buy a departing owner's share of the business; what events will trigger a buyout; and what price will be paid for an owner's interest in the business

C

capital contribution

The contribution of capital, in the form of money, services or property, that someone provides to a business in exchange for an ownership interest in the business

caselaw

Law established by judicial decisions

click wrap

The terms and conditions of use for a website or other downloadable product that are posted on the website, and do require the user's express manifestation of assent (typically by clicking an "I Agree" button or something similar)

Code of Federal Regulations (CFR)

The official compilation of all regulations and rules promulgated by the agencies of the United States government

code

A systematic compilation of statutes that are consolidated and classified according to subject matter (there can also be codes of rules and regulations)

compilation

In copyright law, a work formed by the collection and assembling of preexisting materials or of data that are selected, coordinated, or arranged in such a way that the resulting work as a whole constitutes an original work of authorship

complaint

The pleading that initiates a civil lawsuit

consideration

In contract law, the agreement, act, forbearance or promise of a contracting party (in simple terms: what the party "gives" to the other party)

consignment

An arrangement whereby the owner (e.g., an artist) transfers goods (e.g., works of art) to a seller (e.g., an art gallery) who then acts as the owner's agent for purposes of selling the goods

construction

In contract law, how terms are interpreted (or "construed")

convention

In international law, another word for "treaty"

copyright

The bundle of exclusive rights relating to the reproduction, distribution, public display, public performance and creation of derivative works, that are accorded to the authors of statutory "works of authorship"

counteroffer

An offer made in response to a previous offer by the other party. Making a counter offer automatically rejects the prior offer, and requires an acceptance under the terms of the counter offer or there is no contract.

Creative Commons

A non-profit organization headquartered in Mountain View, California devoted to expanding the range of creative works available for others to build upon legally and to share (www.creativecommons.org)

cross-purchase buyback

In a buy-sell agreement, an arrangement permitting the continuing owners of the business to purchase the departing owner's interest, in proportion to their current holdings (see entity-purchase buyback)

D

declaratory judgment

A binding judgment from a court defining the legal relationship between parties and their rights in the matter before the court; it states the court's opinion regarding the exact nature of the legal matter without requiring the parties to do anything

defamation

The communication of a statement that makes a claim, expressly stated or implied to be factual, that may give the subject of the statement a negative or inferior image. There are many types of defamation, such as: calumny, vilification, traducement, slander (for transitory statements), and libel (for written, broadcast, or otherwise published words).

defendant

The person or entity against whom a civil or criminal action is brought in a court of law; the one being sued or accused

derivative work

In copyright law, a work based upon one or more preexisting works, such as a translation, musical arrangement, dramatization, fictionalization, motion picture version, sound recording, art reproduction, abridgment, condensation, or any other form in which a work may be recast, transformed, or adapted. A work consisting of editorial revisions, annotations, elaborations, or other modifications, which, as a whole, represent an original work of authorship, is a "derivative work" (17 USC §101).

design patent

A type of patent issued in the United States for an original design of purely ornamental or aesthetic nature made for an article of manufacture (35 USC §171). Design patents protect the appearance of an article of manufacture (rather than the article itself), from infringement.

dilution

In trademark law, a concept giving the owner of a famous trademark standing to forbid others from using the mark in a way that would lessen its uniqueness

disclosure invasion of privacy

Publishing information about someone's personal life that has not previously been revealed to the public, that is not of legitimate public concern, and the publication of which would be offensive to a reasonable person

diversity of citizenship jurisdiction

The subject matter jurisdiction of United States federal courts to hear a civil case because the persons that are parties are citizens of different states or non-U.S. citizens

domain name

A unique name, consisting of an alphabetical or alphanumeric sequence followed by a suffix indicating the top level domain (e.g., .com), that serves as the address for a website

donee

The recipient of a gift

droit de suite

A right granted to artists or their heirs, in some jurisdictions, to receive a royalty on the resale of their works of art

E

eCo

Electronic Copyright Office: the United States Copyright Office's system for registering works online

Employer Identification Number (EIN)

A (usually 9-digit) number assigned by the Internal Revenue Service to identify tax-paying business entities in the United States. Also known as a federal tax identification number.

entity-purchase buyback

In a buy-sell agreement, an arrangement permitting the business itself (as opposed to the remaining owners) to purchase the departing owner's interest (see cross-purchase buyback)

exclusive license

A license whereby the licensor agrees not to authorize others to exercise the same rights as those authorized under the license

executive branch

In the United States federal government: the President, the Cabinet and independent federal agencies, charged with implementing and enforcing the laws written by the legislative branch

F

fair use

In copyright law, a doctrine that permits limited use of copyrighted material without permission from the copyright owner, pursuant to a four-factor balancing test (17 USC §107)

false light invasion of privacy
Publishing offensive and false facts about a person

federal question jurisdiction
The subject matter jurisdiction of United States federal courts to hear a civil case because the plaintiff has alleged a violation of the United States Constitution, federal law, or a treaty to which the United States is a party

first sale doctrine
In copyright law, a doctrine that permits lending, reselling, disposing, etc. of the physical copy in which a work of authorship is embodied, but does not permit engaging in any of the rights reserved for the copyright holder (17 USC §109)

fiscal sponsorship
The practice whereby a tax-exempt nonprofit organization provides its tax-exempt status to a project related to the organization's mission. Fiscal sponsorship typically involves a fee-based contractual arrangement between the project and the tax-exempt non-profit.

Framers
Delegates to the 1787 Constitutional Convention; also known as the Founding Fathers of the United States of America

G

gift tax
A federal tax on the transfer of property by one individual (the donor) to another (the donee) when the donor receives nothing, or less than full value, in return. The tax applies whether the donor intends the transfer to be a gift or not, and payment of the tax is the responsibility of the donor.

H

Harry Fox Agency
An agency that collects and distributes mechanical license fees on behalf of music publishers in the United States (www.harryfox.com)

I

inalienable

Absolute; inherent; incapable of being surrendered or transferred

indemnification

A guarantee by one party (the indemnitor) to compensate the other (the indemnitee) for any loss, damage or expense the indemnitee might suffer as a result of specified occurrences. Contract example (plain English): "You're swearing to me this work is original and won't infringe on the rights of anyone else. If it turns out that's not true, and I get sued, you're going to pay my expenses and make me whole."

independent creation

In copyright law, one of the requirements for originality (see minimal level of creativity)

indictment

The formal accusation charging someone with having committed a crime

industrial design

The ornamental or aesthetic aspect of an article; it may consist of three-dimensional features, such as the shape or surface of an article, or of two-dimensional features, such as patterns, lines or color

innocent infringement

In copyright law, a claim that the defendant did not realize that the work was protected. An innocent infringement defense can result in a reduction in damages that the copyright owner would otherwise receive.

intestate succession

The law that dictates who will inherit property when the person who died (the decedent) did not have a will

intrusion invasion of privacy

An intentional interference with a person's interest in solitude or seclusion, either as to his/her person or as to his/her private affairs or concerns, of a kind that would be highly offensive to a reasonable person. The invasion may be by physical intrusion; it may be by the use of the defendant's senses, with or without mechanical aids, to oversee or overhear the plaintiff's private affairs; it may be by some other form of investigation or examination into the plaintiff's private concerns.

J

joint work

In copyright law, a work prepared by two or more authors (**joint authors**) with the intention that their contributions be merged into inseparable or interdependent parts of a unitary whole. Unless there is a written agreement to the contrary, joint authors share equally in copyright ownership of the joint work.

judicial branch

In the United States federal government: the Supreme Court, lower courts, special courts and court support organizations

jurisdiction

Three different meanings: a government's general power to exercise authority over the persons and things within its territory (personal jurisdiction); a court's power to decide cases involving certain subject matter (subject matter jurisdiction); and a geographic area (like a state) within which political or judicial authority may be exercised.

L

legislative branch

In the United States federal government: Congress (consisting of the United States House of Representatives and the United States Senate)

libel

Defamation by written or printed words, pictures, or in any form other than by spoken words or gestures

license

Permission to commit some act that would otherwise be unlawful, such as reproducing copyrighted material. Licenses can be **exclusive** (meaning the licensor cannot grant the license to anyone other than the exclusive licensee) or **nonexclusive** (meaning the licensor may grant the same license to multiple parties). Licenses can also be **revocable** or **irrevocable**.

limited liability company (LLC)

An unincorporated legal entity – statutorily authorized by a state – in which owners (called members) have limited personal liability for the debts and obligations of the company. LLCs also feature management by the members or managers, limitations on ownership transfer, and the option to be taxed either as a partnership or a corporation.

litigant

A party to a lawsuit

litigation

The process of resolving a legal dispute in a formal court action or lawsuit

lottery

A promotion in which participants furnish some kind of consideration for the opportunity to win a prize that is awarded by chance

low profit limited liability company (L3C)

A for-profit, social enterprise venture that has a stated goal of performing a socially beneficial purpose, not maximizing income. It is a hybrid structure that combines the legal and tax flexibility of a traditional LLC with the social benefits of a nonprofit organization. The L3C is designed to make it easier for socially oriented businesses to attract investments from charitable foundations as well as from private investors.

M

master use license

An agreement by which the copyright owner of a sound recording grants permission to use the sound recording, usually in an audio-visual work such as a movie or television production

material breach

A breach of contract substantial enough (as opposed to a technical breach) to allow the innocent party to pursue legal remedies

mechanical license

A license that permits the making and distribution of phonorecords of musical works. Mechanical licensing is compulsory if the musical work has already been distributed to the public under the authority of the copyright owner.

member

An individual or entity with an ownership interest in a limited liability company

merger doctrine

A principle of copyright law stating that, when there is only one or a limited number of ways to express an idea, copyright law will not protect the expression because it has "merged" with the idea

metatags

Searchable code that contains descriptive information about a webpage

minimal level of creativity

In copyright law, one of the requirements for originality (see independent creation)

moral rights

In copyright law, the rights of attribution and integrity (17 USC §106A)

musical work

A category of work protected by copyright law but (interestingly) not defined in the law. Generally: a composition.

N

net income

Income remaining after the deduction (from gross income) of specified expenses

nondisclosure agreement (NDA)

A legal contract through which the parties agree not to disclose confidential material, knowledge, or information that the parties wish to share with one another for certain purposes, but wish to restrict access to or by third parties

O

offer

In contract law, a promise to do or refrain from doing some specified thing; a display of willingness to enter into a contract on specified terms, made in a way that would lead a reasonable person to understand that acceptance will result in a binding contract

operation of law

Rights and liabilities that are cast upon a party by the law, without any act by the party or a court

ordinance

A law passed by a municipality (such as a city, town, village, or borough)

original expression

In copyright law, a requirement for a work's eligibility for copyright protection

orphan works

Works protected under copyright whose owners are difficult to locate

P

partnership

A voluntary association of two or more persons who jointly carry on a business for profit. Under the Uniform Partnership Act, a partnership is presumed to exist if the persons agree to share proportionally in the business's profits or losses. Unlike LLC members, general partners are personally and fully liable for all business debts and obligations of the partnership.

patent

The right to exclude others from making, using, offering for sale, or selling an invention in the United States or importing the invention into the United States. What is granted is not the right to make, use, offer for sale, sell or import, but the right to exclude others from making, using, offering for sale, selling or importing the invention.

performing rights society

An organization that collects and distributes royalties on the behalf of the copyright owner of a musical work, for nondramatic public performances of the musical work

phonorecords

Material objects in which sounds, other than those accompanying a motion picture or other audiovisual work, are fixed by any method now known or later developed, and from which the sounds can be perceived, reproduced, or otherwise communicated, either directly or with the aid of a machine or device (17 USC §101)

plaintiff

The party who brings a civil action in a court of law

preemption doctrine

A doctrine based on the Supremacy Clause of the US Constitution stating that federal laws preempt or take precedence over inconsistent state laws

pro bono

Professional work undertaken voluntarily and without payment, as a public service

pro se

Representing oneself in court, rather than being represented by a lawyer

pseudonym

A fictitious name

public domain

In copyright law, any work of authorship not (or no longer) protected by copyright. This includes work published before 1923 and work for which the term of copyright protection has expired.

publication

In copyright law, the distribution of copies or phonorecords of a work to the public by sale or other transfer of ownership, or by rental, lease, or lending. The offering to distribute copies or phonorecords to a group of persons for purposes of further distribution, public performance, or public display constitutes publication. A public performance or display of a work does not of itself constitute publication. Generally, publication occurs when copies of the work are first made available to the public. If a work has not been made available to the public in this manner, it is considered unpublished.

punitive damages

Damages that may be awarded to a successful plaintiff, in addition to actual damages, for the purpose of punishing the defendant's conduct

Q

QR code

A two-dimensional barcode (consisting of small squares with black and white patterns) used to deliver information such as text or a URL to smartphones and other devices with scanning capability. "QR" stands for "quick response."

R

Register of Copyrights

The director of the United States Copyright Office

regulations

The rules and procedures created by administrative agencies

remedies

In contract law, a type of redress available for a breach of the contract. The five types of remedies are: money damages, restitution, rescission, reformation, and specific performance.

reporters (caselaw)

A series of publications containing the judicial opinions of selected courts

S

samples

Segments taken from one sound recording and inserted into another

scenes a faire

In copyright law, a term that refers to characters, places, story elements, etc., that are standard to a general topic or theme

second level domain (SLD)

The portion of a domain name that is located immediately to the left of the dot

security interest

A property interest created by agreement or by operation of law to secure the performance of an obligation

Shallus, Jacob

The engrosser of the original copy of the United States Constitution

short code

A short numeric code to which text messages can be addressed from a wireless device

signatory

In international law, a nation that joins a convention or treaty

slander

Defamation by spoken words or gestures

sole proprietor

Someone who owns an unincorporated business by himself or herself

sound recording

A work that results from the fixation of a series of musical, spoken, or other sounds, but not including the sounds accompanying a motion picture or other audiovisual work, regardless of the nature of the material objects, such as disks, tapes, or other phonorecords, in which they are embodied

SoundExchange

The non-profit performance rights organization that collects statutory royalties from satellite radio, internet radio, cable TV music channels and similar platforms for streaming sound recordings

statute

An act of the legislature that has been codified (see code)

summary judgment

A final judgment granted before trial on a claim about which a judge has determined there is no genuine issue of material fact, and upon which the movant (the party requesting summary judgment) is entitled to prevail as a matter of law

Supremacy Clause

Article VI, Clause 2 of the United States Constitution. The Supremacy Clause establishes the US Constitution, federal statutes, and US treaties as "the supreme law of the land." The text provides that these are the highest form of law in the United States legal system, and mandates that all state judges must follow federal law when a conflict arises between federal law and either the state constitution or state law of any state.

synchronization license

A license authorizing the synchronization of a musical composition in timed relation with audio-visual images on film or videotape

T

technical breach

A breach of contract not substantial enough (as opposed to a material breach) to allow the other party to pursue legal remedies

top level domain (TLD)

The right-most label in a domain name (for example, ".com")

trade dress

A product's physical appearance, including its size, shape, color, design, and texture; protectible under trademark law if it is non-functional and serves the same source-identifying function as a trademark

trade secret

Information, including a formula, pattern, compilation, program, device, method, technique, or process; that derives independent economic value, actual or potential, from not being generally known to or readily ascertainable through appropriate means by other persons who might obtain economic value from its disclosure or use; and is the subject of efforts that are reasonable under the circumstances to maintain its secrecy

trademark

A distinctive word, phrase, design, smell, sound or other indicator of source used by a seller or service provider to distinguish its goods and services from those of others

U

unconstitutional

A law that is contrary to a provision in the Constitution; contrary to the manner in which a court has interpreted the Constitution; or passed by a legislative body without proper authority or in violation of Constitutional procedures

United States Constitution

The supreme law of the United States of America

USPTO

The United States Patent and Trademark Office (www.uspto.gov)

utility patent

Patent protection granted to one who invents or discovers any new and useful process, machine, article of manufacture, or composition of matter, or any new and useful improvement thereof

V

venue

The locality in which a court proceeding will be heard

W

work made for hire

In copyright law, an exception to the general rule that the person who creates a work of authorship is its author. A work qualifying as work made for hire is either a work prepared by an employee within the scope of his or her employment; or a work specially ordered or commissioned – but only in certain narrow circumstances specified by statute. When a work qualifies as a work made for hire, the employer, or commissioning party, is considered to be the author.

work of authorship

In copyright law: literary works; musical works, including any accompanying words; dramatic works, including any accompanying music; pantomimes and choreographic works; pictorial, graphic, and sculptural works; motion pictures and other audiovisual works; sound recordings; and architectural works (17 USC §102)

Index

In this index page references in **bold** type refer to glossary entries; page references followed by "Fig." refer to a figure or illustration; and page references followed by '*n*' refer to footnotes

A

B

C

E

F

G

H

I

J

K

L

M

N

O

P

Q

R

S

T

U

V

W

Z

About the Author

This book is for real people, and I have attempted to use real-world characters to tell stories and share information. So it seems only right that this space should share something about me the person, as opposed to me the lawyer.

Several of the Conversations in this book feature a character named TS. That's me. My entire middle name is the single letter T (that's true) and it stands for Tuna Sub (also true). Don't blame my parents; it's not their doing. I chose T as my middle name all on my own, later in life, in connection with a seemingly endless string of changes in marital status.

I narrowed it to T because even I could appreciate the downside of adopting Tuna Sub as my actual legal name.

I'm not crazy; there's a reason for the goofy name. When I was in college I met three women who became – and to this day remain – the greatest friends a person could ever have. One day, while we were in a deli waiting for sandwiches, they decided somewhat arbitrarily that my given name was not sufficiently distinctive. My response: "OK. Call me something else." The closest thing in view was the menu board. They chose quickly and declared, "We shall call you Tuna Sub." I chuckled, confident the moniker would be forgotten before our next meal.

It wasn't. To those friends and a surprisingly wide circle of others, for decades, I have been known as TS.

I dedicated this book to all of my friends. TS owes a little bit more to Drane, MJ and Vert.

Elizabeth T Russell
www.erklaw.com

ORDER FORM

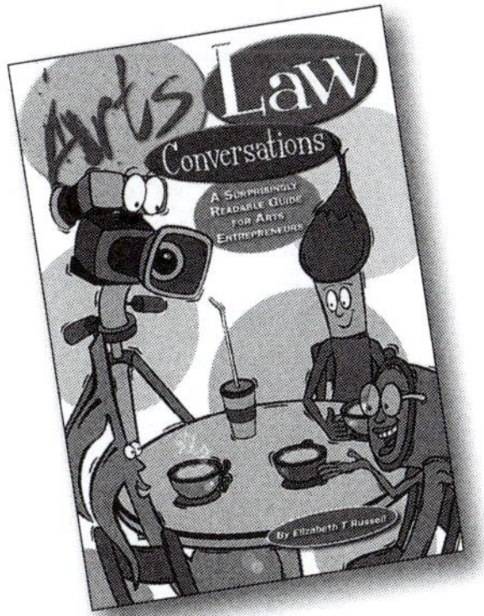

Ruly Press
6907 University Ave., #227
Middleton, WI 53562
info@rulypress.com

$21.95 PLUS SHIPPING

Discounts available for bookstores

ARTS LAW CONVERSATIONS

By Elizabeth T Russell

Qty	Price	Preferred Method of Shipping	Total
______	______________	______________________________	______
______	______________	______________________________	______
______	______________	______________________________	______
______	______________	______________________________	______

Subtotal: ______

Sales tax @5.5%: ______
(WI residents only)

We will contact you with final shipping cost, based on your indicated preference.

TOTAL: _____

CUSTOMER INFORMATION

Name ______________________________

Company ______________________________

Street Address ______________________________

City ______________ State ________ Zip ______________

Phone (_____) ______________ Fax (_____) ______________

Email ______________

PAYMENT METHOD

❒ Check ❒ VISA ❒ MasterCard

Credit card #______________________ Exp. Date _______ CVC ___

Billing Address: ______________________________

COMMENTS

____

____

TALK TO US

Conversations With You

WE WANT TO KNOW WHAT YOU THINK. REALLY.

Ruly Press
6907 University Ave., #227
Middleton, WI 53562
info@rulypress.com

HOW DID YOU HEAR ABOUT ARTS LAW CONVERSATIONS?

____

____

____

____

____

WHAT DID YOU THINK ABOUT THE BOOK?

____

____

____

____

WHAT OTHER TOPICS WOULD YOU LIKE US TO PUBLISH?

____

____

____

____

NOBODY'S PERFECT!

Please let us know how we can improve future editions of this book.